The *ULTIMATE* SOCCER DICTIONARY of American Terms

An extensive glossary for players, coaches, parents, and fans of soccer in the United States

This dictionary (in PAPERBACK, ***complete***) includes **over 4,000 defined terms** – and ***all*** appendices with ***all*** *"Quick-Start"* (▫) terms and ***all*** *"Oral Communication"* (▶) terms.

JOHN C. HARVES

CoachingAmericanSoccer.com®

Edited by **Neil Gillespie**

GillespieConsulting.net

Copyright

The *ULTIMATE* SOCCER DICTIONARY of American Terms
by John C. Harves

Published by: CoachingAmericanSoccer.com®

Editor: Neil Gillespie, GillespieConsulting.net
Email: neil@gillespieconsulting.net

Graphics, cover, and interior design by Neil Gillespie
Website Assistance by William R. Iandolo, Extreme Systems, LLC

Four versions of this dictionary are available:

→ **ISBN: 978-0-9969806-0-9 Paperback, Complete version**
ISBN: 978-0-9969806-1-6 Kindle eBook, Complete version
ISBN: 978-0-9969806-2-3 Kindle eBook, "Condensed" version
ISBN: 978-0-9969806-3-0 Kindle eBook, "Basic" version

Books may be purchased in paperback or electronic form (Kindle eBooks) at Amazon.com or at either of the author's websites, CoachingAmericanSoccer.com and SoccerDictionary.biz

Library of Congress Control Number (Paperback): 2016909422
First Edition: September 2016 – v1.1 September 2017

About this book ...

The ULTIMATE SOCCER DICTIONARY includes definitions for more than 4,000 soccer terms and is available in a softbound edition and as a Kindle eBook. It is also available in two abridged Kindle eBook versions: a "Condensed" version with definitions for over 1,600 terms and a "Basic" version with over 800 terms.

Soccer is widely recognized as ***the most popular sport in the world*** – for players *and* fans. Soccer is one of the ***fastest-growing*** major sports in the United States, for both genders, at all levels – youth, collegiate, and professional. During the past 50 years, the number of soccer players in the U.S. has risen dramatically, from under 100,000 in 1967 to over 13 million today, with more than 25 million enthusiastic fans. ***More than 20% of all American households now include at least one soccer player or avid fan!***

The ULTIMATE SOCCER DICTIONARY of American Terms is the largest and most complete U.S. soccer glossary ever published. Written by John Harves – successful collegiate player, coach, and experienced referee – this dictionary is ***the*** vital resource to help players, coaches, parents, fans, administrators, and journalists learn ***American soccer terminology and current jargon*** and better understand the game and the rules.

What other coaches and experts are saying about this book:

"*The Ultimate Soccer Dictionary* is a great resource for all soccer fanatics, from those just being introduced to the game to the higher education coaches looking for an edge or angle in teaching all components of the game."

- Marc Reeves, Men's Soccer Coach, Elon University

"*The Ultimate Soccer Dictionary* is a must for all youth coaches and parents who really want to learn the game."

- John Sullivan, Recreation and All-Star Coach and former Soccer Club Manager and Referee

"I am astounded by the amount of detail that has gone into this book. Every coach and fan should own one, it will give them insights into the nuances of the game and raise their soccer IQ."

– Jim Bruno, NSCAA National Private School Girls Coach of the Year, Our Lady of Good Counsel High School, Olney, MD

To Will, Tom, Neil and all of my family, friends, players and assistant coaches who have supported my passion.

– John Harves

Photo by
Jeffrey L. Brockman ©

Preface

In addition to being a reference book, this dictionary is intended to help players, coaches, parents, and fans ***enjoy*** soccer more – and ***learn more about the game*** – even while watching matches on TV, during practice sessions, or on game day. It provides brief explanations of words and phrases applied to the outdoor sport of soccer, as used in the United States of America. This book is particularly useful when you hear coaches, advanced players, and TV commentators make references that are unfamiliar to you. **Additional information and detailed explanations for most of these words and phrases are available on the author's website at:**

www.CoachingAmericanSoccer.com

Also, the "Laws of the Game" published by the International Football Association Board (IFAB) is most helpful. The complete version of this dictionary includes a brief outline of the content of these Laws. **The "Laws of the Game" may be found at:**

www.theifab.com

Further, information contained at the International Federation of Association Football (FIFA) is most helpful.
The FIFA website may be found at:

www.fifa.com

Regarding gender equity, when definitions refer to "he" or "she," both "she" and "he" are implied, if applicable.

We welcome your suggestions for additional words or phrases for possible inclusion in future editions (or suggested alternate definitions, hyperlink breaks, or other corrections). We will greatly appreciate your input, "likes and dislikes," comments, and other feedback, which may be submitted to:

HeadCoach@CoachingAmericanSoccer.com

Thanks!

Acknowledgements

Special thanks to:

Neil Gillespie, GillespieConsulting.net, for his personal dedication and extensive involvement in the editing and professional presentation of this book.

William R. Iandolo, Extreme Systems LLC, for his unwavering support and technical assistance with CoachingAmericanSoccer.com from which this book is derived. Also, for the majority of the game photographs used within the book.

Tom Lillard, for recruiting me to coach at Radford University.

Russell Mark Pusateri, RussellPusateri.com, for the photographs included in this book which represent the contact surfaces of the soccer shoe.

Jeffrey L. Brockman, for the Dedication photograph.

With gratitude,

John

Introduction

Welcome to this first edition of **The *ULTIMATE* SOCCER DICTIONARY of American Terms!** I hope your use of this dictionary adds greatly to your enjoyment and your understanding of soccer!

THERE ARE FOUR DIFFERENT VERSIONS OF THIS DICTIONARY:

The four versions of this dictionary are:

1. **This ULTIMATE… (complete version, paperback)**
2. **The ULTIMATE… (complete version, Kindle eBook)**
3. **The "Condensed" ULTIMATE… (Kindle eBook)**
4. **The "Basic" ULTIMATE… (Kindle eBook)**

- ✓ The **COMPLETE** versions – **paperback** or Kindle (over 400 pages) – include more than 4,000 defined terms: ALL "Basic" terms and ALL "Condensed" terms plus about 2,500 additional terms.
- ✓ The "**Condensed**" version has over 1,600 entries (40% of the complete version), which includes ALL the "Basic" terms plus over 800 additional terms.
- ✓ The "**Basic**" version has over 800 defined terms (20% of the complete version).

The Kindle versions provide hundreds of dynamic ***hyperlinks*** that greatly enhance the usefulness of the dictionary. In most instances, **the paperback versions retain the underline**, as a visual cue to the existence of the linked content.

The "**Condensed**" and "**Basic**" Kindle versions are intended to make these ***abridged*** versions of the dictionary ***more affordable*** for as wide an audience as possible – especially for young players! With that goal in mind, we are planning Special Promotions at least twice a year during which we will provide customers with the opportunity to download the "Basic" version for FREE!

Each of these versions may be purchased through the author's websites, CoachingAmericanSoccer.com and SoccerDictionary.biz. All four versions are also available at Amazon.com and at various other websites and book distributors.

SYMBOLS KEY

for symbols used in this dictionary:

▫ "**Quick-Start**" terms: 230 terms, listed in **"Appendix 1" (the "*Quick-Start Guide*")**. Selected from the 800 "BASIC" terms. (In electronic versions, ***hyperlinked*** with Appendix 1.)

■ Terms in the "**BASIC**" version. Includes all "Quick-Start" terms. **(Shaded medium gray.)** ("BASIC" terms are also in the "Condensed" version, so ***both*** symbols appear: ■□.)

□ Terms in the "**Condensed**" version (Shaded light gray.)

► ***On-field Oral Communication*** *(in Appendix 4)*. (In electronic versions, hyperlinked to and from definitions.)

These symbols are intended to help: (a) to facilitate coaches' use of the dictionary for instructional purposes; and (b) to simplify usage among team members who have different versions of this dictionary – e.g., when players using the "Basic" version can't find terminology the coach uses (from the complete version).

Coaches: For beginning players, you may find it helpful to start with "Quick-Start" terms (Appendix 1) ▫. Also, the ***complete*** version shows which terms are in the "Condensed" or "Basic" versions (and which ***are not***). If some of your players own different versions, you may wish to let them know in advance which terms you will be using that are ***not*** in their version.

The dictionary also includes useful tools for teaching new concepts and teamwork to your players, including more than 160 ***On-field Oral Communication*** directives. (See Appendix 4.)

EXAMPLE: If you plan to teach how to use "**Back passes**" and verbal communication ("**Back**"), the ***complete*** dictionary shows entries for:

Back pass, Back-pass ▫ □

To pass the ball to a teammate who is behind the player with the ball.

Back; Drop; or Drop It – ►

► *On-field Oral Communication:* There is a teammate open for a back pass.

However, from the symbols used in these entries, you can see that the ***Oral Communication*** term **Back; Drop; or Drop It** is ***not*** in the "Condensed" or "Basic" versions, so you can adjust your teaching plans for players using those versions.

That brings us to another symbol used in this dictionary: ▶ This symbol ▶ indicates terms related to ***verbal communication:***

"ON-FIELD ORAL COMMUNICATION"

Some of the most useful and helpful entries in this dictionary are those that relate to "***On-field Oral Communication***." All such entries are shown with the symbol "▶." For example:

Far post (1) – ▶

▶ ***On-field Oral Communication:*** Pass or shoot the ball toward the part of the goal farthest from you.

For your convenience, a LIST of more than 160 "*On-field Oral Communication*" terms are included in Appendix 4, HYPERLINKED in electronic versions to each definition (and reverse-linked back to Appendix 4). Players and teams that are able to learn and effectively use these communication skills give themselves a *big advantage!*

Coaches: These terms can help you teach and encourage your players to use verbal communication more effectively during matches, which can contribute to major improvement in team play.

Players: You can improve your team play (and your team's success) by using these oral communication tools during game play (and by recognizing and applying such use by your teammates).

Parents (family, friends, and fans): Please provide your child (and the coach and entire team) with all of your great support and encouragement, for which you will be remembered and appreciated! The better you understand the lingo, the more fun you will have – watching, cheering for your favorite team and players, and enjoying the game! However, for the purposes of this section, please remember: **During game play, "*On-field Oral Communication*" is intended to be used *only by the Coach and the Players!***

Note: This dictionary usually refers to spoken communication as "oral" instead of "verbal" simply because "verbal communication" may be ***either*** written ***or*** spoken, whereas "oral communication" clearly means **"*spoken.*"** Many coaches and players often ***correctly*** refer to spoken communication as "verbal" – as I often do too – but in this dictionary, look for it as: ▶ ***On-field Oral Communication***.

SOCCER "QUICK-START GUIDE" ◘

Each version of this dictionary includes ***ALL*** of the "Quick-Start" terms – more than 230 terms selected (from the 800 BASIC■ terms) ***especially*** to help ***anyone new to the game of soccer*** quickly become familiar with basic soccer terminology. These "Quick-Start" terms are listed together in Appendix 1. ***In the electronic versions of this dictionary, each "Quick-Start" term in Appendix 1 is LINKED to its definition, and each "Quick-Start" term throughout the dictionary is underlined and is indicated by the symbol ◘. From each of these definitions, clicking on the underlined link (with the symbol ◘) will take you to the complete "Quick-Start" list in Appendix 1. Using these links can be a fun and effective way to learn these terms.***

UNFAMILIAR TERMINOLOGY:

Some obscure terms are included in this dictionary that many coaches and players rarely (or never) use. This includes terms that I have come across through the years from various sources, including players, coaches, TV sports commentators, soccer blogs, and elsewhere. The inclusion of such terms is ***not*** intended to promote the use of obscure, archaic terminology. My intent is simply to help soccer fans better understand what they hear (on TV, at practice, or at the game) or read (e.g., on the Internet) – and hopefully enjoy soccer even more!

I hope you really enjoy using this book!

John H.

Table of Contents

(Hyperlinked in Kindle versions)

Academy programs; U.S. Soccer Development Academy

"The Development Academy is a partnership between U.S. Soccer and the top youth clubs around the country to provide the best youth players in the U. S. with an everyday environment designed to produce the next generation of National Team players. The Academy's programming philosophy of increased training, less total games and more competitive games is based on U.S. Soccer's Best Practices utilized by the U-17 U.S. National Team Residency program." – U.S. Soccer; USSF

Accelerate, Acceleration □

Increase in speed from a standing or slow-moving position to a fast run or sprint.

Accident ■□

Collision typically involving two players.

Accumulation of yellow cards

In a competition, a specified number of yellow cards given to a player over a certain number of games leads to a suspension from the next game.

Across the goal, Across the goal mouth ■□

A path of the ball roughly parallel to the end line from one side of the goal to the other.

Acting ■□

Faking having been fouled; diving; flopping.

Active ■□

A player who is demonstrating a high energy level and making the most of the minutes made available to him while playing in a game.

Active duty

Player returns from injury and is available to the team.

Acute angle

Shooting from a difficult angle, from a position outside of the goal post and close to the end line.

Ad boards

Painted or electronic signs surrounding a field used for advertising; dasher boards which keep a ball from going too far out of play.

An extensive glossary for players, coaches, parents, and fans of soccer in the United States

The *ULTIMATE* SOCCER DICTIONARY of American Terms

AARS *(Abbrev.)*
Additional Assistant Referees.

Abandon the game plan
To switch to a different type of attack and/or defense during the course of a match, other than the original plan designed before the start of the match, usually due to going down by a number of goals.

Abandoned match, Abandon the game, Abandonment □
Law 7 of the Laws of the Game. A game which has to be terminated before completion, due to such things as loss of daylight or lightning. Game is to be replayed unless competition rules specify otherwise.

Absent, Absence ■□
Player not available to perform for a team (e.g., due to injury, illness, national team duty, or suspension).

Absorb, Absorb pressure, Absorbing pressure □
With respect to a team's defensive performance – To resist, withstand, and defend against attacks without being scored on.

Academy (Soccer academy)
A formal program of education for soccer players, often in-residence, usually combining traditional schooling with intensive soccer training and instruction, provided by a team or institution, to develop its own players from youth to advanced teams.

NOTE: Page numbering begins here with p.15 to match Kindle's pagination.

SYMBOLS KEY

for symbols used in this dictionary:

▫ "**Quick-Start**" terms: 230 terms, listed in **"Appendix 1"** (the **"*Quick-Start Guide*."**) Selected from the 800 "BASIC" terms. In the electronic versions of this dictionary, these terms are ***hyperlinked to and from*** Appendix 1.

■ Terms in the "**BASIC**" version. Includes all "Quick-Start" terms. **(Shaded medium gray.)** ("BASIC" terms are also in the "Condensed" version, so ***both*** symbols appear: ■□.)

□ Terms in the "**Condensed**" version (Shaded light gray.)

▶ ***On-field Oral Communication*** *(Appendix 4)*.
Each of these terms is listed in Appendix 4. In electronic versions each term is ***hyperlinked to and from*** Appendix 4.

... Table of Contents (continued)

Adaptive compression shoe uppers

The tops of next generation shoes, with "sock-like" features, designed to be extremely light-weight and to uniquely mold to the foot of the wearer.

Added time, Additional time (Allowance for time lost) ◘ □

At the discretion of the referee, playing time is extended at the end of each half for substitutions, injury, time wasting, or other events which caused an unnecessary or excessive loss of playing time during that half.
Commonly referred to as Stoppage Time; Time Added On; includes Injury Time; described in Law 7 of the Laws of the Game.
(Note: "Added Time" is NOT the same as "Extra Time." See: Extra Time.)

Remember: Each "**Quick-Start**" term has this symbol ◘ and in the electronic versions is ***hyperlinked*** to Appendix 1, which lists all these terms together, ***linked back*** to each definition. This can help make it much easier to quickly learn these terms.

Additional Assistant Referees

Discussed in Law 6 of the Laws of the Game, additional assistant referees may help the referee with goal-line outs, if a goal is scored, which team is awarded corner kick or goal kick, and, for a penalty kick, if the goalkeeper moves off the goal line before the kick is taken.

Additional balls

Law 2 of the Laws of the Game, The Ball, permits extra balls to be placed around the field of play as long as their use is under the control of the referee.

Adjustable goals

Soccer goals that are designed to allow for modification to their height and width.

Adjustments □

(1) Changes made by the coach, including substitutions, during play or at halftime, to address offensive or defensive needs observed in a match. (2) Tactical changes made by players during a game, to adapt to new and unexpected challenges, opportunities, or situations.

Administration

All activities, other than coaching, that relate to running or managing a team or soccer organization.

Administrative rules

Those guidelines governing the conduct of the organization that oversees leagues or competitions.

Administrator

League executive officer.

Adult players, Adult soccer leagues

Players, 19 years old or older; matches played by participants 19 years old or older.

Advanced clinic

(1) Intense, short-term, technique-specific programs designed to rapidly develop soccer knowledge and advanced skills;
(2) Similar short-term programs of instruction for referees (e.g., for referees working adult games).

Advancement

For leagues having multiple divisions, there is a procedure for winning teams to move up from lower divisions to higher divisions after a competition has been completed. Contrast with losing teams which move down due to "relegation."

Advancing

(1) Goalkeeper coming out to meet an opponent;
(2) Team moving on in a tournament.

Advantage (1) (playing the advantage) ◘ □

The application of the Advantage Rule by the referee. Generally, when the attacking team has a potential opportunity to advance or score but the opposing team commits a foul that did not alter the course of play, the referee chooses not to call the foul. Calling the foul might otherwise give the infringing team an unfair '**advantage**' by stopping the attack. See: Advantage Rule.

Advantage (2) (statistical advantage: shots, corners, ...) □

In a count or statistical analysis of certain actions in a game, when one team has better results than the other team, they have a statistical advantage related to those actions (e.g., more shots on goal, more assists, fewer fouls, or more big chances).

Advantage (3) (advantage in number of players)

One team has a greater number of players on the field than the other team, usually due to the opponent removing an injured player or having had a player ejected. Example: Due to an injury where an opposing player was not immediately replaced, the team still with eleven players has a "one-man advantage."

Advantage rule, Advantage clause ◘ □

The referee shall refrain from penalizing an infringement of the Laws of the Game when doing so would result in unfairly giving an **'advantage'** to the infringing team. Contained in Law 5 of the Laws of the Game. See: Advantage.

Aerial □

Related to activities occurring while the ball is in the air (and associated with the ball in flight). The flight of, or any activity associated with, the ball when it is in the air.

Aerial battle, Aerial challenge

Two players contest for a ball that is in the air, competing against each other to control the ball.

Aerial game

The strategy and tactics applied by an attacking team to effectively utilize the ball when putting it into the air.

Aerial skills

Ability of a player to properly play the ball when it is in the air.

Aerobic capacity

The level at which a physical activity can be performed by an individual without experiencing oxygen debt.

Aerobic power

Period of performance of a strength activity prior to oxygen debt.

AET, A.E.T., a.e.t. *(Abbrev.)*

"***After*** Extra Time" – Additional time (Added Time) for stoppages (due to injuries, penalties, etc.) or excessive delays, which occurred ***during*** Extra Time (overtime).

AF, A.F. *(Abbrev.)*

Association Football; soccer.

AFC *(Abbrev.)*

Asian Football Confederation; FIFA confederation of nations in Asia.

Affiliated organizations

Administrative bodies recognized by, and under the jurisdiction of, the United States Soccer Federation. See: USSF.

AG *(Abbrev.)*

Artificial Grass; soccer shoe with cleats designed for use on artificial grass.

Again – ▶

▶ ***On-field Oral Communication:*** Repeat a shot, run, or pass. **EXAMPLE:** After your teammate attempts a shot that is deflected back toward herself, you shout, ***"Again!"*** – thus telling her ***not*** to waste time considering other options – such as looking around, passing to a teammate, or dribbling to a new location. Just go ahead and immediately ***take another shot on goal!***

> Remember: Each "***On-field Oral Communication***" term has this symbol ▶ and in the electronic versions is ***hyperlinked*** to Appendix 4, where all of these terms are listed together. Each term is linked ***back*** to its definition, which makes it easier to learn these terms.

Against the run of play; Scoring a goal against the run of play

A team that has been on the defensive for a large portion of a match suddenly scores.

Age groups (U# Age Groupings) ■□

Classification system for youth soccer, based on birth year or birth date, used for age-appropriate competitions. The two approaches commonly used are:
(1) the "calendar-year" system (a.k.a. "birth-year" system), and
(2) the "school year" system.
See: U# - Age Groups
See also: Appendix 6: Age Group Charts

Age-appropriate instruction

Teaching those skills and techniques of soccer that will be understood by players based on their physical and mental development and cognition as they grow up.

Age-group instruction

Programs of learning for the skills and techniques of soccer, from instructional to advanced, based on the chronological age of players; for example, U4, U6, U8, U10, U12, U14, U17, and U19 would each have their own objectives. See: Appendix 6: Age Group Charts

Aggregate, Aggregate goals

Total goals for each team in a home-and-home aggregate-goal competition. Generally, if each team wins one game, the team with the most total goals advances.

Aggression, Aggressive, Aggressor □

Forceful actions made by a player, intended to dominate an opponent.

Aggressive receiving

Player moving quickly to the ball in order to intercept it or collect it, instead of waiting for the ball to come to him.

Agility □

Ability of a player to react and move quickly and easily, under control.

Agility shoe upper

The tops of next generation shoes, with "sock-like" features, designed to be extremely light-weight and to uniquely mold to the foot of the wearer.

Aglet

The end, usually made of plastic, of shoe laces that keeps them from unraveling. Players need to ensure that they remain intact.

Air ball ■□

A pass or kick intentionally lofted or chipped; any ball not on the ground.

Air gauge ■□

Device for measuring air pressure in a ball.

Air horn ■□

Signaling device which may be used to identify halftime or the end of the game when time is not kept by the referee.

Air pressure ■□

The amount of air forced into a ball to keep it inflated; must conform to Law 2 of the Laws of the Game, "The Ball."

Air pump ■□

A device, powered by hand or electricity, used to put air into a ball; requires a ball needle.

Airborne

Player jumping or otherwise leaving his feet to get to a ball; player sent flying through the air after being undercut.

Algarve Cup

Women's tournament conducted in Algarve, Portugal.

Alignment ◘ □

Formation designating the number of backs, midfielders, and forwards, e.g., 4-4-2 from the goal out; the goalkeeper is assumed; always adds up to 10 for full-sides play.

See: Formation.

Remember – You can go to the "**Quick-Start**" list in Appendix 1 simply by clicking on the ***hyperlinked*** term (with the ◘ symbol). Each term is linked back to its definition.

All ■□

Tie; tied score; equal number of goals for both teams; example, one-all is a 1-to-1 tie, either a current or final score.

All ball □

Implies that a tackler did not touch any part of the opponent during a tackle, only the ball (but does not necessarily mean that the tackle was fully legal).

Allowance, Allowance for time lost □

Additional time for time lost; stoppage time; allowance for time lost in accordance with Law 7 of the Laws of the Game.

Also called: Added Time.

All-star

A player selected from among a number of teams by an administrative body for special recognition due to the player's performance during the course of a season; usually identified by position on an all-star team, which may or may not play in an actual all-star game.

All-star game

An actual match utilizing the all-star designees from the teams in a league; may be played between two teams of all-stars or a team of all-stars against some other team.

AM *(Abbrev.)*

Attacking Midfielder; shorthand for the attacking midfielder player position.

Amateur ■□

Any player who is not paid to play the game; a player who does not demonstrate professional training.

Amendments

Changes made each year by the International Football Association Board (IFAB) to the Laws of the Game.

American football

Game most identified with the National Football League (NFL) and widely played throughout the United States. This name is often used to distinguish that game from soccer-football.

American terms

Soccer words and phrases used in the United States by coaches, players, fans, administrators, journalists and commentators.

Amnesty

Wiping out the possible suspension effects of cards received prior to the semi-finals in a tournament; eliminating the effects of any yellow or red cards received in any competition.

Amped, Amped up

Mentally and psychologically prepared to play at the optimum level during a match; psyched; psyched up.

Anaerobic activity

Brief periods of intense exercise performed during oxygen debt (from Greek ***an-*** "without" + ***aer-*** "air," i.e., not dependent on oxygen). Anaerobic exercises are typically intended to develop strength, power, speed, and/or muscle mass.

Analysis

Breakdown of a team or individuals into their component parts, such as system of play, re-starts, and tendencies, in order to capitalize on potential defensive lapses or to defend against offensive threats. Also used to identify areas for improvement or to confirm what was done well. See also: Match Analysis.

Analytics

Data, metrics, or statistics associated with a player, usually aggregated over more than one practice or game; the use of data and statistics to evaluate players.

Anchors

Any of a number of plastic, metal, concrete, or weighted devices designed to keep the backstays of a goal firmly attached to the earth, in order to keep the goals form tipping over; goal anchors.

And back – ►

►***On-field Oral Communication:*** Requests a return pass, as in the second pass of a give-and-go.

Angle of a pass ☐

Direction or path of a pass from a passer in relationship to the touchline, a defender, or a teammate.

Angle of a run ☐

Direction or path of the run of a teammate seeking a pass.

Angle of approach ☐

The direction a defender takes when running to meet an opponent in possession of the ball.

Angle of pursuit

Direction taken by a defender to obtain a proper defensive position against the offensive player he is marking when the offensive player makes a run.

Angle of recovery

Direction taken by a defender to re-establish defensive position against either: (a) An offensive player with the ball who has beaten him; or, (b) Another offensive player due to a defensive switch.

Angles ◘ ☐

Usually associated with the relative position of a shooter to the goal. A goalie coming out to meet a shooter may be "cutting down the angle."

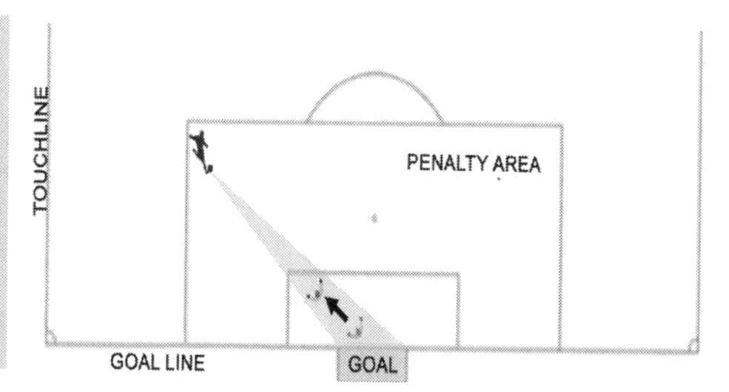

Animation software

Computer graphics video application that allows the user to generate and present moving pictures of soccer players, positions and actions, ball movement, equipment, and plays, for demonstration and instructional purposes.

Ankle (shin guard)

A type of shin guard, with an attached securing mechanism, designed to be held in place by a sock-like sleeve, usually involving a stirrup and ankle protection.

Announcer

A person who orally describes a sports event for television or radio; a person who orally provides information over a loudspeaker at a stadium.

Anticipation

To successfully analyze a situation, usually involving a specific opponent, and to project in advance what is most likely to happen next, thereby being able to react in advance.

Appeal

Usually, an attempt by a player to get the referee to make or change a call; a formal challenge by a team to an organizational body regarding a result or ruling.

Appearances

The number of times a player has been on the field for a team; usually refers to the national team.

Approach (to a PK)

The run up to the ball used just before the kick, including speed and angle.

AR *(Abbrev.)*

Assistant Referee. Law 6 of the Laws of the Game; formerly "linesman." The Assistant Referee assists the Referee with touchline outs, offside, goal-line outs, goals, fouls and other duties.

AR1 *(Abbrev.)*

Assistant Referee number one, assigned to the side of the field with the team benches.

AR2 *(Abbrev.)*

Assistant Referee number two, assigned to the side of the field opposite the team benches.

Arc

The semi-circular line just outside the Penalty Area marking 10-yards from the Penalty Spot; also referred to as the "D" or the "bubble." Penalty Arc.

See: Appendix 3 – Field Diagram.

Area ☐

Typically refers to the Penalty Area; The Area/
("Area" is also sometimes used to refer to the Goal Area, if applicable.)

Armband

Elastic cloth worn on the upper arm by the team captain to designate his position.

Around the edge

Turning around a defender near the end-line and moving toward the goal, after having dribbled the ball along the sideline.

Arriving late

A mistimed tackle, usually resulting in a foul, whereby the defender makes contact after the ball has been touched away.

Artificial surface, Artificial turf ☐

Addressed in Law 1 of the Laws of the Game; a non-grass, synthetic playing surface; must be green; e.g., "AstroTurf™".

Artistic

Deft and clever skills demonstrated by a player with the ball, usually dribbling.

ASRA *(Abbrev.)*

Assistant State Referee Administrator.

Assessment

Evaluation of referee performance.

Assessment of injured player

A stoppage of play by the referee to check on a player who is down on the field due to an apparent injury. Based on an initial review, the referee may summon a trainer or medical personnel from the sideline for a quick examination to see if the player requires treatment. If so, the player is to leave the field, possibly by stretcher.

Assessor

Experienced referee designated to perform assessments of the performance of other referees.

Assignment

Designation of a referee to officiate a match.

Assignor

An individual authorized to designate referees to officiate games.

Assist ◘ □

Recognizes the player that passed the ball to the teammate who scored. In a common point system for attacking prowess, players are awarded two points for a goal and one point for an assist.

Assistant Referees ◘ □

Discussed in Law 6 of the Laws of the Game. Formerly called "linesmen." The Assistant Referees assist the Referee with touchline outs, offside, goal-line outs, goals, fouls and other duties. *Abbrev.*: ARs.

Assistant Referees' lanes, ARs' lanes

Four running spaces, just outside the field of play, used by the Assistant Referees. These include the two portions of shoulders of the field, just outside the touchlines (sidelines), from the halfway line to the corner, and the two portions of the field just outside the goal lines, from one corner to the nearest goalpost.
See: Appendix 3A – Soccer Field Diagram.

Association Football

Formal name for soccer. The term "soccer" is widely recognized to be derived from the word "association" (from the abbreviation "assoc.").

AstroTurf™

Original artificial, synthetic, playing surface used instead of grass.

Athlete

A person who is trained in, or good at, games or exercises that require physical skill, strength, and/or endurance.

Athletic play

Demonstration of strength and agility in the performance of skills. May refer to an individual or a team.

Athletic supporter

Clothing designed to support male genitalia; jock; jockstrap; (may include a "cup" or "athletic cup" for protection, if made of plastic).

Athletic tape □

A narrow, adhesive, woven cloth used to help support joints, prevent injury, or secure bandages.

Athletic, Athleticism □

Vigorous, strong and active.

Attack staller

Generally the first defender, expected to take on the opponent in possession of the ball and delay, jockey, or control him in such a way as to allow more defenders to arrive.

Attack, Attacking ◘ □

Offensive action against the opponent; the team with the ball strives to ultimately obtain a shot on goal by running and passing and getting the ball to a free teammate who can take the shot; collectively, the style or type of play a team is using to score a goal.

Attacker □

Any player on offense actively engaged in trying to score, or help score, a goal.

Attacking and defending box-to-box

A team with the fitness and the willingness to effectively and repeatedly get upfield to attack and back to defend, from the top of one penalty area to the other.

Attacking cone

Imaginary, triangle-shaped portion of the field, similar to a funnel, approximately 30 yards wide starting from about 7 yards outside the penalty area and narrowing to the goalposts.

Attacking first touch

A player with the vision and the execution to intercept or receive a ball and to immediately direct it or pass it into dangerous offensive space.

Attacking goal

The goal currently being attacked. Any reference to the 'attacking goal' refers to the goal currently being attacked, from an offensive perspective. (Similarly, a reference to 'defending goal' takes a defensive perspective, referring to the goal being defended.)

Attacking half □

The half of the field with the goal the opponent's team is defending.

Attacking Midfielder □

Midfield player position expected to play closest to the opponent's goal, be the first to support strikers, and then join in the attack; shorthand for the position is "AM."

Attacking plan

Approach to be used to attack a future opponent; part of a Game Plan.

Attacking soccer, Attacking tendency

The tendency of a team to try to stay on attack; offensive soccer; contrast with defensive soccer or maintaining possession.

Attacking space □

An open area, within the attacking third of the field, that is not otherwise defended and is available for exploitation.

Attacking style

General type of offensive scheme preferred by a coach and implemented by a team. E.g.: long ball, possession, short-passing, or counterattack.

Attacking team ◘ □

The team in possession of the ball.

Attacking third ◘ □

The forty yards of a full-sized field of play in front of the goal at which the offense is trying to score. (Also called the final third or Zone 3.) Coaches commonly characterize the field as divided into three parts: the attacking third, the middle (or transition) third, and the defensive third.

Attacking-minded players □

Individuals who intuitively and effectively press forward to score.

Attempts ■□

Shots taken by a player or team.

Automatic berth

Format of a competition which provides for a team to participate without having to go through a qualifying process, such as a host country.

Automatic booking

A yellow or red card foul or situation required to be applied to a player by the referee according to the Laws of the Game.

Availability □

A player who is present and ready for a coach to use in a game.

Award ■□

Referee decision to call a foul and create a free kick for a team, particularly a penalty kick.

Awareness ■□

A player's perception, knowledge, and understanding of how a match is progressing around him, how he fits into it, and how to properly respond; soccer awareness; game awareness.

Away (1) □

Not playing at home; playing at the opponent's location.

Away (2) – ►

►***On-field Oral Communication:*** Goalkeeper is telling the defensive teammate to kick or head the ball out from goal.
EXAMPLE: The goalie sees a situation where his teammate might typically control a loose ball or perhaps even pass it to the goalie. However, this time, the goalie sees danger from an attacker and simply wants the ball cleared, so he shouts, **"Away!"**
See also: "Clear (2)"

Away Goals Rule

In home-and-home series, a tie-breaking procedure where, when both teams have scored the same number of goals, the team that scored more goals in its away match is declared the winner.

Away kit

Players' uniforms to be worn at away games.

Away leg

Playing at the opponent's location in a home-and-home (home-and-away), or "two-leg," series.

Away-and-to

Potential recipient of a pass first moves away from his teammate who has the ball and then moves toward him; check back.

Axis, Axes (plural)

Reference to the sideline-to-sideline orientation of the soccer field as "horizontal" and the goal-line-to-goal-line orientation as "vertical."

AYSO *(Abbrev.)*

American Youth Soccer Organization.

B *(Abbrev.)*
Back; shorthand for the fullback player position.

Back (1) ◘ □
Back defender; fullback; a player in back defense.
See: Appendix 2: Player Positions.

Back (2) □
In the direction of the goal being defended.

Back (3) – ▶
▶ ***On-field Oral Communication:*** Goalkeeper or defensive organizer is telling defenders to quickly return to their deep defensive positions.

Back across the goal
During an attack, a second pass of the path of the ball roughly parallel to the end line from one side of the goal to the other after having just done so in the other direction.

Back and face – ▶
▶ ***On-field Oral Communication:*** Goalkeeper or defensive organizer is telling teammates to return by sprinting, get goal-side, and then turn around to confront oncoming opponents.

Back and left – ▶
▶ ***On-field Oral Communication:*** Player who is open and available for a back-pass is telling his teammate (who has the ball) where he is located.

Back and right – ▶
▶ ***On-field Oral Communication:*** Player who is open and available for a back-pass is telling his teammate (who has the ball) where he is located.

Back door □
Opposite side of the goal from the ball, when the ball is in the attacking third of the field.

Back four
The back defenders in a four-back formation.

Back four, "Back 4"

Utilizing or referring to a team with four back defenders; four back defenders as a unit; the back four.

Back header

Use of the head by a player to send the ball on a path behind him.

Back heel

A back pass executed by kicking the ball backward with the heel of the foot.

Back in play; Putting it back in play; Putting the ball back in play □

Any re-start after the ball is out of play; commonly a throw-in or a goal kick.

Back line

Group of back defenders playing just ahead of the goalkeeper; the back defenders in any given formation.

Back of the net; In the back of the net □

A goal has been scored; referring to the ball, "It's in the back of the net!"

Back on

A player returns to the field after having previously gone off due to an injury.

Back pass rule, Back-pass to keeper

Violation of Law 12 of the Laws of the Game, Fouls and Misconduct, where the goalkeeper illegally handles a deliberate kick or a throw-in directly from a teammate.

Back pass, Back-pass □ □

To pass the ball to a teammate who is behind the player with the ball.

Back post

The upright of the goal farthest away from the ball; the far post.

Back tackle

An attempt by a defender, coming from behind or beside a dribbler, to dispossess the ball using a motion that takes his foot from behind to the front of the ball.

Back three, "Back 3"

Utilizing or referring to a team with three back defenders; three back defenders as a unit; the back three.

Back to the goal

Striker facing away from the goal he is attacking, usual as he receives the ball.

Back; Drop; or Drop It – ▶

▶ ***On-field Oral Communication:*** There is a teammate open for a back pass.

Back-and-forth ☐

A game which is not dominated by one team or the other; the ball is routinely obtained by the opponent and sent toward the other end of the field.

Back-heel volley

A skill rarely used or attempted in games whereby the ball goes over the kicker's head and then is struck with the heel from behind.

Backing

Foam or synthetic material attached to the front plate of a shin guard to absorb contact and keep the front plate from rubbing against the skin. Cushion.

Backing in

To move backward into an opponent, usually instead of going up for an air ball, thereby committing a foul.

Backpack

Carrying case to be worn on the back using shoulder straps specifically designed to handle soccer gear, often including a mesh attachment to carry a soccer ball.

Backpedal

To retreat or move backward without turning around, generally on the balls of the feet, in order to cover the moves or expected run of an opponent.

Backs ◘ ☐

Players specifically identified in a formation as defenders; back defenders; fullbacks. See: Appendix 2: Player Positions.

Back-side ☐

Weak side; on defense, the side of the field opposite the side with the ball.

Backstays

Supports attached to, and behind, the goal in order to reinforce and maintain the goal's stability and location; may also be used to support the nets.

Backstopper

A term sometimes used to refer to the Goalkeeper.

Backswing, Back swing

The pullback of the leg of a kicker prior to kicking the ball; The articulation of the leg at the knee and hip by a player contracting the hamstring muscles and glutes in order to prepare to kick the ball.

Back-to-defender □

Any offensive player, marked by an opponent, who is facing away from the attacking goal.

Back-to-goal

Any player, usually an attacker in the attacking third, who is facing away from the attacking goal, whether marked or not.

Bad bounce ■□

An incoming ball hops or otherwise moves in an unexpected way just as it contacts the ground in front of a player.

Bad foot, Bad leg

The opposite foot or leg of a naturally right- or left-handed person; weak foot, weak leg.

Bad pass, Bad ball ■□

A pass that is so poorly struck, either in direction or pace, that it is easily intercepted by the defense.

Bad touch ■□

Misplayed ball.

Badge □

Team emblem worn by players on their jerseys; association emblem worn by referees.

Bait

(1) To badger an opponent, usual verbally, into committing an offense; (2) To fake a foul in such a way as to obtain a call from the referee. Also see: <u>Baiting</u>.

Bait the referee

Setting up the referee to call a foul which did not occur.

Baiting

Setting up an opponent to expect a certain move and then using another; setting up an opponent to make them react in an illegal manner.

Balance (1) ◘ □

A team's ability to cover all space on defense; a team's ability to use all available options on attack.

Balance (2) ■□

An individual's ability to maintain his/her center of gravity while performing skills; to shift body mass in order to maintain equilibrium.

Balanced attack □

Ability of a team to offensively go at the opponent's goal in a variety of ways, including dribbling, through balls, chips, fast counters, or crosses, from all parts of the field.

Ball (1) ◘ □

The spherical object of play in the game of soccer; described in Law 2 of the Laws of the Game, "The Ball", including material requirements, dimensions (spherical/circumference), weight, and pressure.

Ball (2) – ► (Calling for the ball) ■□

►On-field Oral Communication:

A player who is not directly covered by a defender yells for his teammate to pass the ball to him.

Ball (3) – ► (Coming to you)

►On-field Oral Communication:

Call to get a teammate's attention, who is concentrating on an opponent, that the ball is nearby or coming to their location soon.

> Remember: Each "***On-field Oral Communication***" term has this symbol ► and in the electronic versions is ***hyperlinked*** to Appendix 4, where all of these terms are listed together. Each term is linked back to its definition, which makes it easier to learn these terms.

Ball and GLT standards

FIFA Quality PRO, FIFA Quality, IMS – International Match Standard.

Ball back

Back pass.

Ball bag ■□

A net or mesh bag of varying sizes sold by soccer-supply stores for carrying a number of inflated soccer balls.

Ball boy / Ball girl ■□

Young people used to provide replacement balls to players during the course of a game when the ball is kicked out of play.

Ball carrier □

The player in immediate possession of the ball; dribbler.

Ball control ■□

The ability of an individual player to keep the ball close to his body and, by his various actions, to place the ball where he wants to and when he wants to.

Ball delivered □

A successful pass.

Ball denial □

The interposition of a defender between an opponent and a passer such that the opponent does not receive the ball.

Ball forward □

To move or pass the ball directly toward the opponent's defense.

Ball gets away □

Due to an unexpected bounce, or due to taking ones eye off the ball, a player misplays the ball and loses control of it.

Ball hop

A bounce, often in an unexpected way.

Ball in play, Ball out of play ■□

Law 9 of the Laws of the Game; the ball is out of play when the whole of the ball goes over the touch line or goal-line, whether on the ground or in the air, and when the referee blows it dead; the ball is still in play if it rebounds back into the field off the goal, the flagposts or the referees, if they are inside the field.

Ball mark ☐

The impression or bruise made in the skin of a player as a result of being struck by a particularly hard ball.

Ball movement ■☐

Successful passes in succession by one team, which maintains possession and probes the defense.

Ball persons ☐

People equally spread outside the perimeter of the game field with extra game balls to be provided when the ball is not easily obtained by players when the ball goes out of bounds; ball boys; ball girls.

Ball rolling off the foot ☐

Due to a momentary loss of control, lack of concentration, or taking one's eye off the ball, the ball slides just to one side of the shoe, keeping the player from performing the next desired skill.

Ball size ■☐

Sizes "1, 2, 3, 4, and 5," from smallest to largest, with Sizes 1 through 4 for youth and Size 5 having the qualities and measurements as described in Law 2 of the Laws of the Game.

Ball too long ☐

A forward pass, often a through-ball, which is hit too hard and goes beyond the intended recipient.

Ball watching ■☐

A player who is observing the action of the game instead of moving into a proper position to react to the dynamics of the match.

Ball work ■☐

Practice, technique and skill with the ball.

Ballistic stretching ☐

A flexibility process intended to lengthen muscles and tendons by the use of sharp bouncing or projection movements. (Not recommended. Can cause injury.) See: Dynamic Stretching.

Ballon d'Or

French for "golden ball" (ball of gold); Annual award to FIFA (professional) player of the year.

Balloon ball □

A light or possibly over-inflated ball that may seem to the players to inordinately float in the air or feel soft when kicked.

Balls of the feet ■□

The front part of the soles of the feet, behind the toes. The actual part of the foot used to support a player's weight when the player has his heels raised off the ground in order to promote proper balance or increase reaction time. Colloquially, the actual part of the foot used when someone says "be on your toes."

Ball-side

A position in which a defender is able to interpose himself between an attacker and the ball as they both chase the ball, going in the same direction.

Banana (...pass, shot, or ball) □

A kick of the ball which imparts spin ("English") causing the ball to curve or "bend" in flight, making the path of the ball look like the curve of that of a banana.

Bang-bang play

An almost instantaneous collision of players and the ball during which the ball usually rebounds or deflects in an unexpected way. (Often occurs near the goal and usually hits a defender's arm or hand without sufficient time to react, thereby not resulting in a foul for handling.)

Bangboard ■□

A solid structure, often made of wood or masonry and usually the size of a goal, which allows a player to kick a ball against it and receive the rebound.

Banner □

Printed or embroidered cloth with the design of the team or organizing body.

Bar ■□

The crossbar of the goal.

Barge ☐

To awkwardly collide with or run into a player (who usually has the ball); to contact an opponent clumsily or to attempt a tackle using little skill, often resulting in a foul being called.

Barricade

More than one player creating a pick.

Baseball throw, Baseball release

After having made a save or otherwise receiving the ball, the goalkeeper throws the ball to his teammate using a motion similar to that of a baseball player; a long goalkeeper release. A.k.a.: Javelin Throw.

Baseline testing

(1) Cognitive assessment of a player if needed for comparison purposes due to a possible concussion;
(2) Skills or fitness assessment of a player to measure future progress.

Battle

Two opposing players contest for the ball.

Be creative

To try unexpected dribbling moves or passes.

Be there – ▶ ☐

▶ ***On-field Oral Communication:*** Encouragement for a teammate to get to a ball or get to a particular spot on the field.

Beat, Beaten (1)

An offensive player with the ball has successfully feinted and gotten around the immediate defender; to get the ball past an opponent by dribbling, passing or shooting.

Beat, Beaten (2)

To have defeated an opponent.

Beating the offside trap

Successfully passing behind defenders who have intentionally moved upfield to try to create a violation of Law 11 of the Laws of the Game, "Offside."

Behind (1) ■☐

Down a goal or more in the score.

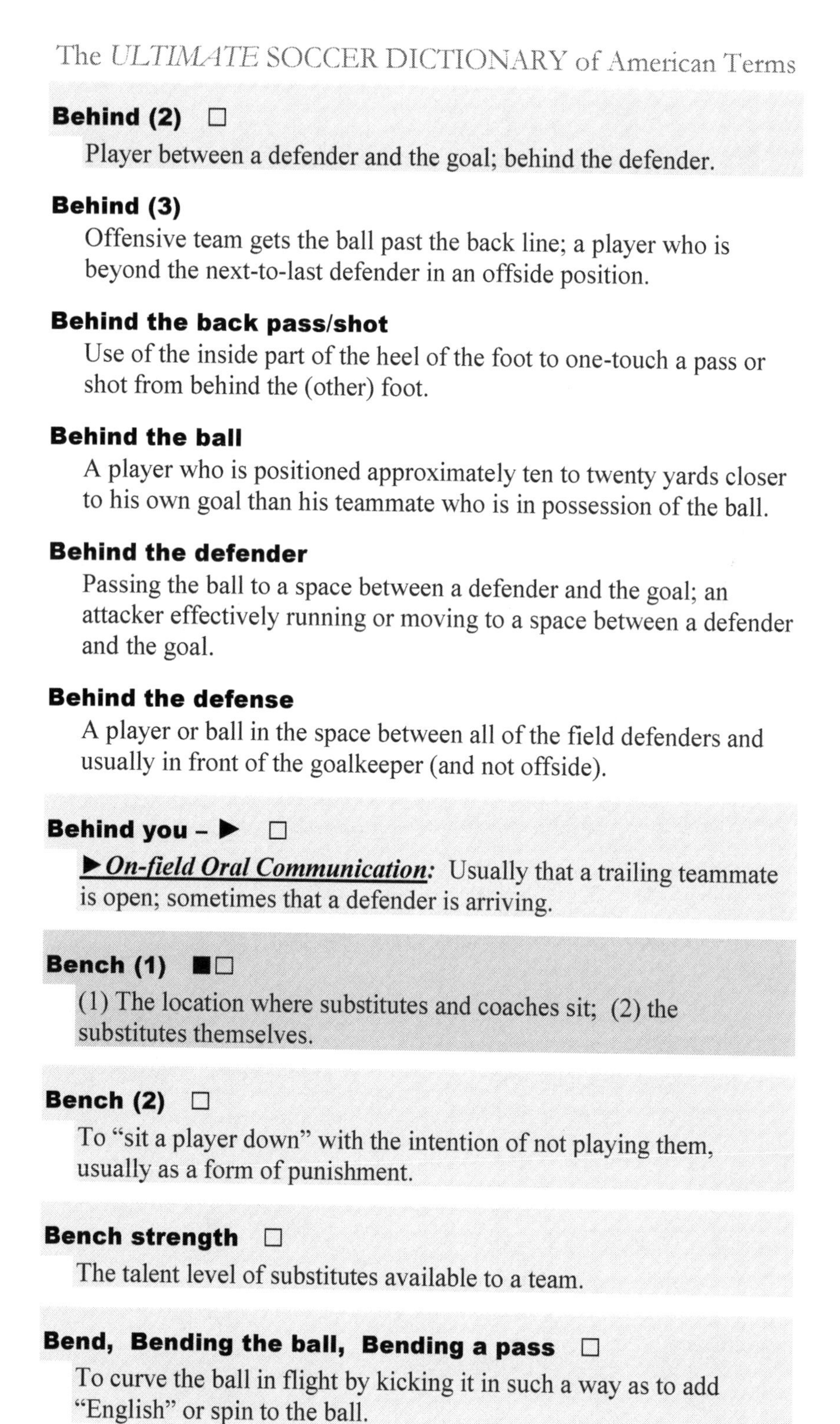

Behind (2) ☐

Player between a defender and the goal; behind the defender.

Behind (3)

Offensive team gets the ball past the back line; a player who is beyond the next-to-last defender in an offside position.

Behind the back pass/shot

Use of the inside part of the heel of the foot to one-touch a pass or shot from behind the (other) foot.

Behind the ball

A player who is positioned approximately ten to twenty yards closer to his own goal than his teammate who is in possession of the ball.

Behind the defender

Passing the ball to a space between a defender and the goal; an attacker effectively running or moving to a space between a defender and the goal.

Behind the defense

A player or ball in the space between all of the field defenders and usually in front of the goalkeeper (and not offside).

Behind you – ► ☐

►***On-field Oral Communication:*** Usually that a trailing teammate is open; sometimes that a defender is arriving.

Bench (1) ■☐

(1) The location where substitutes and coaches sit; (2) the substitutes themselves.

Bench (2) ☐

To "sit a player down" with the intention of not playing them, usually as a form of punishment.

Bench strength ☐

The talent level of substitutes available to a team.

Bend, Bending the ball, Bending a pass ☐

To curve the ball in flight by kicking it in such a way as to add "English" or spin to the ball.

Bending run, Bent run

A run that creates a path that looks like a semi-circle, as made by a player trying to get open for a pass, usually made to open space behind an opponent.

Between the sticks, Between the posts □

The goalkeeper's position in the middle of the goalposts on or just ahead of the goal-line. (A.k.a.: "Between the pipes")

Bib □

A vest (a.k.a. "pinnie"); a cover designating a potential substitute or someone not actively playing in a game.

Bicycle kick ◘ □

A ball skill whereby the non-kicking leg is thrust high into the air in order to raise the path of the kicking leg as it is thrust higher into the air to strike the ball immediately thereafter, above the original level of the head, with the player landing on his shoulders. Also known as an overhead volley or a scissor kick.

Bi-line (Byline, By-line, Bye-line) ◘ □

Either of the two halves of the goal-line (end-line), outside of the goal itself, extending from each goal-post to the corner.

Bite (1) ■□

To be fooled or to react to a fake, feint, or juke by shifting body weight or stabbing at the ball; to take a fake.

Bite (2) ■□

To actually bite an opponent, resulting in an ejection and administrative disciplinary action.

Bladder □

Bag or sack inside a ball that contains air.

Blast □

A particularly hard-hit shot.

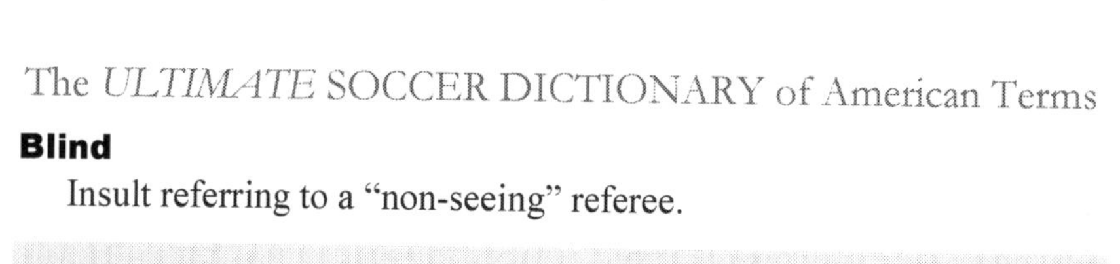

Blind

Insult referring to a "non-seeing" referee.

Blind side □

(1) Usually, the area behind a player which cannot be seen without turning the head;
(2) Sometimes, the side of the field opposite the ball.

Blind-side run

A run by an offensive player, hoping for a pass from a teammate, into the area behind his opponent where his opponent is not looking.

Block tackle

See: Front Block Tackle.

Block, Blocked

A defender, either a field player or the goalie, interposes a part of his body into the path of a shot, resulting in the ball being deflected away from goal.

Blood problem □

Bleeding; bleeding such that a player is required to leave the field to address the blood rule.

Blood rule

Law 5 of the Laws of the Game; a player who is bleeding must promptly leave the field and not may not return until the bleeding has stopped and any affected clothing has been replaced. (Incorporated after the advent of HIV/AIDS.)

Blood stop

Chemical compound used to coagulate blood.

Blow the call □

Referee misses a foul or makes the wrong decision on a foul.

Blow the whistle ■□

Referee stops play, usually to call a foul; referee calls for halftime or full-time.

Blowout □

Dramatic difference in the number of goals scored in a game by one team over the other; an "unwritten rule" of soccer is to stop scoring in a game that has become a blowout.

Blunder □
A very poorly executed skill; a bad mental mistake.

Bobble, Bobbled, Bobbling □
A ball not handled cleanly by the goalkeeper.

Bodied
Legally moved off the ball by strong (should-to-shoulder) body contact.

Body save
Goalkeeper intentionally or unintentionally blocks a close-in, hard shot with his chest.

Bomb
A particularly long and strong shot, punt, or clearance.

Bone bruise
Localized injury to a bone and the sheath surrounding the bone, usually without a fracture, often resulting from a traumatic, direct strike, but may result from repetitive contact, such as on the heel of the foot.

Booked, Booking
Having been given a yellow or red card, the player's number and offense are recorded by the referee.

Boom ball □
A usually not-very desirable or effective style of play in which the ball is kicked as far and as long downfield and the attacking team runs after it.

Boot, Booted; To boot ■□
To kick the ball.

Booter (archaic) □
Soccer player.

Boots □
Old, traditional, name for a player's soccer shoes; cleats.

Bounce, Bounced ■□
The rebound or reflection of a lofted ball after striking the ground.

Boundary, Boundary lines ■☐

The outer-perimeter lines of the field; the goal-lines and the Touchlines; the end-lines and the side-lines.

Bowl, Bowling throw, Bowling release ☐

After a save or otherwise obtaining the ball, the goalkeeper sends it to a teammate along the ground using a motion that looks like that of throwing a bowling ball.

Box out ☐

To legally establish a position as a defender that keeps an opponent from getting directly to a ball.

Box, Boxing ☐

The goalkeeper punches the ball away from the goal usually using just one hand as a fist.

Box; The Box

Unspecified references to "**the box**" usually refer to the Penalty Area – but in some contexts, it may refer to the Goal Area. However, any nonspecific references to "the box" must be used correctly, in the specific context. E.g.:
• **Example #1**: "The Keeper handled the ball outside **the box**." – This clearly refers to the Penalty Area (a.k.a. Penalty Box).
• **Example #2:** "When a goal kick is to be taken: (a) the ball is kicked from any point within **the box**; and, (b) Opponents must remain outside **the box** until the ball is in play." – To be correct (according to the rules): (a) is referring to the Goal Area (a.k.a. Goal Box.); and (b) is referring to the Penalty Area (a.k.a. Penalty Box).

Box-to-box

The area of the field from the top (18-yard line) of one Penalty Area to the other.

Box-to-box midfielder

A midfielder with the endurance to run during a game from the top (18-yard line) of one Penalty Area to defend to the top of the other Penalty Area to attack.

Brace

To score two goals in a game by the same player.

Brave

A goalkeeper who is willing and able to go into a crowd to save or clear a ball, generally implying a degree of risk.

Brazilian drill, Brazilians

A set of practice skill drills using two teammates where one teammate serves the ball to the other for headers, volleys, or other skills, either standing or moving.

Brazilian Soccer

A reference to a style of play that is particularly attractive, clever, and skillful and demonstrates great individual spontaneity.

Break (1) ◘ □

A counter-attack by an opponent marked by speed or swift action; fast break; fast counter.

Break (2); The break ■□

Halftime; Intermission.

Breakaway

A striker with the ball has gotten behind the defense.

Breakdown

A defense loses its ability to mark and defend all of the opponents on attack, usually allowing a player to run free and to shoot and possibly score.

Breaking down

Player whose skills or emotional state is starting to deteriorate; team with a defense that is starting to fail.

Breaking down a defense

Probing passes and runs designed to find weaknesses in a defensive structure.

Breaking down film

Analysis of videos of practice, games, or opponents' games.

Breaks down

Attack falls apart.

Breakthrough

The first goal of a match, usually after an extended period of scoreless play.

Brick hands, Bricks for hands

A goalkeeper who has difficulty holding onto the ball or frequently drops it.

Bring it forward, Bring it up ☐

To move the ball into attacking space.

Bring someone down

To intentionally or unintentionally contact an opponent in such a way that they go to the ground.

Broken down

Injured.

Broken up

A defender stops an attack, usually by intercepting a pass.

Bronze Ball

Designation or award to a person voted the third-best player of a tournament.

Brush

See: Pick (1).

Brutality

Physical assault by one player against another; savage, ruthless or deliberately violent behavior covered under Law 12 of the Laws of the Game.

B-team

Reserve players.

Bubble

The penalty arc; the "D."

Build a counter

To quickly add players to a fast break or counter-attack.

Build from the back

(1) To create a team or formation that starts by placing the strongest players in defense and then moving upfield;
(2) A possession-style of play that brings the ball upfield, and generates numbers, by passing from defenders through the midfield to the strikers.

Build Up, Buildup, Build-up, Build an attack, Build up of

the attack, Building the attack

The ball movement and possession by the attacking team which allows it to involve and send more players forward.

Bulletin board material

Comments made by opponents used to excite or psych up one's own team.

Bumping, Bumped ☐

Usually shoulder to shoulder contact that results in an opponent giving up the ball; sometimes contact, with the ball not present, which alters the path of an opponent.

Bunch, Bunched, Bunching ◘ ☐

Too many players, too close together, to engage in effective passing.

Bundesliga

German premier professional soccer league.
[Pronunciation: BOON-des-LEE-guh]

Bunker, Bunkering

To place a majority of players in defense with little attempt to go on offense or to move the ball forward. (See also: Catenaccio.)

Burn out ☐

In the short term, too tired to continue due to physical exhaustion; in the long term, too much soccer such that a person is no longer excited about playing the game.

Burst ☐

A quick application of speed by an offensive player, usually with the ball.

Bury, Buried, Bury it

To dramatically score by hitting the back of the net with the ball.

Bye-line

See: Bi-line; each of the two parts of the goal-line (end-line), not including the portion between the goalposts, extending from the goalpost to the corner.

By-line, Byline

See: Bi-line; each of the two parts of the goal-line (end-line), not including the portion between the goalposts, extending from the goalpost to the corner.

CAF *(Abbrev.)*
Confederation of African Football; FIFA-recognized confederation of nations in Africa.

Call (1), Calling ◘ □
Any type of oral communications by players on the field during a game; Generally, yelling to a teammate that you are open for a pass.

Call (2) ◘ □
Referee's decision.

Call off
(1) To tell a teammate you are getting or keeping the ball; "mine."
(2) To cancel a game.

Called up
Player is asked to join the next higher level of the team; player is asked to join the national team.

Called, Called off
A game is cancelled, terminated, or postponed due to such things as inclement weather, darkness or fan misbehavior.

Calm finish
The ability to perform the technique necessary to score without getting excited or emotional and possibly blowing the attempt.

Calmness
The ability to perform skills under great pressure, particularly shooting.

Cameo
To make a brief appearance in a game.

Camp (1)
To go to a camp; to attend a program of days dedicated to soccer; summer camp; soccer camp; pre-season practice.

Camp (2), Camp out, Camping out
Generally, a striker setting up at the top of the penalty area with little movement until teammates bring the ball near.

Cannon □

A particularly strong leg or shot.

Cap, Caps ◘ □

One figuratively "awarded" for each time a player plays for his national team in an international game; old term still in common usage; players used to physically receive caps (hats/headgear) for each time they represented their country. The total number of caps equals the total number of international appearances.

Capitalize, Capitalizing

To take advantage of a mistake made by an opponent; to score as a result of a defensive mistake.

Captain □

The member of the team designated as its leader for a match; usually calls the coin toss for the visiting team; upon approval, speaks for the team to the referees; wears the captain's armband during the match. (Skipper.)

Captain's armband

Elastic ring of cloth worn on the upper arm during a match by the team captain, usually a contrasting color to the jersey and containing the letter "C" or the word "Captain."

Carbohydrate loading, Carbs, Carb intake

A dietary technique which stresses the intake of carbohydrate-rich foods for two to five days before a match in order to try to improve performance.

Card ◘ □

To issue a yellow card (caution) or red card (ejection) to a player.

Cards

The actual yellow and red cards carried by the referee.

Careless

Allowing the ball to go to the other team due to not paying enough attention to the proper execution of a pass or reception.

Carried off

Injured player removed from the field on a stretcher by medical personnel.

Carry (1)

To dribble.

Carry (2) – ►

► ***On-field Oral Communication:*** Take the ball (dribble) upfield; i.e., individually attack open space.

Carrying a (yellow) card

A player still playing in a match after having received a Caution.

Carrying the ball

Goalkeeper foul for taking more than six seconds to release the ball from his hands after taking possession.

Catch ■□

Goalkeeper grasps and holds on to the ball with his hands.

Catch up

To run down a ball that is moving away quickly.

Catenaccio

A style of play that heavily emphasizes defense. Italian for "door-bolt" and "chain;" the Catenaccio is a historical approach popularized by the Italian national team which places the majority of field players in defensive positions and looks for a fast break or quick counter-attack for offense. (See also: Bunker); incorporates a "libero" or "sweeper" behind the back line who does not have a direct marking function and double marks or obtains loose balls. [Pronunciation: CAHT-eh-NAH-chyo]

Caught

Whistled for being offside.

Caught flat

Back defenders all in a straight line, right at the moment attackers put a ball past them.

Caught flat-footed □

Defender in a one-on-one situation is not able to effectively react to a dribbler's move due to their weight being heavily placed on the full soles of both feet.

Caught in possession

Dribbler who is unable to move to space or pass the ball is tackled and the rest of the team may not be prepared to quickly go into defense.

Caught looking ☐

Failure to see and react to a developing situation due to watching somewhere or someone else; didn't see a defender arrive.

Caught offside ☐

A player unwittingly is in an offside position when a pass is made to him, or is the victim of an offside trap, such that they are called for offside.

Caught out of position ☐

Goalkeeper is not in the proper place to maximize the chance of a proper save when a shot is taken.

Caught sleeping, Caught napping

Failure to see and react to a developing situation due to watching somewhere or someone else.

Caught square

Back defenders in a straight line, right at the moment attackers put a ball past them.

Caution, Cautionable offenses ◘ ☐

Law 12 of the Laws of the Game; a player is cautioned and shown a yellow card for unsporting behavior, dissent by word or action, persistent infringement of the Laws, delaying the restart of play, failure to respect the required distance when play is restarted with a corner kick, free kick or throw-in, entering or re-entering the field of play without the referee's permission, or deliberately leaving the field of play without the referee's permission.

CB *(Abbrev.)*

Center Back. Shorthand for the center back or center fullback position.

CD *(Abbrev.)*

Central Defender. Shorthand for center fullback or stopper position.

Celebration

An act of exuberance demonstrated by a player or team just after scoring a goal; goal celebration; an "unwritten rule" of soccer is to not engage in a celebration that demeans the opponent.

Center (1) ◘ ☐

To pass the ball into the middle of the field from near the sideline.

Center (2) – ►

►*On-field Oral Communication:* Send the ball in the air or on the ground to the middle of the field.

Center (3)

The imaginary bisector of the field running from one goal to the other. (Not synonymous with "Middle.") See: Center Line (2).

Center Back □

Position name for a middle player of the back defenders; center fullback. See: Appendix 2: Player Positions.

Center backs □

The pair of central defenders, usually in a four-back system; central pairing. See: Appendix 2: Player Positions.

Center circle ■□

Law 1 of the Laws of the Game; the ten-yard-radius circle marked in the center of the field of play, with the radius emanating from the center mark.

Center Forward ■□

Position name for a middle player of the attacking strikers; central striker. See: Appendix 2: Player Positions.

Center Fullback ■□

Position name for the middle player of the back defenders; center back. See: Appendix 2: Player Positions.

Center Halfback ■□

Position name for the middle player of the midfielders; center midfielder. See: Appendix 2: Player Positions.

Center line (1) ■□

Halfway Line; field marking from sideline to sideline (at midfield), dividing the field in half (i.e., into two ends).

Center line (2) □

Imaginary line (the length of the field) from the middle of one goal to the middle of the opposite goal. Divides the field into two sides – left side and right side – dependent upon which goal a team is defending.

Center Mark, Center Spot ■□

Law 1 of the Laws of the Game; the midpoint of the halfway line in the field of play; where a kickoff occurs.

Center midfielders; Central midfielders ■□

Position names for the middle players of the halfbacks, often split as an attacking midfielder and a defensive midfielder.

Center Referee

The Referee; the referee in the middle of the field; Law 5 of the Laws of the Game.

Center Striker, Central striker, Center Forward ■□

Position name for the middle player of the attacking forwards; often a target player on attack. See: Appendix 2: Player Positions.

Center the ball ▫□

To send the ball from near the sideline toward the middle of the field.

Centerback

The position name "Centerback" is sometimes used when a specific Center Back has primary responsibility to control and coordinate the overall team defense (in addition to his regular upfield responsibilities). [Compare with the American Football designation 'quarterback' (even though that term applies to the offense).]

Centerback's in charge – ►

►On-field Oral Communication: Goalkeeper announces that he has relinquished control of the overall defense to the upfield defensive coordinator (if a specific centerback is used).

Centering pass □

Generally, a square pass from the sideline to the middle of the field, usually in the attacking third of the field, and directed to an oncoming striker or attacking midfielder.

Central □

In the middle of the field.

Central back

Position name for a middle player of the back defenders; center fullback.

Central defender ☐

Position name for the back defender directly in front of the goal. See: Appendix 2: Player Positions.

Central pairing

The two center defensive backs playing beside and with each other.

Ceremonies

Any of a number of pre-match activities which may include handshakes with the referees and opponents, exchange of team banners, pictures, and the playing of national anthems.

Certification; Recertification

Annual referee registration and delegation of authority to officiate games.

CF *(Abbrev.)*

Center Forward; shorthand for the center forward position.

CFB *(Abbrev.)*

Center Fullback; shorthand for the center fullback position.

Chaining

Combining a number of dribbling moves, one after the other.

Chalk on your shoes

Old saying to remind a player to stay as wide as possible (closest to or even on the sideline), used when fields were marked with chalk or lime.

Challenge (1) (the challenge, a challenge, to challenge) ☐

A defender takes on or engages an opponent with the ball; attempts a tackle.

Challenge (2) – ►

►On-field Oral Communication: As a supporting defender, this tells a teammate that support in defense has arrived and that a solid attempt to take the ball away may be made. This generally comes shortly after a Jockey or Contain call.

Challenging player

Defender taking on the player with the ball and going in for a tackle.

Chance ☐

An opportunity to shoot or score.

Chances

Multiple opportunities to score.

Change ends ◘ □

In the second half of a match, teams attack the opposite goals from the first half, in accordance with Law 8 of the Laws of the Game.

Change jerseys □

If there is too much similarity in jerseys, one team (usually the home team) is required to switch to a different color. Also applies to goalkeepers.

Change; Changes

Substitution or substitutions; modifications to a team's lineup, formation, or system of play.

Changes at halftime

Substitutions made by a team during the interval.

Changing the point of attack, Change the point of attack

Generally, switching the ball from one side of the field to the other on offense using a series of passes among midfielders and/or back defenders.

Channel, Channeling

Defender moving in such a way as to force a dribbler to move toward the outside of the field or into stronger defense.

Channels

Areas on either side of the field, approximately 15-yards inside of each sideline; open lanes available for passing anywhere in the field, usually between defenders, that parallel the sidelines.

Chaos

The mess created when a ball starts bouncing around among players in front of the goal.

Charge □

To physically contact an opponent, legally or illegally.

Charging (1) ◘ □

Legal contact, shoulder-to-shoulder, either front-to-front or side-to-side.

Charging (2), Charges an opponent illegally

Violation of Law 12 of the Laws of the Game, Fouls and Misconduct; illegal contact resulting in the award of a direct free kick.

Chase; To give chase

The active and usually proper first response to being beaten by an offensive player.

Chasing

Defensive players constantly running behind the player with the ball or offensive players making runs; indication of a breakdown in the defensive system of play or poor technique by defensive players.

Chasing the ball

A defender ineffectively running after the ball as it is being passed around.

Chasing the game

Down at least one goal, team trying to come from behind, generally implying trying to gain possession with some difficulty.

CHB *(Abbrev.)*

Center Halfback; shorthand for the center halfback position.

Cheating, Cheating up, Cheating over

Defensive line or the goalkeeper moving forward or to one side in order to try to gain an advantage before a shot, possibly leaving the other side or over-the-top more vulnerable.

Check – ►

► ***On-field Oral Communication:*** You will likely be a passing option if you move away from your current location (usually toward your teammate with the ball), draw your defender, and then return to the spot you left.

Check away

That portion of a checking run in which a teammate moves away from his teammate with the ball.

Check to, Check back

That portion of a checking run in which a teammate, who has moved away from his teammate with the ball, turns and comes back for a possible pass.

Checking off

See: Checking run.

Checking run

Any of a number of runs by a player trying to set up a passing option for a teammate involving moving in one direction to influence the defender to follow and then quickly changing direction and moving into open space.

Checklists

Device used by coaches to ensure completion of tasks, such as game preparations or teaching skills.

Cheeky

Performance of an unexpected or clever skill; a player with the audacity to pull off the skill.

Chemistry

A strong interaction and mutual attraction among players which results in a higher level of team play.

Chest pass

Use of the chest to re-direct a ball, which has arrived at chest-height, to a teammate.

Chest save

Goalkeeper blocks a shot with his upper body due to proper positioning and insufficient reaction time to use his hands.

Chest trap □

The skill of receiving a ball in the air, taking the pace off the ball by extending and then deflating the chest, and then collecting the ball at the feet in order to make the next move.

Chested down

To make a chest trap to the one's own feet or a chest pass to the feet of a teammate.

Chip (1) ◘ □

A variation of the instep drive in which the foot is pointed out to the side like the head of a golf club and then swept under the midpoint of the ball in order to arc the ball over a defender and place backspin on the ball so that it won't run when it hits the ground.

Chip (2) – ►

► ***On-field Oral Communication:*** Pass the ball over a defender or shoot the ball over the goalkeeper with a chip instep kick.

Chipping

The act of using a chip (i.e., with loft and backspin) to pass or shoot the ball.

Chippy

(1) Unnecessarily combative (as if trying to agitate, annoy, and stir up trouble), e.g., ticking an opponent's heels, barging into opponents, and/or jawing at each other (talking trash), often leading to fouls; (2) A game where behavior has started to deteriorate.

Choice, Choices ☐

The selection of, or the variety of selections available to a player, whether or how to run, shoot, pass, or otherwise perform with the ball; decisions made by a player.

Chop

The act of a dribbler whereby he pivots slightly on one foot in order to turn a leg at the hip and knee to hit the ball from near its opposite side and deflect it beyond a 90-degree angle from its forward path.

Circuit training

The use of a number of stations established around a practice field where each station promotes a different skill or fitness objective; players rotate among the stations.

CK *(Abbrev.)*

Corner Kick.

Claim, Claiming the ball

Goalkeeper moves to collect and secure a ball that was not a shot requiring a save.

Clash

Jersey color conflict; game between two rival teams.

Classic soccer ☐

A level of youth soccer above recreational which usually selects players and plays matches that are as close as possible to the traditional Laws of the Game.

Clean sheet

No goals allowed during a match.

Clean strike

Shot taken without a defender immediately impeding or blocking the shooter.

Clean tackle

A completely legal tackle according to the Laws of the Game and the referee, even if the dribbler goes down to the ground.

Cleaned up

A defender arrives who clears a ball that has been bouncing around dangerously in front of the goal.

Clear (1); To clear ◘ □

A defender kicks the ball long, far and as wide as possible away from goal to end an immediate threat.

Clear (2) – ► □

► ***On-field Oral Communication:*** Get the ball out of danger, away from the goal, immediately. (Tells the defender to kick the ball as far upfield, toward the sideline, and out of bounds if necessary.)

Clear (3)

Points above an opponent in the standings, given an equal number of games played.

Clearance, Clearing, Cleared away

An emergency action to kick the ball away from the defensive goal, as far upfield as possible, toward the sideline, or out of bounds, in order to quickly get the ball out of a dangerous scoring opportunity for the opponent.

Cleared out

Opened up an area for attack.

Clearing off the line □

A defender manages to kick the ball safely away from the goal just before the ball passes completely over the goal-line.

Cleats ◘ □

A player's game shoes with molded or replaceable studs designed to grip the turf; the studs themselves.

Cleats up □

A player who makes a tackle with the sole of the foot (showing the cleats) directed at an opponent. Very dangerous; usually results in a card. Sliding at or tackling an opponent with the soles of the shoe facing directly at him; illegal tackle; violation of Law 12 of the Laws of the Game; studs up.

Clever, Clever run
To sneak in to an open space unexpectedly or without being picked up in order to receive a pass.

Climb one's back
Player jumping up and onto an opponent's shoulders in order to get to a head ball.

Clinic (1) ☐
A one-time demonstration of soccer skills, tactics, or fitness, to an interested group of players or coaches.

Clinic (2); To give a clinic
To demonstrate overwhelming skills and tactics in a match, either as an individual or as a team.

Clinical
To perform any skill in a way that it is coached or exactly as expected.

Clinical goal
A scoring shot deemed to have been a "perfect" shot, performed with great technical competence, which had no chance of being stopped by the goalkeeper.

Clinician
The coach presenting a clinic.

Clip, Clipped feet
Defender running behind a ball carrier taps the heel(s) of the carrier with their foot.

Clogged midfield
(1) A defensive strategy placing a large number of defenders in the middle of the field to disrupt possession and attacks;
(2) Attacking players bunching in the middle of the field and failing to use the space on the wings;
(3) A whole lot of players jammed up in a small space in the center of the field.

Close out the game ☐
To take those actions near the end of a match to ensure victory, usually by maintaining good possession of the ball or taking the ball into the corner to kill time.

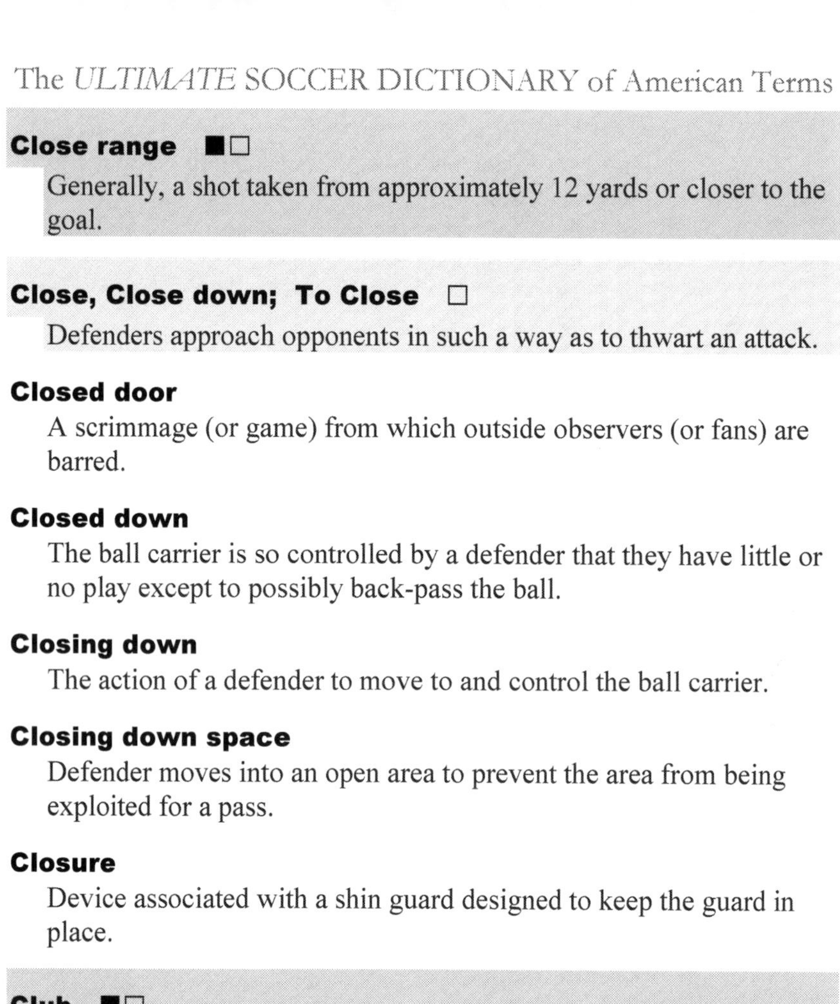

Close range ■□

Generally, a shot taken from approximately 12 yards or closer to the goal.

Close, Close down; To Close □

Defenders approach opponents in such a way as to thwart an attack.

Closed door

A scrimmage (or game) from which outside observers (or fans) are barred.

Closed down

The ball carrier is so controlled by a defender that they have little or no play except to possibly back-pass the ball.

Closing down

The action of a defender to move to and control the ball carrier.

Closing down space

Defender moves into an open area to prevent the area from being exploited for a pass.

Closure

Device associated with a shin guard designed to keep the guard in place.

Club ■□

A soccer team or organization supporting or sponsoring a soccer team or a number of teams.

Club linesmen □

A soccer team or supporting organization provides individuals to act as Assistant Referees when only one Referee is available.

Club World Cup

FIFA-sponsored international competition for the best club teams.

Clumsy

A very poorly executed tackle.

Clumsy touch □

An attempt to receive and control a ball that just winds up bouncing off the player.

CM *(Abbrev.)*

Center Midfielder; shorthand for the center or central midfielder position.

Coach ■□

(1) A trainer or director of an athletic team, teacher; (2) to provide instruction in a technique or skill.

Coach contract

A formal document specifying an agreement between a coach and his players, players' parents, and/or an employer.

Coach notebook, Coach's notebook, Coach files

A formal storage location to keep coaching material, practice plans and documents for reference or future use.

Coach's box, Coaching box, Coaching area ■□

Areas designated near the Halfway Line and outside of the Touchline which delineate the location where coaches must remain during a match; Technical Area.

Coach's Kit

Equipment, clothing or any other devices necessary or used to perform the duties of a coach.

Coachable moment ■□

An opportunity during practice for a coach to stop action and provide brief instruction.

Coaching ■□

Teaching, imparting or training knowledge and experience about a game.

Coaching aids

Any of a number of products or devices to assist a coach in the presentation of material to players, including such things as white boards, electronic screens, and computer software.

Coaching books

Traditional written hardback or softcover texts providing instruction for soccer coaches.

Coaching classes, Coaching courses, Coaching training

Formal instruction made available to coaches to learn how to teach soccer.

Coaching DVDs

Digital Video Disks providing visual and oral instruction for soccer coaches.

Coaching opportunity ■□

See: Coachable moment.

Coaching ovals

Small, colored plastic discs used by coaches to delineate practice space and drills; saucers.

Coaching philosophy

A formal presentation or document outlining the over-arching ideas, creed, or motto, of a coach for his direction of a team or program.

Coaching posts/flags

The same as, or similar to, corner posts/flags, but used for drills or to represent the positions of players.

Coaching school

An organization formally established to provide soccer instruction, often for remuneration, including the USSF and NSCAA.

Coaching sticks

Short, colored rods or poles used by coaches for fitness routines.

Coachspeak

Platitudes or generic phrases sometimes uttered by a coach, which might be of little use either for instruction, inspiration, or other actual benefit to the players or team. (E.g., "Winning isn't everything – It's the only thing!"; "In this game, there is no 2nd place – Either you're 1st, or you're last!". Even Vince Lombardi later improved upon his own sayings: "Winning is ***not*** everything – but making the effort to win ***is***.")

Coast-to-coast

A run by a player, or a player who dribbles the ball, from one end of the field to the other; any activity taking place from one end of the field to the other.

Cock (cocking the kicking leg back; preparing to kick)

To draw back the leg to prepare to kick the ball – like "cocking a gun."

Coerver method (Coerver coaching, Coerver system)

A skill and technique program developed and promoted by Dutch coach Wiel Coerver.

Cognitive testing

Evaluation of a player's ability to think and reason, usually quickly; evaluation of a player's responses following a possible concussion.

Coin toss, Coin flip ◘ □

Law 8 of the Laws of the Game; prior to match, winner of coin toss by referee chooses which goal to attack first; loser takes opening kickoff; teams change ends at halftime; winner of coin toss takes kickoff to start second half.

Collapse diving

Goalkeeper technique whereby a leg is pulled up in order to let gravity get the body down to the ground as quickly as possible.

Collar (sock-like part of shoe)

Fabric sewn to next generation "adaptive compression" soccer cleats, designed to help pull the shoe on.

Collect, Collecting

Initial receipt of a ball, whether on the ground or in the air, in order to get it under control, often as a result of a pass; trap; receive.

College Cup

Term used for the NCAA Division I final four annual championship.

Collision □

Two players running into each other, not necessarily involving a foul.

Combination goals □

Field equipment designed as both soccer and American football goal posts in one unit. Local rules should require that if the ball should hit the American football crossbar or uprights, it is out of play and a corner kick or goal kick be awarded.

Combination play, Combination passes, Combo play □

Multiple passes among players on the same team, usually within a small area, which generally sets up a through pass, a centering pass, or a cross to a teammate in another part of the field.

Come – ►

► ***On-field Oral Communication:*** Tells a teammate who is free with the ball to dribble toward him (with the expectation that the caller is going to then break a run).

Come back – ▶

▶ ***On-field Oral Communication:*** When a defender sees a situation where there are too many teammates who have moved forward to cover potential attackers should the ball change teams, this tells defensive teammates that they must return to mark opponents or cover space.

Come back *(verb),* Comeback *(noun)* ■□

To come from behind and score to tie or win a game; A comeback.

Come off defender/man

To quickly sprint away from an opponent to start a run.

Come out of the tunnel

Players entering the field of play before the start of a match.

Comes on (or in), Comes/goes out (off); Goes on (or in) ■□

Player substitution; one player enters the field after another player leaves. (E.g., "Chris, go in for Matt." "Matt, come off.")

Comes up big, Coming up big □

Goalkeeper makes a particularly strong, physical and significant save.

Comfortable

Striker who does not get nervous and accepts the pressure of playing in front of the goal; defender or goalkeeper who does not get nervous and accepts the pressure of defending in front of the goal.

Comfortable on the ball

Any player exhibiting freedom and relaxation while dribbling.

Coming forward □

Defender moves into the attack.

Coming off the line, Coming off his line □

Goalkeeper leaves the proximity of the goal to go into the field after the ball.

Commentator

Sportscaster reporting on or discussing a soccer match.

Commissioner

An official given the authority to administer the operation of a league or an organization of referees.

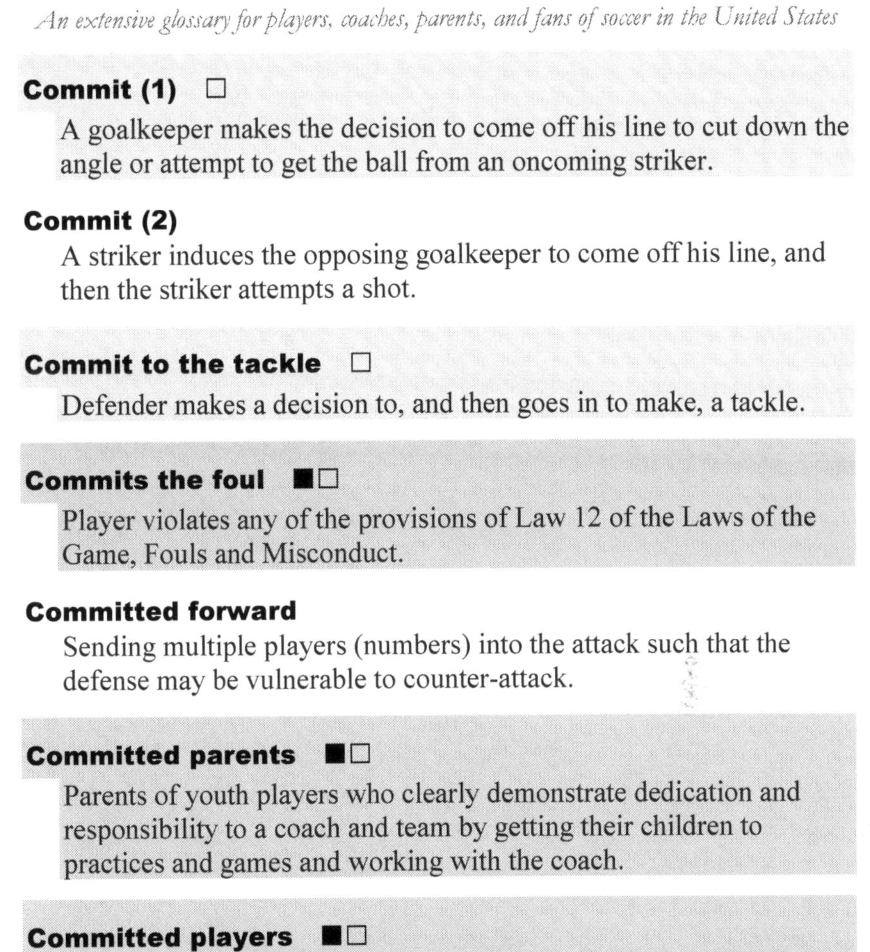

Commit (1) ☐

A goalkeeper makes the decision to come off his line to cut down the angle or attempt to get the ball from an oncoming striker.

Commit (2)

A striker induces the opposing goalkeeper to come off his line, and then the striker attempts a shot.

Commit to the tackle ☐

Defender makes a decision to, and then goes in to make, a tackle.

Commits the foul ■☐

Player violates any of the provisions of Law 12 of the Laws of the Game, Fouls and Misconduct.

Committed forward

Sending multiple players (numbers) into the attack such that the defense may be vulnerable to counter-attack.

Committed parents ■☐

Parents of youth players who clearly demonstrate dedication and responsibility to a coach and team by getting their children to practices and games and working with the coach.

Committed players ■☐

Individuals who clearly demonstrate dedication and responsibility to a coach and team.

Committee

Colloquial expression for the group of attacking players surrounding the ball prior to taking a free kick.

Committing the defender

Action caused by a ball carrier to force a defender to come toward him.

Committing to the challenge ☐

Defender decides to make and then goes in for a tackle.

Communication ■☐

(1) Oral or non-verbal interchange between players or coaches to transmit important information regarding the game;
(2) discussion between any interested parties associated with a team or team activities.

Compact

A tight grouping of players on offense or defense.

Compact defensively

Good coordination among back defenders that keeps gaps from forming.

Competing for positions □

Second-tier players working as hard as possible to get on the field as a starter.

Competition (1) ■□

Opponent; opposing team (or teams).

Competition (2) □

Format of a schedule of play among teams.

Competition Authority

The administrative organization responsible for overseeing a schedule of play among teams.

Competition Rules

Administrative procedures and modifications to the Laws of the Game enacted for the conduct of a tournament of schedule of play for a group of teams.

Competitive soccer ◘ □

Any of a number of forms of organized soccer which is otherwise not recreational or just "kicking around" where game results and standings are maintained.

Complacent, Complacency □

A player or team not playing up to standard because they are satisfied with the status quo of a match, generally having a sizable lead and letting up; Seeming to not care about the result of a match.

Complexion

The overall feeling or tenor of a match.

Compliance

Players and administrators abide by team and league rules.

Composure (player), Composed on the ball

Individual who handles pressure well.

Composure (team) ☐

As a group, the team doesn't over-react or lose its cool after being scored upon.

Compress – ▶

▶ ***On-field Oral Communication:*** Goalkeeper or defensive organizer is directing defenders or the defense to force play toward the sideline.

Compress the field ☐

Defenders push out away from the goal or toward the sidelines in order to restrict the space available to the attacking team.

Compressed

Multiple players close together resulting in a narrowing of space.

Compression-fit shoe uppers

The tops of next generation shoes, with "sock-like" features, designed to be extremely light-weight and to uniquely mold to the foot of the wearer.

Compression shorts

A skin-tight undergarment of an elastic nature worn under game shorts generally intended to support the hamstrings; when worn in games, must be the same color as the game shorts; also known as "slide pants;" protect the upper leg and hips during slide tackles or other contact with the ground.

CONCACAF *(Abbrev.)*

The Confederation of North, Central American and Caribbean Association Football. Division of FIFA confederations which contains the United States.

CONCACAF Gold Cup

Tournament conducted every four years involving the national teams of the CONCACAF confederation; winner competes as the regional representative in the FIFA Confederations Cup.

Concede, Concede a goal, Conceding a goal ☐

To give up a goal; to be scored upon; giving up goals.

Conceding the equalizer

Giving up a goal that allows the other team to tie, usually near the end of a game.

Concentrate

To send a group of players into a relatively small area.

Concentration ■□

The ability to give full attention and thought to the technique that needs to be performed with the ball without being distracted.

Concussion ■□

A damaging injury to the brain, causing a lack of function.

Concussion protocol ■□

Process to be followed if a concussion is suspected.

Condition

A player's fitness level versus the optimum.

Condition of the field □

Status or playability of the pitch.

Conditional play □

Restrictions placed on players during a drill or scrimmage; example: 2-touch; restricted play.

Conditioning ■□

Physical fitness for playing the sport of soccer.

Conditioning coach □

Assistant coach to a team specializing in physical fitness.

Conditions (1) ■□

Aspects of the weather or the field which may affect play.

Conditions (2)

See: Conditional play.

Cone ball

Players getting together to play informal soccer by placing two cones to form small goals at each end of a patch of ground.

Cone cart

Device used to hold and transport practice cones.

Cones ◘ □
Plastic devices, usually available in different colors, used to delineate practice spaces or for drills.

Confederation
Group of soccer associations, recognized by FIFA, which belong to the same continent or relative geographic region (e.g., six Confederations in FIFA: CONMEBOL, AFC, UEFA, CAF, CONCACAF, OFC).

Confederations Cup
FIFA competition between Confederations winners, held every four years, one year before the World Cup.

Confidence ■□
An individual's self-assurance in his/her own skills; a team's self-assurance in its ability to overcome adversity.

Conflict
Two teams wearing the same color jerseys; one team must change. Also applies to goalkeepers.

Conflicted □
Player can't make up his mind about what to do.

Congested (1), Congestion □
Too many players too close together to engage in effective passing.

Congested (2)
A tight schedule with many games close together.

CONMEBOL *(Abbrev.)*
Confederation of South American Football; FIFA-recognized confederation of nations in South America.

Conservative tactics □
A conscious decision on the part of a coach to implement more defense and less attack in a match.

Consistency ■□
A player's ability to perform skills accurately and repetitively; a referee's ability to make the proper call the same way each time in a match.

Consolation match □

Game between the losers of the two semi-final matches of a single-elimination tournament; third-place game.

Constitution

A formal, approved, document guiding the conduct and administration of a league or soccer organization. Example, the Constitution of an Open Soccer League.

Contain – ►

► ***On-field Oral Communication:*** As a supporting defender, this tells a teammate to defend a dribbling opponent by standing ground and confining the opponent to a small space. By not tackling and attempting to take the ball, thereby avoiding the possibility of being beaten, this buys time so the defense can return, reorganize, balance and cover.

Containment

Defender keeping a ball handler in a restricted space.

Contest (1) ***(noun)*** ■□

A game or match.

Contest (2), Contested ***(verb)*** ■□

To challenge or compete for the ball.

Contingencies □

Planning in advance for any number of events, from weather to injuries to playing a man short.

Contract □

(1) An agreement to serve as a paid, professional coach;
(2) Agreement to play as a paid, professional player;
(3) Agreement to play a game;
(4) A document used as a "device" to obtain performance understandings from players or parents.

Control (1), Controlling the ball ◘ □

The ability to receive, collect, and manipulate the ball in the way desired.

Control (2) ☐

The ability of a defender to influence an offensive player to go in a direction he does not want to go.

Control (3), Controlling the game

The ability of the referee to properly apply the Laws of the Game and to ensure that players maintain proper conduct.

Controlled scrimmage

A structured, planned way to practice game situations. Either with one's own team members or with a 'cooperative' opposing team, setting up and practicing game situations (such as offensive and defensive restarts). May also include a period of free play (basically unstructured).

Controlling surface ☐

The part of the body used to receive the ball.

Controlling the match

The ability of a team to maintain possession of the ball and dictate the flow of the game.

Convert, Converted

To score on a penalty kick.

Conviction

Individual who makes a decision and does not hesitate when going for a ball or into a tackle.

Cool down ■☐

Exercises and drills intended to reduce body temperature and heart rate in a controlled manner after a practice session; The time period after a practice used for stretching and to return the body to a resting state.

Cooling break

Administrative stoppage of play, authorized by the referee, to permit players to briefly rest and obtain fluids.

Coordination ☐

(1) General physical ability to perform skills; (2) Understanding between coaches and players on tactics; (3) Agreement between players on how to react to certain situations.

Core conditioning

The overall strength and fitness of the abdomen and chest (torso, trunk) of the body.

Corner (1) ■□

Corner kick.

Corner (2) ■□

To be awarded a corner kick.

Corner (3) ■□

In an area of the field close to a corner flag.

Corner (4) – ▶ ■□

▶ ***On-field Oral Communication:*** Pass the ball in the direction of the offensive near corner of the field, usually directed toward the corner flag.

Remember: Each "***On-field Oral Communication***" term has this symbol ▶ and in the electronic versions is ***hyperlinked*** to Appendix 4, where all of these terms are listed together, Each term is ***hyperlinked back*** to its definition.

Corner Arc

Law 1 of the Laws of the Game; a quarter circle with a radius of one yard from the corner drawn inside the field of play from goal-line to touch line.

Corner flag bag

Container for carrying a set of four corner posts.

Corner flag, Corner flagposts, Corner posts; Flags ■□

See: Flagposts.

Corner Kick ■□

Law 17 of the Laws of the Game; a re-start awarded when the whole of the ball passes over the goal-line either on the ground or in the air having last touched a player of the defending team (as long as a goal has not been scored in accordance with Law 10); taken from the Corner Arc nearest to the point where the ball crossed the goal-line.

Corner kick defense

The tactical approach and placement of players used to defend an opponent's corner kick.

Corner kick mark, optional

Law 1 of the Laws of the Game; marks may be made just outside the field of play at right angles to the goal-lines and touch lines 10 yards from each corner arc; helps referee and assistant referees ensure that defenders are the proper distance away from a corner kick.

Corner kick offense

The tactical approach and placement of players used to try to score a goal from a corner kick.

Corner kick options

Tactical choices available to a team or player on how to execute a particular corner kick; includes "near post," "far post," etc.

Corner taker, Corner kick taker, Corner kick specialist

A player designated to take corner kicks under certain circumstances.

Count-down clock ☐

Match timing device which starts at full time and runs to zero; may be halted temporarily for stoppages.

Counter, Countering, Counter attack ☐

A defending team obtains possession of the ball and swiftly transitions to offense.

Courtesy

Sportsmanship of kicking a ball out when an opponent is injured and then the other team giving it back on the ensuing throw-in.

Cover ☐

(1) To mark an opponent defensively. (2) To get on the goal-line to backstop the goalkeeper when he comes out. (3) To fill open space defensively.

Cover the net, Cover the goal ☐

One or more defenders goes back to the goal-line, between the uprights of the goal, when the goalkeeper goes out to try to make a save, in order to try to stop the ball if it gets past the keeper.

Coverage

Sufficient number of players to defend the space and the attackers in front of the goal.

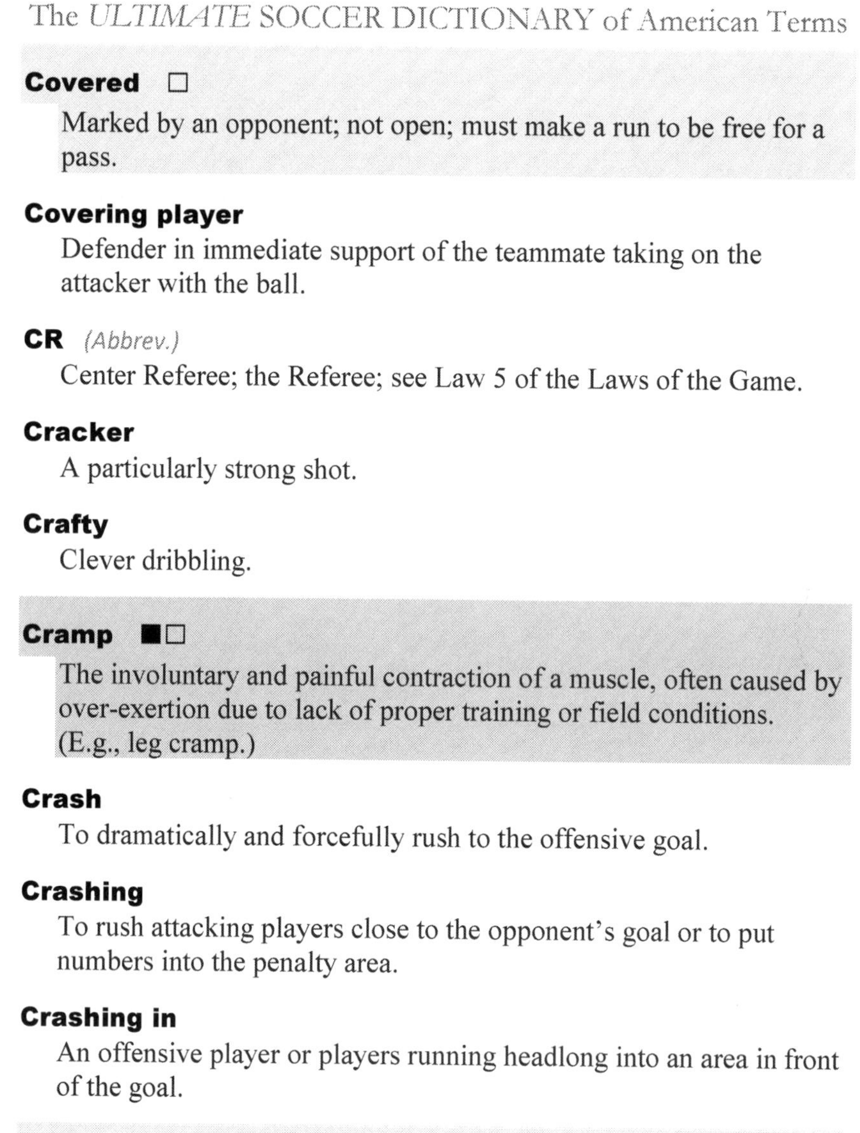

Covered □

Marked by an opponent; not open; must make a run to be free for a pass.

Covering player

Defender in immediate support of the teammate taking on the attacker with the ball.

CR *(Abbrev.)*

Center Referee; the Referee; see Law 5 of the Laws of the Game.

Cracker

A particularly strong shot.

Crafty

Clever dribbling.

Cramp ■□

The involuntary and painful contraction of a muscle, often caused by over-exertion due to lack of proper training or field conditions. (E.g., leg cramp.)

Crash

To dramatically and forcefully rush to the offensive goal.

Crashing

To rush attacking players close to the opponent's goal or to put numbers into the penalty area.

Crashing in

An offensive player or players running headlong into an area in front of the goal.

Create, Creating chances, Create opportunities □

To make a move or a run which generates an opportunity to shoot or score.

Creating space ■□

Ball movement or player runs which influence defenders to move to a certain location so that an area is vacated which can then be exploited on attack.

Creative play

Clever, innovative, or unexpected movement of the ball by a team.

Creativity

Clever, innovative, or unexpected movement of the ball by a player.

Creep up, Creeping up

Back defenders moving farther upfield than usual in an effort to support the offense, which may create space behind them which could be exploited by the opponent.

Crest

Team badge worn on a jersey.

Criticism

Coaching delivered and received in an unconstructive manner.

Cross (1), Crossing ◘ □

The use of an instep drive kick to pass the ball from an outer area of the field into the middle of the field in front of the offensive goal in order to try to create an opportunity for a shot; includes kicks to teammates or locations, far post, near post, etc.

Cross (2) – ▶ ■□

▶ ***On-field Oral Communication:*** Send the ball in the air to the center, to the opposite field, or to the opposite outer corner of the penalty area.

Crossbar □

Law 1 of the Laws of the Game; horizontal component of the goal; sits atop the two goalposts.

Cross-field pass

Sending the ball long from one side of the field to the other.

Cross-over

See: Offensive switch.

Crossover run

Two players making an offensive switch, with or without the ball, in order to create a passing opportunity.

Crown

The slightly higher elevation of the middle of the field along its length, with the two sideline areas slightly lower (e.g., by perhaps 12” or more), to allow for drainage.

Cruel game

Sometimes in soccer, things happen where the better team does not win; an incorrect referee's decision that improperly influences the outcome of a match.

Crumb rubber

Infill of small pellets, made from used tires, placed within an artificial surface to absorb shock.

Crunches

An exercise designed to strengthen the abdominal muscles using fast, intense contractions through a short range of motion.

Cruyff

Soccer ball dribbling move created and used by Dutch player Johan Cruyff.

CS *(Abbrev.)*

Center Striker or Central Striker; shorthand for the center striker or central striker position.

Cues

Subtle movements or actions by an offensive player which may tip off a defender about what the offensive player is going to do next.

Cup

(1) Trophy for a tournament; (2) See also: Athletic Supporter (plastic apparel to protect male genitalia).

Curl

Spin (a.k.a. "English") imparted to the ball by a player, causing the trajectory of the ball to curve ("bend," i.e., hook or slice) while in flight.

Curl it in

To kick a bending ball to the area in front of the goal.

Curled

To have shot, passed, or otherwise kicked a ball with spin on it such that it curves in flight.

Curled in

To pass a ball in the air with spin on it such that is curves toward the goal.

Curls

Exercises designed to strengthen various muscles using slow, deliberate contractions through the full range of motion. Abdominal curls mainly work the abdominal muscles. Leg curls mainly work the hamstrings (and the calves). Arm curls mainly work the biceps.

Curving pass

Curving, bending, or putting "English" on the ball so that is goes around a defender to a teammate.

Curving the ball

Use of the outside or inside portions the instep during an instep drive kick to impart spin or "English" to the ball so that it arcs left or right in flight; see Banana, Bending.

Cushion (1), Cushioning the ball ☐

The act of taking the pace off the ball while receiving it.

Cushion (2) ☐

Having a 2-goal lead or more.

Cushion (3)

Foam or synthetic material attached to the front plate of a shin guard to absorb contact and keep the front plate from rubbing against the skin. Backing.

Cut

(1) To make a run or move in a significantly different direction;
(2) To chop the ball.

Cut back

To pass to a trailing teammate, usually from the end-line.

Cut inside

To make a sharp turn and quick run toward the middle of the field, usually around the penalty area.

Cut it back

To use the "chop" feature in dribbling to direct the ball beyond a 90-degree angle.

Cut it off – ►

►***On-field Oral Communication:*** Tells a teammate to intercept an opponent's pass (because he has coverage).

Cut off ☐

Intercept a pass; a pass is intercepted; a player is kept from receiving a ball.

Cut outside

To make a run toward the sideline of the field.

Cutback (1)

See: Chop. A type of dribbling soccer move.

Cutback (2)

A cross.

Cuts (1) ☐

Fakes, feints or sharp lateral moves; a group of tryout players being released from a team.

Cuts (2)

The release of current or try-out players prior to finalizing a team roster.

Cutting down the angle; Narrowing the angle ☐

The act of the goalkeeper coming off his line toward an oncoming dribbler in order to reduce the amount of the goal available for a shot.

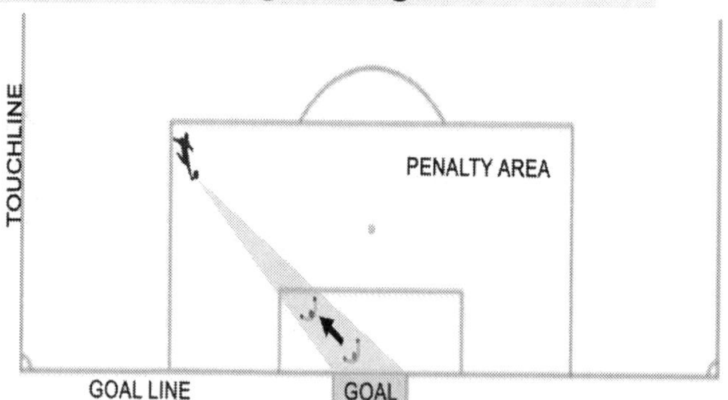

Cutting it back

A dribbler originally going down the touchline turns the ball and heads toward the middle of the field.

Cutting off the passing lane

A defender recognizes the existence of, and moves into, space which the opponent could have exploited to get the ball to a runner.

D (1) *(Abbrev.)*
Defense; shorthand for defense or a defender.

D (2) *(Abbrev.)*
Draw; shorthand for a tie or a number of ties.

D (penalty arc) *(Abbrev./Symbol)*
Law 1 of the Laws of the Game; that portion of a circle with a radius of ten yards marked on the field outside the penalty area from the penalty spot; looks like the capital letter "D" of the alphabet when combined with the intersecting line of the penalty area.

Dance
Dribbler moving on or around a ball with repetitive foot moves that look like dancing.

Danger area, Danger zone
Area immediately in front of the goal from which it seems most goals are scored.

Dangerous ☐
Creating a situation that could result in a possible shot on goal.

Dangerous attackers
Generally, opponents who are currently residing in the Danger Zone.

Dangerous cross ☐
A well-struck cross directed toward multiple teammates in front of the goal.

Dangerous play ◘ ☐
Law 12 of the Laws of the Game; generally kicking too high, heading too low or failing to get up when on the turf and engaged with an opponent; results in an indirect free kick.

Dasher boards
Indoors, walls that keep the ball in play. Outdoors, low barricades – mostly containing advertising – outside of the field of play that restrain the ball from going too far away from the perimeter lines.

Data Collection

(1) Gathering and measuring pertinent information about opposing coaches, players and teams as part of scouting;
(2) Gathering pertinent information about one's own players as part of making improvements.

Date of game □

The actual calendar date a match is played.

Dead ball ◘ □

The referee has blown his whistle and stopped play.

Dead leg, Dead legs

Showing no strength in the leg or legs due to injury or exhaustion.

Dead-ball situations

The initiation of a restart by the offensive team after a stoppage of play, and the response to it by the defensive team, based on the location of the ball and the players on the field.

Dead-ball specialist

A player who is particularly good at taking free kicks, especially closer to the goal when there is a better chance of scoring directly.

Deadening the ball

Taking the pace off the ball when receiving it.

Debut

The first time a player plays in a match for a particular team, usually the national team.

Deceive

To intentionally try to mislead or trick the referee.

Decision; No decision □

A call, or the lack of a call, given on the part of the referee.

Decisions

The choices a player makes associated with all aspects of a game.

Decisive □

Goalkeeper making a quick decision and a strong move to go for the ball; striker making a quick decision and taking a fast shot.

Deck; On the deck

The playing surface; to keep the ball in contact with the ground.

Decoy

A player specifically placed, usually during a free kick near the goal, who defenders might reasonably expect to receive the ball, but who will not; a player designated to attract defenders away from the ball.

Decoy call

Oral communication intended to influence the actions of an opponent, such as calling for the ball in order to draw a defender instead of actually expecting to receive a pass.

Decoy run

A run made by a member of the attacking team, intended to draw a defender toward the runner (and away from the ball handler), creating more space and opportunity for the intended attack – i.e., allowing the ball handler to more-easily attack or to pass to a (now-more-open) attacking teammate. See: Creating Space.

Deducted

Points administratively removed from a team in the standings due to misconduct.

Deep

Sending the ball long and far into the attacking third of the field; attackers setting up well into the attacking third with the ball far away; defenders setting up well into the defensive third with the ball far away. (Contextual.)

Deep Corner

A corner kick sent well to the opposite side of the goal from the corner from which it was taken.

Deep throw in ☐

A long (offensive) throw-in going well into the Penalty Area, usually taken from within 18-yards of the corner flag.

Deep-lying midfielder

Usually a central, defensive midfielder who may join an attack under certain conditions.

Defective ball, replacement of

Law 2 of the Laws of the Game; stop match, obtain suitable replacement; if during field play, restart with drop ball; otherwise with appropriate restart, e.g., throw-in.

Defend deep

Defenders staying closer to their own goal.

Defend, Defending ◘ □

To keep the opponent from putting the ball in your goal; to place players on the field and have them move in a way to keep the other team from scoring.

Defender arriving or closing late

Mistimed tackle, usually resulting in a foul.

Defender getting turned

Offensive player gets around a defender such that the defender must chase back toward their goal.

Defenders ◘ □

Any or all of the players trying to stop an attack; generally, the goalkeeper, the fullbacks, and the defensive midfielders.

Defending champion, Defending their title

The tournament or cup winner from the previous season or competition.

Defending plan

That part of an overall Game Plan designed to defend against the players and attacking scheme of a specific opponent.

Defending soccer, Defending tendency

The tendency of a team to stay on defense; defensive soccer searching for counter attacks for offense; contrast with attacking soccer or maintaining possession.

Defending team ◘ □

Team not in possession of the ball.

Defense, Defensive ◘ □

Collectively, the style or type of play a team is using to protect its goal.

Defensive containment

The ability of a team to keep the opponents far enough away from their own goal so that they can't get off good shots.

Defensive half □

That half of the field of play containing the goal that a team is defending.

Defensive header □

A head ball struck by a defender which sends the ball away from the goal.

Defensive midfielder ■□

A player designated in a formation (or system of play) who plays in a midfield position but whose primary responsibilities are defensive in nature. See: Appendix 2: Player Positions.

Defensive Midfielders □

Pairing or multiple central midfield positions occupied by players in a system of play where they rarely go into the attack. See: Appendix 2: Player Positions.

Defensive Organizer

A defender, usually the goalkeeper or the center fullback depending on the position of the team on the field, responsible for providing instruction to ensure opponents are covered and to maintain defensive integrity.

Defensive pressure ■□

The amount of force applied to respond to or repel an attack. Generally ranges from hard, going immediately to take the ball and tightly marking opponents, to soft where defenders give ground.

Defensive stance

Body position of a defender going against a dribbler where weight is equally distributed on the balls of the feet, knees are bent for quick reaction, distance is close to occupy the dribbler but not so close to be beaten, and a lead foot is closer to the midline of the field.

Defensive style

General type of defensive scheme preferred by a coach and implemented by a team, for example: zone versus man-to-man defense.

Defensive switch

An offensive player beats a defender, causing a teammate of the defender to have to cover his man, resulting in the original defender covering the teammate's man, effectively exchanging positions.

Defensive third ■□

The one-third of the field closest to the goal the team is defending.

Defensive transition

The switch to defense that a team must make immediately upon losing the ball to the opponent.

Defensive vulnerability

Gaps or weaknesses in a team's defense that can be exploited.

Defensive zone

The area of the field that a defender is assigned to cover in a zone defense.

Deficit

The number of goals by which a team is behind in a match.

Deflate ■□

To release or lose air from inside a ball.

Deflection, Deflected

The change in the path of the ball after it strikes, rebounds or bounces off of a player, usually a defender.

Dehydration ■□

Failure to take in enough fluids to allow for proper sweating. NOTE: It is vitally important to stay properly hydrated during all vigorous exercise and activity.

Deke

To fake, feint or juke while in possession of the ball.

Delaying □

Defensive techniques used to slow down a dribbler.

Delaying the restart of play

Cautionable, yellow card offense; violation of Law 12 of the Laws of the Game.

Deliberate hand ball □

Intentional handling of the ball in violation of Law 12 of the Laws of the Game, usually calculated to kill an attack; based on circumstances, may result in a yellow card or red card, in addition to a direct free kick.

Deliberately leaving

Deliberately leaving the field of play without the referee's permission; Violation of Law 12 of the Laws of the Game; Cautionable, yellow card offense.

Deliver, Delivery, Deliver the ball, Delivery service
A service or pass to a teammate that attempts to optimize his opportunity to shoot.

Demands of the Game ☐
Includes such elements as dedicated time, fitness, skills, tactical understanding, and motivation.

Demonstration, Demonstrate ☐
The physical or visual act of showing players how to perform a skill or technique.

Demonstrator, Demonstrators
Person or persons who show players how to perform a skill or technique; may be a coach or a player.

Denied ☐
A shot which appeared to have a good chance of scoring is stopped by the goalkeeper.

Deny service, Deny shot
Defender is able to block the ball, intercept the ball, or otherwise keep the ball carrier from passing or shooting when they want to.

Deny, Delay, Destroy
The so-called "Three D's of Defense:" Intercept or cut off the ball, otherwise slow down the attack, then kill the attack by getting the ball.

Denying an obvious goal-scoring opportunity
A violation of Law 12 of the Laws of the Game, "Fouls and Misconduct," where a defender deliberately handles the ball, or holds, pulls, pushes, or charges an opponent without attempting to play the ball or having no possibility to play the ball, and stops the play or the opponent when, in the opinion of the referee, the attacker had a high chance of making a goal; DOGSO.

Depth ☐
A team with substitutes who are almost as skilled and talented as its starters.

Depth in defense
Multiple layers of defenders in a system of play.

Designated home team, Designated away team ☐

When games are played on a common-use field, teams are designated as "home" and "away" for such things as which jerseys to wear and who calls the coin toss.

Desperation defending

As a team, defensive players sprinting to get goal-side or make tackles after being overwhelmed by numbers of attackers or after having been beaten by a fast break; as a team, bunkering to try to overcome waves of attack while attempting to run out the clock.

Determining the Outcome of a Match

Law 10 of the Laws of the Game.

Development

(1) An unexpected occurrence during a match;
(2) Player progress.

Development Academy

U. S. Soccer program to identify and school youth players for national teams.

Developmental team; B team

An organization's group of feeder players, usually younger, who are working to be promoted to the top team.

DFK *(Abbrev.)*

Direct Free Kick.

Diagonal ball ☐

An angled pass which is neither perpendicular ("square") to the sideline nor parallel to ("down") the sideline.

Diagonal defense

A system of positioning a series of defenders along an imaginary line, angled backward from one sideline to the other with the lead defender closest to the ball, allowing each person in turn to provide support in defense.

Diagonal run ☐

An angled run by an offensive player without the ball which is neither perpendicular ("square") to the sideline nor parallel to ("down") the sideline.

Diagonal System of control

Traditional three-man approach to officiating a game, using a center referee, who runs inside the field generally from the outside corner of one Penalty Area to the corresponding outside corner of the other Penalty Area, and two assistant referees.

Diagonal, on the diagonal

A positioning of defensive players on an imaginary line, running into the field approximately 45-degrees to the ball handler and toward the defensive goal, which provides for defensive support should the first defender be beaten or the ball passed.

Diagram, to diagram

Coach shows player positions, system of play, a drill, and/or player movement on a chart, board, paper, or electronic screen.

Diamond formation

Certain shape of midfielders within a system of play, sometimes designated as the lead, trail, right and left, that looks like four points of a diamond.

Diamond, Diamond midfield

Part of a formation in which four midfielders are positioned at four points, like a diamond, as lead, trail, left, and right.

Dictating play ☐

A team which is consistently retaining possession and winning the ball such that the opponent has few opportunities to go on attack.

Dictating the speed of play

A team which is consistently maintaining possession determines whether the runs being made and the pace of the ball will be fast or slow.

Die, Dying

(1) The unexpected stop of a moving ball, usually in a water puddle; (2) Poor play due to exhaustion.

Difficult conditions ☐

Aspects of a very challenging set of circumstances surrounding a game, usually involving an away match, a hostile crowd, and a poorly-maintained field of play.

Dig

A defender's attempt to dislodge the ball from an opponent, usually by trying to get under it with the toes of the foot and pulling it upward.

Digging the ball out of the corner

Dribbler who seems trapped by two defenders next to the corner flag is able to escape.

Dimensions ■□

The length and width of the field of play; Law 1 of the Laws of the Game. See: Appendix 3: Field Diagram.

Dink

A soft chip pass.

Dip, Dips, Dipping ball (due to spin)

As a result of top-spin being applied to be ball at the time of a shot, the ball drops or dives in flight as it approaches the goal.

Diploma program

Graduated series of certificates offered by the NSCAA as a result of successful completion of training courses.

Dipping; Ball dipping

The flight of a shot taken with topspin which causes the ball to dive down toward the ground.

Direct Free Kick ■□

Law 13 of the Laws of the Game. A re-start taken as a result of certain fouls. A goal may be scored directly from the kick, without the ball being touched by any other player.

Direct kick ■□

See: Direct Free Kick.

Direct play

An attacking style which promotes the use of long passes, through balls, and attacks straight at the opponent's goal.

Direct red card

A player is ejected from a match for an egregious foul without having first received a yellow card (caution).

Direct score

To score a goal by kicking the ball from a direct free kick, without the ball being touched by anyone other than the kicker.

Direct score corner kick

To score a goal by kicking the ball from a corner kick without the ball being touched by anyone other than the kicker.
A.k.a.: "Olympic goal."

Direction of attack □

The movement of play away from the goal a team is defending.

Dirty

A player or team exhibiting constant fouling.

Dirty match

A team or both teams exhibiting constant fouling during the course of a game.

Dirty work

Generally, the unheralded play of a defensive midfielder, effectively stopping attacks and initiating counter-attacks.

Disallowed goal, Disallowed, Disallow □

An apparent score called back by the Referee due to the call of an infraction.

Disappearing spray

Liquid used by referees at the time of a free kick to mark the location of the ball and a line 10-yards away from the ball, which evaporates shortly after the kick is taken.

Disappointment, Disappointed ■□

A player's frustration – typically due to failed expectations (e.g., in not successfully scoring on an easy, open shot).

Disc holder

A strap or device for stacking and carrying practice discs.

Disciplinary record

The official administrative tracking of a player's yellow and red cards, or other misconduct, and the associated penalties.

Discretion

Judgment by the referee or another match official used when making a decision.

Discipline (1) ■□

Mental control.

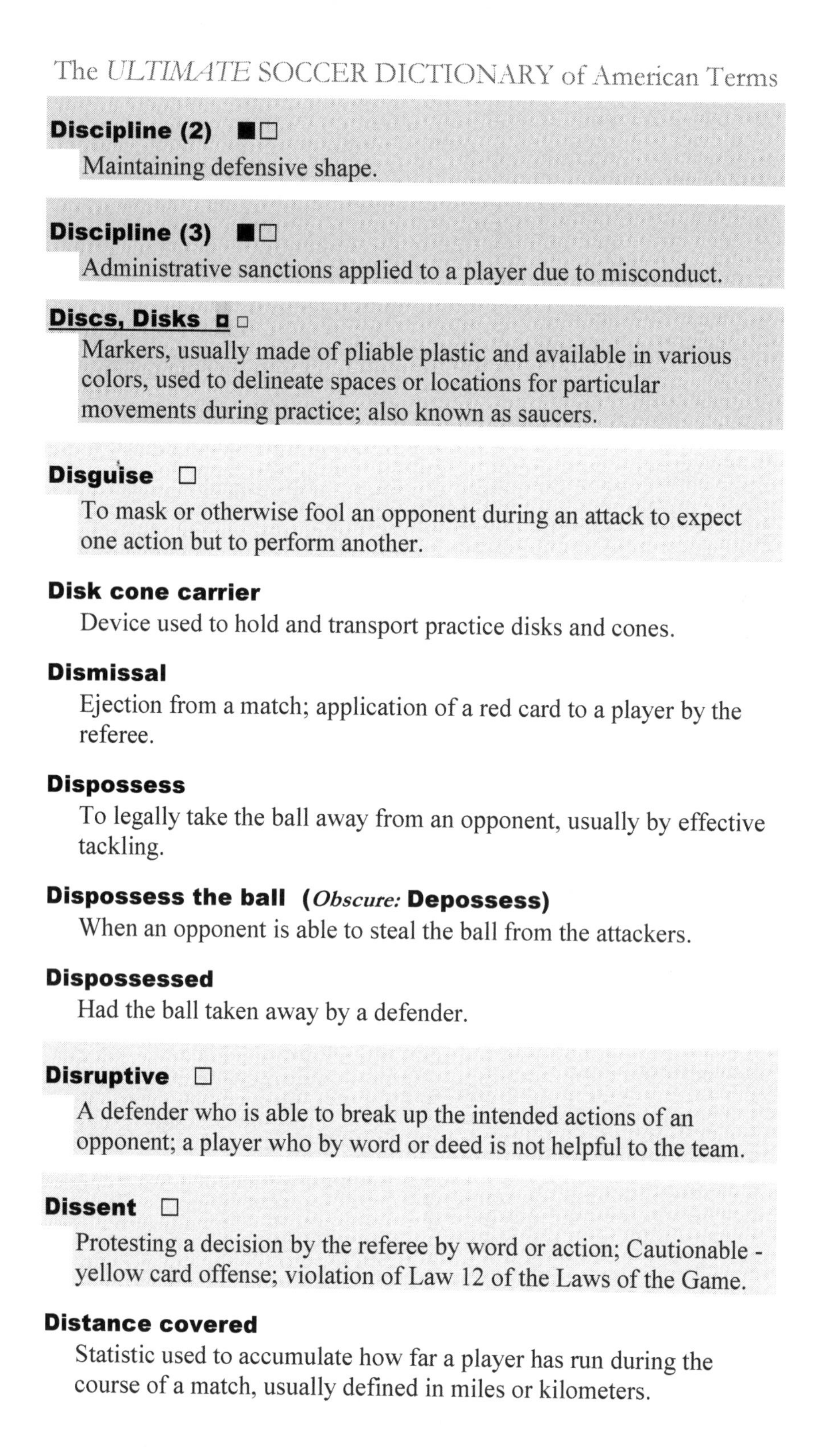

Discipline (2) ■□

Maintaining defensive shape.

Discipline (3) ■□

Administrative sanctions applied to a player due to misconduct.

Discs, Disks ◘□

Markers, usually made of pliable plastic and available in various colors, used to delineate spaces or locations for particular movements during practice; also known as saucers.

Disguise □

To mask or otherwise fool an opponent during an attack to expect one action but to perform another.

Disk cone carrier

Device used to hold and transport practice disks and cones.

Dismissal

Ejection from a match; application of a red card to a player by the referee.

Dispossess

To legally take the ball away from an opponent, usually by effective tackling.

Dispossess the ball (*Obscure:* **Depossess**)

When an opponent is able to steal the ball from the attackers.

Dispossessed

Had the ball taken away by a defender.

Disruptive □

A defender who is able to break up the intended actions of an opponent; a player who by word or deed is not helpful to the team.

Dissent □

Protesting a decision by the referee by word or action; Cautionable - yellow card offense; violation of Law 12 of the Laws of the Game.

Distance covered

Statistic used to accumulate how far a player has run during the course of a match, usually defined in miles or kilometers.

Distracter

Players, cones, or other devices, used in a drill to deliberately force a player to concentrate on technique while avoiding the devices.

Distractions □

The placement and movement of attacking players intended to take the goalkeeper's attention away from the ball or intended targets.

Distribute, Distribution □

The goalkeeper's selection of the player and part of the field to release the ball to in order to start an attack after receiving or saving a ball.

Distributing

Midfielders and back defenders conducting the flow of the attack by passes to the left and right and up the middle of the field.

Dive, Diving, Diving save (1) ◘ □

Goalkeeper jumping outward and landing on the ground in order to make a save.

Dive; To take a dive (2) ◘ □

Faking a foul by going headlong into the turf after a supposed trip, in an attempt to draw a penalty call by the referee.

Diving header □

A head ball performed around the level of the knees by launching the body parallel to the ground.

Diving pit

An area, often filled with foam blocks or sand, used by goalkeepers to practice diving saves.

Divot (1)

The piece of grass and dirt dug out of a natural turf field by stubbing one's toe or point of the shoe in the ground.

Divot (2) - To take a divot

To stub one's toe or point of the shoe in the ground.

DM *(Abbrev.)*

Defensive Midfielder. Shorthand for the Defensive Midfielder position.

DMF *(Abbrev.)*

Alternate abbreviation for the Defensive Midfielder position.

DOC *(Abbrev.)*

Director of Coaching.

DOGSO *(Abbrev.)*

Denying an Obvious Goal Scoring Opportunity.

Domes

Half-spheres, usually made of hard plastic approximately six inches in diameter, to mark practice spaces or for drills.

Dominant foot, Dominant leg □

A natural preference for one extremity over the other, such as being right-handed or left-handed.

Dominant team, Dominated, Domination, Dominating

Team with the better of the play, most possession, regularly in the opponent's half of the field, that isn't chasing the ball, and usually scores the most goals.

Dominate □

A player or team having more control or power over another player or team.

Don't appeal (1) – ►

►***On-field Oral Communication:*** Tells a teammate to keep playing the ball and not challenge the referee for a call that isn't going to come.

Don't appeal (2) – ►

►***On-field Oral Communication:*** Requests that a teammate who has just been called for a foul get away from the referee and keep quiet in order to not get carded for dissent.

Don't quit (1) – ► ■□

►***On-field Oral Communication:*** Tells a teammate to keep playing the ball and not stop because of a mistake, misplay, or tiredness.

Don't quit (2) – ►

►***On-field Oral Communication:*** Encourages the entire team not to suffer a let-down after a goal has been scored against them.

Double

Player scores two goals in a game; brace.

Double mark

Two defenders marking one offensive player, usually front and back.

Double pass

In context, a give-and-go or "one-two" where a player passes to a teammate and immediately receives a return pass, or two give-and-go passes performed one right after the other.

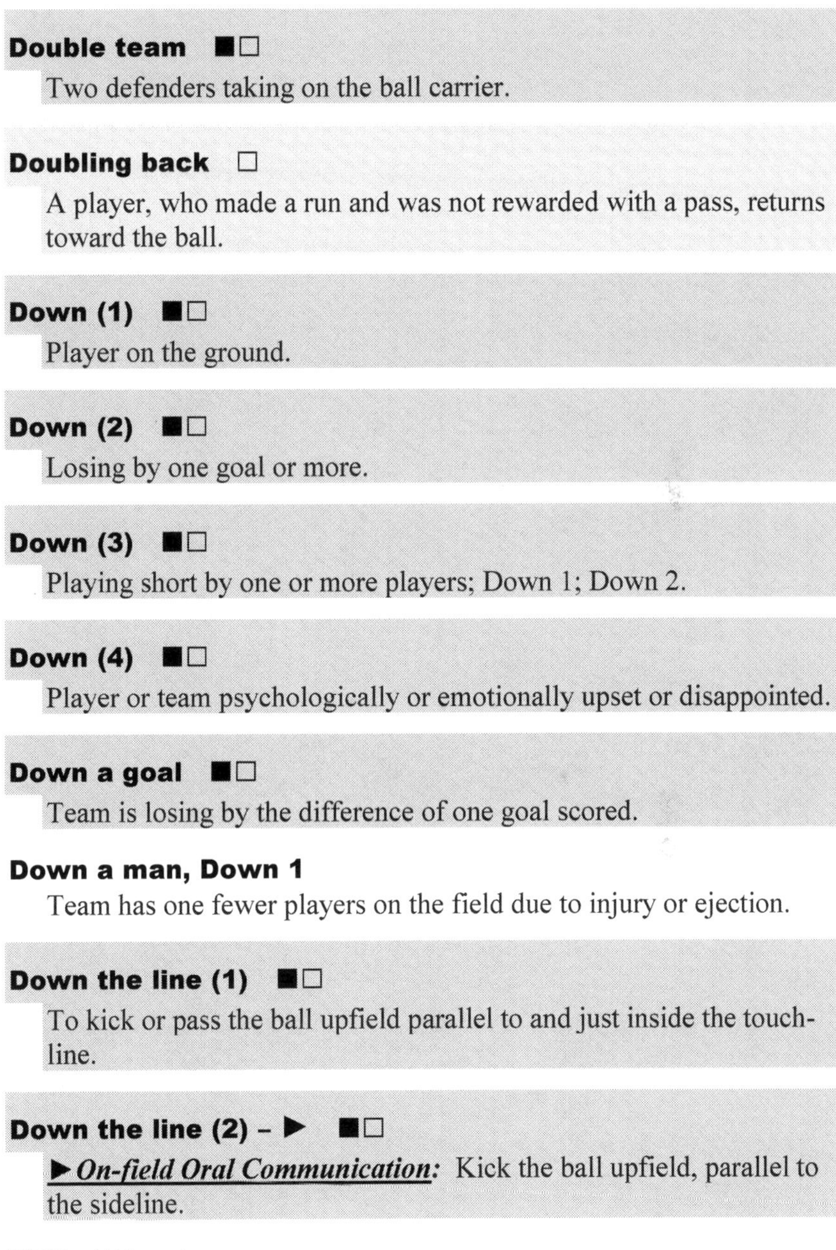

Double team ■□

Two defenders taking on the ball carrier.

Doubling back □

A player, who made a run and was not rewarded with a pass, returns toward the ball.

Down (1) ■□

Player on the ground.

Down (2) ■□

Losing by one goal or more.

Down (3) ■□

Playing short by one or more players; Down 1; Down 2.

Down (4) ■□

Player or team psychologically or emotionally upset or disappointed.

Down a goal ■□

Team is losing by the difference of one goal scored.

Down a man, Down 1

Team has one fewer players on the field due to injury or ejection.

Down the line (1) ■□

To kick or pass the ball upfield parallel to and just inside the touch-line.

Down the line (2) – ▶ ■□

▶ ***On-field Oral Communication:*** Kick the ball upfield, parallel to the sideline.

DPD *(Abbrev.)*

Director of Player Development.

Draft; Player draft

A system by which players may be selected to join teams.

Drag a defender

Overlapping run that pulls a defender away from the goal area with the effect of creating space.

Drag back

Dribbling move, fake or feint where the ball is first pulled backward using the sole of the foot; "pull back" or "V-cut."

Drag, Dragging the ball

Use of the sole of the foot to move the ball slowly in front of a defender before making a dribbling move, fake or feint.

Draw □

(1) Law 10 of the Laws of the Game; game resulting in a tie. (2) Procedure for establishing seedings in a tournament.

Drawing fouls

A player or team attempting to tactically create situations which result in calls being made against the opponent.

Drawing level, Draw level, Draw even □

Scoring a goal that ties the game.

Drawing the foul □

A player puts himself in an optimizing position where illegal contact is likely to be made by an opponent.

Dressing room ■□

Locker room; location for changing from/to soccer gear and street clothes.

Dribble, Dribbling ◘ □

The skill of moving the ball around the field by use of the feet, unassisted by other players.

Dribbler ◘ □

The player in immediate possession of the ball who is dribbling; ball carrier.

Drifter □

Attacking player specifically allowed to roam during corner kicks or offensive restarts who looks for rebounds or opportunities to score who is not part of the set play; Roamer.

Drifting around

Forwards that make moves at the top of the area, but aren't decisive about making runs or taking on a defender.

Drilled, drilled in

A particularly hard shot or cross.

Drills ◘ □

Practice routines designed to introduce or reinforce skills, tactics, or techniques which are expected to be used properly in games.

Drive, Drive the ball ■□

Instep drive; often a hard, low instep drive shot on goal or cente3ring pass.

Driven across the goal mouth

A particularly hard pass, usually on the ground, that crosses in front of the whole goal from post-to-post without being touched by an attacker, defender, or the goalkeeper.

Driven, Driven in, Driven pass

A strong, hard, offensive, usually diagonal, pass directed toward a group of forwards in front of the goal.

Driving the ball ■□

A particularly hard and straight instep kick, low to the ground – typical for many shots.

Driving the service

A particularly hard and straight instep kick, low to the ground, which is a pass to a teammate, usually trying to set up a shot.

Drop ball, Dropped ball ◘ □

Law 8 of the Laws of the Game; if the referee has to stop play for any reason not involving a re-start as identified in the Laws, play is resumed with a dropped ball at the point where the ball was when play was stopped; the ball is in play as soon as it hits the ground.

Drop kick, Drop-kick ☐

An instep drive performed by the goalkeeper by releasing the ball from his hands to the ground and then kicking it a split second after it bounces; intended to remove the friction of the turf to increase distance and accuracy.

Drop, Drop the ball, Drop pass ☐

A back pass to a trailing (following) teammate.

Dropping

Making a back pass.

Dropping back ■☐

Retreating to play defense.

Dropping off

Defenders falling too far back from their opponents, allowing for uncontested shots from distance.

Dropping together ☐

Defenders retreating as a unit to play defense.

Dry erase board

Coaching tool which facilitates diagramming of plays and runs.

Duffle, Duffle bag ■☐

Bag used for balls or equipment.

Dugout

A depression in the ground outside the sidelines of a game field, usually covered for protection, where a coach and substitutes may sit.

Dummy (1)

The action of an offensive player to look, feint, or otherwise fake like he is going to receive a pass, only to let the ball continue on its path to a teammate without touching it.

Dummy (2)

A mannequin or full-sized representation of a person used in practice, usually positioned with other mannequins to simulate a defensive wall.

Dummy (3)

A dribbling move, fake or feint where a player runs toward a pass, as if to receive it, lets the ball go through his legs or just past him, turns 180-degrees, and proceeds in the opposite direction.

Dummy (4)

A "no-look" pass where an offensive player with the ball directly stares at, and continues to stare at, one teammate and then passes to a different teammate. A "blind" pass.

Dummy (5) – ►

►***On-field Oral Communication:*** Do not touch the ball. Instead, run over it or near it to create a distraction and let it continue on its path to a following teammate nearby, ready to receive/shoot the ball; sell the dummy.

Dummy run

Sprinting to an area to distract an opponent's attention from a pass going to a teammate.

Dumped it back; Played it back

A back pass, often to the goalkeeper, usually employed because a clear opportunity to pass the ball forward did not materialize.

Durability

(1) The ability of a player to play many games over a long period of time;
(2) Quality or feature used in the evaluation of a goalie glove.

Duration

The length of time of a match.

Dutch soccer

A more recent form of play involving high energy levels and skills demonstrated by all players; origin of "Dutch Whirlwind" and "Total Football" (Total Soccer).

DVDs ☐

a.) Videos of soccer training, courses, games, practices or scouting;
b.) Movies about soccer.

Dying moments

The last minutes of a match.

Dynamic stretching

A form of stretching utilizing the momentum from basic, well-controlled movement. (Caution: Dynamic stretching can be beneficial. However, when performed incorrectly, it may result in injury. Learn and use proper technique. "Do not bounce your stretches. Ballistic (bouncy) stretching can cause injury." – American Academy of Orthopedic Surgeons)

Early goal □

Generally, a goal which is scored within the first ten minutes of a match.

Early service

Passing a ball quickly for a possible shot, not waiting for a buildup.

Early, Early ball, Early pass □

A quick pass, usually a through ball, made to exploit space behind a defense, usually as a result of a turnover.

Earn a corner, Earns the corner

A forward has forced the ball off an opponent over the end line.

Economic (or economical) training

Effectively combining two or more aspects of the game in a practice drill or exercise. For example: involving shooting and sprinting combines skills with fitness.

Edge of the area □

Just outside the 18-yard line of the penalty area.

Education

Formal instruction available to soccer coaches, generally through the NSCAA or USSF.

Effective range of defender

The space a defender can cover in the time available before a pass goes beside or over him.

Efficiency

Goals per shot statistic.

Efficiency of training

Making the best use of the time available during practice; examples, no standing around, no lines, no gaps between drills or exercises.

Efficient ■□

One-or-two-touch play; simple, keeping the ball on the turf; calm possession; a comfort zone.

Eighteen (1) ◘ □

The outermost line of the Penalty Area, parallel to the goal-line; 18; the eighteen.

Eighteen (2) – ▶

▶ ***On-field Oral Communication:*** Send the ball to the outer line (top) of the penalty area. Generally, this is a specific target location established for a cross.

Ejection ◘ □

To be shown a red card and sent off the field of play.

Ejection offenses ■□

The fouls or misconduct for which a player may be sent off (red-carded) during a match; Under Law 12, "Fouls and Misconduct," of the Laws of the Game, sending-off offenses include serious foul play, violent conduct, spitting at a person, denying a goal-scoring opportunity by deliberate handling of the ball, denying a goal-scoring opportunity by a person with a foul punishable by a free kick or penalty kick, offensive language or gestures, or receiving a second caution in the same game.

Electrolytes ■□

Chemicals (salts) used by the body, particularly during heavy physical exertion for muscle movement, that should be replaced as part of hydration during a match or practice.

Electronic Player Tracking System

Devices worn by players which transmit data regarding physical and health attributes. May not be worn in a match if determined by the referee to be in violation of Law 4 of the Laws of the Game; EPTS.

Elevate, Elevated

Jumped very high to make a header (field player), or a catch (goalkeeper).

Eleven ■□

A full team of players for a regulation match.

Eliminated □

To lose a game or a number of games such that the team fails to advance according to the rules of a tournament.

Elite clubs national league

ECNL; designed to be the most competitive youth soccer league for girls in the U. S.

Embellishment, Embellishing

Acting to make contact or a foul appear worse than it was.

Emblem

Crest or badge of the team or soccer organization worn on the jersey.

Emergency defending

Players having to sprint back to cover their own goal due to an unexpected loss of the ball or quick counter-attack.

Empty net ■□

The goalkeeper is out of position to defend his goal due to: (a) moving far away from the goal to try to make a stop; or, in rare cases, (b) joining the attack in a desperate attempt to score.

Encounter

Game or match.

Encroachment ◘□

Defenders are less than 10 yards away prior to a re-start; sneaking up; Violation of Law 12 of the Laws of the Game; Cautionable - yellow card offense; Failure to respect the required distance when play is restarted with a corner kick, free kick or throw-in.

End (1) ◘□

The half of the field a team is defending. ("Our end." "Their end.")

End (2) ■□

Conclusion or termination of a match.

End Line ◘□

The goal-line from corner to corner, at each end of the field of play.

End to end

A game in which both teams repeatedly attack and defend.

Endanger the safety of an opponent

An act that puts an opponent at significant risk of injury.

End-line cross

A forward or midfielder dribbles the ball almost to the goal-line, usually near the corner, and then passes it in the air to the front of the goal.

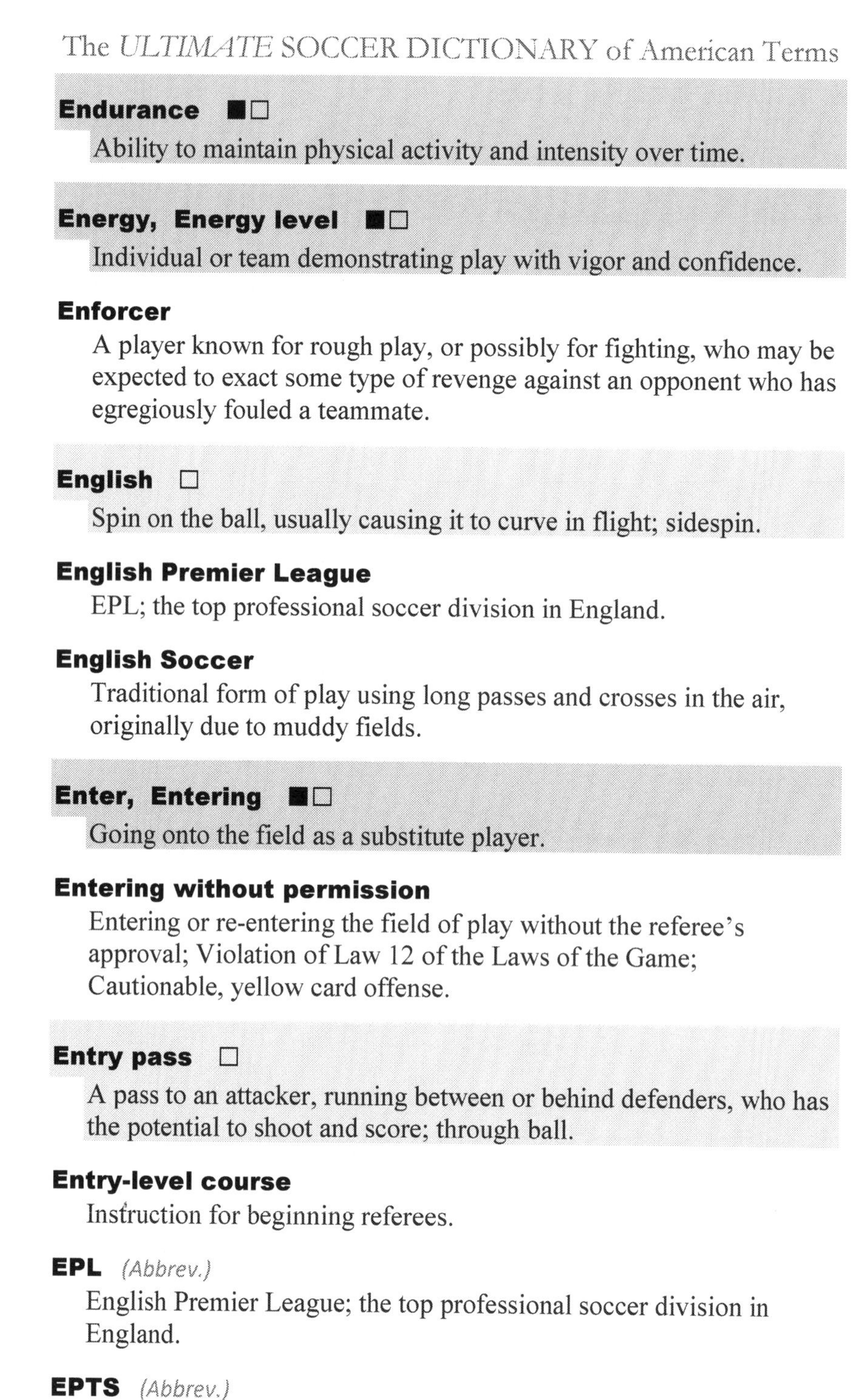

Endurance ■□

Ability to maintain physical activity and intensity over time.

Energy, Energy level ■□

Individual or team demonstrating play with vigor and confidence.

Enforcer

A player known for rough play, or possibly for fighting, who may be expected to exact some type of revenge against an opponent who has egregiously fouled a teammate.

English □

Spin on the ball, usually causing it to curve in flight; sidespin.

English Premier League

EPL; the top professional soccer division in England.

English Soccer

Traditional form of play using long passes and crosses in the air, originally due to muddy fields.

Enter, Entering ■□

Going onto the field as a substitute player.

Entering without permission

Entering or re-entering the field of play without the referee's approval; Violation of Law 12 of the Laws of the Game; Cautionable, yellow card offense.

Entry pass □

A pass to an attacker, running between or behind defenders, who has the potential to shoot and score; through ball.

Entry-level course

Instruction for beginning referees.

EPL *(Abbrev.)*

English Premier League; the top professional soccer division in England.

EPTS *(Abbrev.)*

Electronic Player Tracking System; Electronic Performance and Tracking Systems.

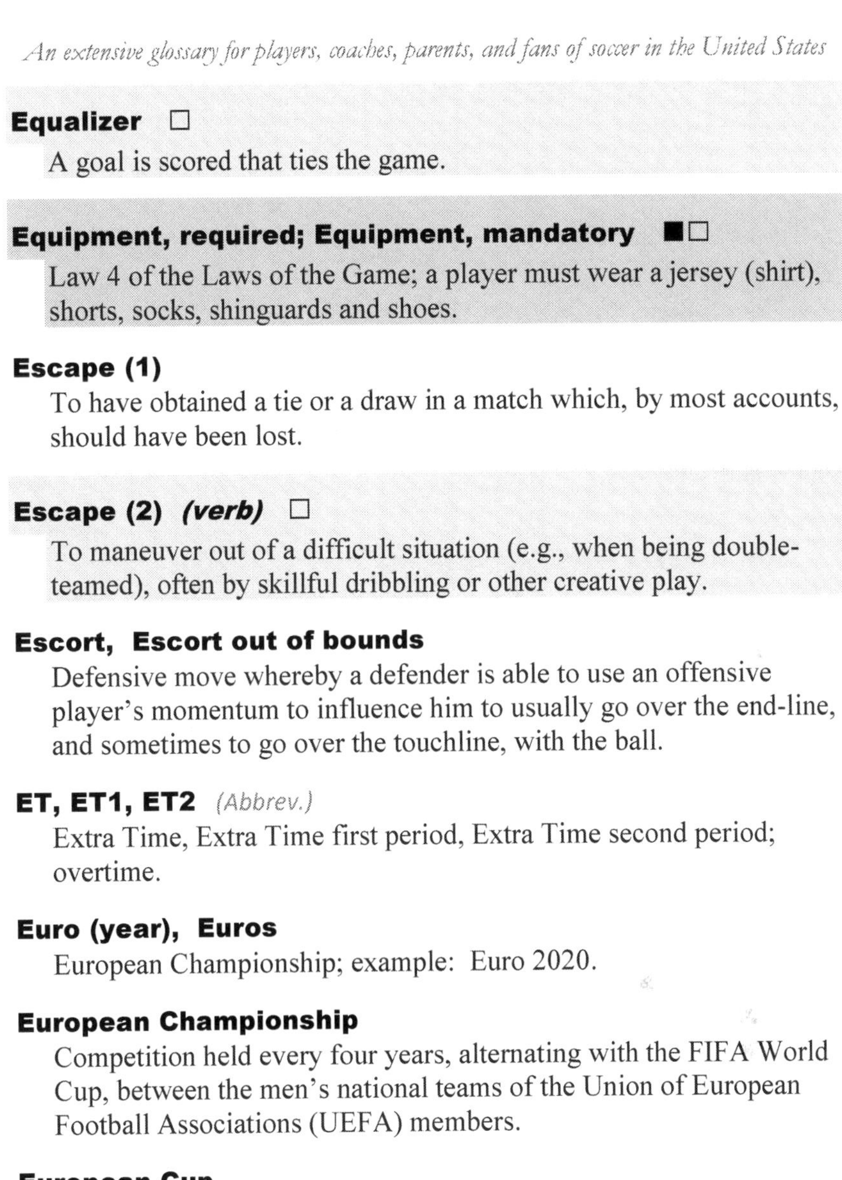

Equalizer □

A goal is scored that ties the game.

Equipment, required; Equipment, mandatory ■□

Law 4 of the Laws of the Game; a player must wear a jersey (shirt), shorts, socks, shinguards and shoes.

Escape (1)

To have obtained a tie or a draw in a match which, by most accounts, should have been lost.

Escape (2) ***(verb)*** □

To maneuver out of a difficult situation (e.g., when being double-teamed), often by skillful dribbling or other creative play.

Escort, Escort out of bounds

Defensive move whereby a defender is able to use an offensive player's momentum to influence him to usually go over the end-line, and sometimes to go over the touchline, with the ball.

ET, ET1, ET2 *(Abbrev.)*

Extra Time, Extra Time first period, Extra Time second period; overtime.

Euro (year), Euros

European Championship; example: Euro 2020.

European Championship

Competition held every four years, alternating with the FIFA World Cup, between the men's national teams of the Union of European Football Associations (UEFA) members.

European Cup

Annual club competition of UEFA.

Even ■□

Tied; sometimes, evenly matched.

Excessive force

A player exceeds the necessary use of force when contacting an opponent to the point where the safety of the opponent is severely endangered; red card offense.

Excuses ■□

Insufficient justification for not performing properly.

Execution ■□

The ability of an individual player to successfully perform a skill; the ability of a team to properly perform a strategy or tactic.

Exercises ■□

Lessons, problems, or drills, designed to advance and improve players' particular functions or skills.

Exhibition

A full game between two teams which is not counted as part of any competition.

Expertise

Knowledge and experience of soccer and soccer coaching.

Exploiting space □

Taking advantage of open space created by making runs or passing the ball into that area.

Explosive strength

Sudden muscle use at the highest level in the shortest period of time.

Explosive training

A type of training for goalkeepers to promote quick, strong and decisive actions.

Exposed (1)

Having a gap in the defense that has been discovered and exploited by the opponent.

Exposed (2)

Goalkeeper has been shown to have a particular weakness, such as not being able to properly catch high balls.

Exposed at the back

By a sequence of attacks, a defense is shown to have a specific weakness in skills at certain positions or in strategy as a team.

Expulsion

Ejection from a game; red carded; sent off.

Extension (1)

The straightening out of a limb of the body at a joint due to muscle contraction.

Extension (2)

The farthest possible reach by a goalkeeper used in an attempt to make a save.

Extra Time ◘ □

Overtime period (or periods) played after a match ends in a tie, usually used in tournaments that require a winner in order for a team to advance or be declared a champion. "Extra Time" (the official term) is also frequently called "Overtime."

Note: "Extra Time" is NOT the same as "Added Time" (a.k.a. "Stoppage Time") – the time added at the end of each half of a game due to injuries and other delays.
See also: Injury Time.

Extra Time Interval

Five-minute rest period between two equal overtime segments.

Extra touch ■□

Taking one dribble too many before getting a shot off, thereby allowing the window of opportunity to close.

Eye contact □

Conscious recognition of the direct view between two people, often setting up a run, a move, or a pass.

Eyesight ■□

Proper 20/20 binocular vision, natural or due to Lasik surgery or contact lenses.

F (1) *(Abbrev.)*
Forward; shorthand for the forward position.

F (2) *(Abbrev.)*
Foul; Fouls; the total number of fouls committed by a team in a match.

F (3) *(Abbrev.)*
Final; Final Result; the final score of a game.

FA *(Abbrev.)*
Football Association; The FA, the governing body of soccer in England.

Face of the crossbar
That part of the crossbar of the goal which can be seen from within the field of play, usually pertaining to rebounds.

Face of the goal
The full plane of the goal mouth from the ground up to the crossbar and from one goalpost to the other.

Face of the post
That part of either upright of the goal which can be seen from within the field of play, usually pertaining to rebounds.

Face up, Face up to ☐
To mark an opponent head on.

Face, Faces, Facing
The goalkeeper against a penalty-kick taker. (E.g., "When **facing** a penalty kick, goalkeepers often have less than half a second to react.")

Facing the goal, Face the goal, Faced up
The body is directed forward with the eyes looking at the goal.

Fail to pull the trigger ☐
To not shoot when one should; to shoot too late.

Failed clearance
A miskick by a back defender, often allowing the ball to be recovered by an opposing striker, sometimes resulting in a goal being scored.

Failed to connect

A pass is not received by its intended target.

Failure to respect

Failure to respect the required distance when play is restarted with a corner kick, free kick or throw-in; Violation of Law 12 of the Laws of the Game; Cautionable, yellow card offense; encroachment.

Fair ■□

An action in accordance with the Laws of the Game.

Fair charge; Legal charge □

See: Charging (1).

Fair Play Rule ■□

One of the "unwritten rules" of soccer that players can play hard but must refrain from hurting or injuring opponents so that everyone can continue to enjoy playing the game (or make a living).

Fake ■□

To feign or simulate an action in order to obtain a reaction from an opponent; deke, juke; a move usually associated with dribbling.

Fakeover

Move where a teammate looks like he is going to take the ball from the ballhandler, but proceeds to run past him, often by stepping over the ball.

Faking, Faking a foul

Simulation; attempting to illegally draw a call by the referee; flopping; diving.

Fall, Fell

(1) To lose the game. (E.g., "The U16 All-stars **fell** to the U15 All-stars 2-1 in their exhibition game."); (2) A goal is scored; usually references the time of the game that a goal is scored. (E.g., "The winning goal **fell** in the 87th minute.")

Falling down

Simulation of having been fouled by going to the ground; to take a dive.

Falling, Falling to

Losing to an opponent.

False 9

Trailing, setback, or withdrawn forward who may fake being a playmaker while actually being a target striker or center forward; the number is a reference to an historical jersey-numbering system (1-to-11) where the number-9 shirt was usually the center forward.

False pressure

Mental pressure applied internally by a player with the ball who thinks that there will be imminent contact by a defender, but it is not happening yet.

Fanwear

Clothing and equipment worn by fans which identifies their support for a particular team.

Far forward

The forward farthest from the ball, usually on the opposite side of the field.

Far fullback

The defender farthest from the ball, usually on the opposite side of the field.

Far midfielder

The midfielder farthest from the ball, usually on the opposite side of the field.

Far post (1) ■□

The upright of the goal farthest away from the ball; back post.

Far post (2) – ▶ ■□

▶ ***On-field Oral Communication:*** Pass or shoot the ball toward the part of the goal farthest from you.

Far side □

The other part of the field or sideline away from the ball; opposite side, opposite post; far post.

Far-post corner □

A corner kick sent well to the opposite goalpost from the corner from which it was taken.

Fast break ■□

A counter-attack by an opponent marked by speed or swift action; fast counter.

Fast counter □

A counter-attack by an opponent marked by speed or swift action, thereby trying to keep the defense from recovering or setting up.

Fast restart

To quickly take a direct or indirect free kick, thereby not allowing the defense to recover or set up.

Fatigue, Fatigued ■□

Weariness or exhaustion on the part of players during a match causing reduced performance.

Favorite, Favored ■□

Team expected to most likely win a match.

FB *(Abbrev.)*

Fullback; shorthand for the fullback position.

FC *(Abbrev.)*

Football Club; soccer team or soccer organization fielding a number of teams.

Fearlessness

Demonstrating bold, brave, or gutsy action involving a high potential for severe contact; usually associated with goalkeepers.

Federation

United States Soccer Federation; FIFA; any of a number of country soccer organizations.

Feed □

To pass a ball to a teammate who has an opportunity to shoot.

Feeder

Player or coach designated to send in balls to players performing a drill.

Feeding

Passing a through ball on to a running teammate.

Feel ■□

The perception, sensory impression, or touch of the ball to a player.

Feet – ▶

▶ *On-field Oral Communication*: Pass the ball directly to my feet; do not lead me.

Feint ◘ □

A movement intended to divert attention or modify the balance of the opponent; juke, deke, fake; usually associated with dribbling.

Feinting

(1) Legal dribbling moves;
(2) Illegal attempts to draw a call of a foul.

Feisty

A colloquialism for a player whose demeanor and actions are just on the edge of committing fouls.

FG *(Abbrev.)*

Firm Ground; soccer shoes with cleats designed to be used on firm ground.

Field ■□

The surface for a game; the pitch; Law 1 of the Laws of the Game.

Field bag ■□

Kit bag carried by players that contains shoes, outer clothing, back-up shoelaces, etc.; Coach's bag containing pinnies, supplies, etc.

Field conditions ■□

Status of the turf and weather that must be taken into consideration during a match; includes such things as wind, rain, mud, puddles, slickness, and hardness.

Field diagram ■□

A graphic representation of the layout (lines) of a soccer field, used as a coaching aid or to guide the actual creation of a soccer field on a piece of ground.
See: Appendix 3 – Field Diagram.

Field maintenance

Keeping a soccer field in playing order, including such things as proper nets, flags, cut grass, elimination of debris, and layout of lines.

Field marker, Field marking wand

Device to hold and spray paint designed for placing lines on a natural grass playing surface.

Field markings

Law 1 of the Laws of the Game; defines the field of play in accordance with the plan of the field; lines are part of the areas they bound; lines must all be the same width, no greater than five inches.

Field of play ■□

Law 1 of the Laws of the Game; must be rectangular; long side is bounded by "touch lines," short side is bounded by "goal-lines;" touch line minimum 100 yards, maximum 130 yards; goal-line minimum 50 yards, maximum 100 yards; the pitch.

Field player

Any player other than the goalkeeper.

Field player gloves

Tight-fitting, non-goalkeeper gloves designed to provide warmth but allow for a proper grip during throw-ins.

Field player's kit

Shoes, equipment, clothing and other articles needed or used by a soccer player other than the goalkeeper.

Field set-up

Installation of nets and flags, and placement of lines on a soccer field prior to play.

Field Size ■□

Determination of the width and length, and interior markings, of a soccer field, usually based on the age of the players who will use it.

Field surface ■□

Law 1 of the Laws of the Game; natural grass or artificial turf, or hybrid.

Field take-down

De-installation of nets and flags, and any other movable items, on a soccer field after the conclusion of play.

FIFA *(Abbrev.)* ■□

Federation Internationale de Football Association (French); International Federation of Association Football (English); world authority of soccer headquartered in Switzerland.

FIFA (YY)

Electronic game of soccer, approved by FIFA, commonly associated with EA Sports; example, FIFA 17.

FIFA 11+ Program

FIFA-designed effort to prevent injuries.

FIFA Age-Group World Cups

FIFA international competitions restricted to players under certain ages; Example, FIFA U-20 World Cup.

FIFA concussion protocol

Outline of steps to be taken by referees when they believe a player may have suffered a concussion during a match.

FIFA Confederations Cup

Tournament for the national teams that won their confederation tournament; played every four years, one year before the World Cup.

FIFA Law

Prior to 2016, shorthand for the "FIFA Laws of the Game" which are now the "IFAB Laws of the Game" or just the "Laws of the Game." See: IFAB.

FIFA Laws of the Game

Prior to 2016, the "Laws of the Game" were published by FIFA but are now published by the International Football Association Board. See: IFAB.

FIFA Women's World Cup

FIFA conducts the largest international soccer competition in the world for women's teams. Held every four years, with play-ins conducted in the two years leading up to the event, every country on earth with a FIFA-recognized soccer governing body is eligible to apply for entry to this competition in order to determine the best women's national team.

FIFA World Cup

FIFA conducts the largest international soccer competition in the world for men's teams. Held every four years, with play-ins conducted in the two years leading up to the event, every country on earth with a FIFA-recognized soccer governing body is eligible to apply for entry to this competition in order to determine the best men's national team.

Fifty-Fifty ball ◘ □

A ball which, during the run of play, is equidistant between two oncoming opponents and is likely to result in a collision unless one player is successful at getting to it first or the other player backs off; 50/50 ball; 50-50 ball.

Figure 8 drill ■□

Two cones set approximately 10-feet apart allow a dribbler to control a ball in a full turn using only the inside of the left foot and then only the inside of the right foot. (Alternatively, the outside of each foot.)

Filling in

Briefly taking a teammate's defensive responsibilities; see Defensive Switch.

Filling space ■□

(1) A defender moves to cover open ground; (2) An offensive player makes a run into open ground; or, (3) *(Derogatory)* A player is standing around, doing nothing useful, just taking up space.

Film

Video of the team's games and practices, or the games of an opponent; term still used from days of actual film.

Film study, Film breakdown

Evaluation or analysis of players or teams from video taken of practices or games.

Final pass

The last pass made to a player who then shoots the ball.

Final passer

The last person to make a pass to a player who then shoots the ball.

Final roster □

List of names, selected from a larger pool or provisional roster, which represents the formal documentation of players available for use in a game or tournament.

Final third □

The one-third of the field closest to the attacking goal; attacking third.

Final threat □
The last attack made before the game ends.

Final whistle ■□
The referee signals the end of a match.

Finances
Accounting for the money needed to run a soccer team, program or organization.

Find a teammate □
To spot an open player and pass them the ball.

Find an opening ■□
To discover and take advantage of attacking space within a defense.

Fingertip touch, Fingertip save
A goalkeeper stretches out to just barely reach the ball and deflect it away from the goal.

Finish, Finishing ■□
To score a goal; the ability of a striker to complete the last action of shooting to score.

Fires
Shoots.

First aid ■□
To provide immediate treatment for an injury before full medical care can arrive.

First aid kit ■□
A container holding supplies and equipment for providing first aid; often includes such items as bandages, topical disinfectant, and chemical cold packs.

First appearance
The initial time that a player has played in a game for a specific team, particularly the national team.

First attacker ■□
Generally, the player with the ball heading for goal; the closest attacker to the goal.

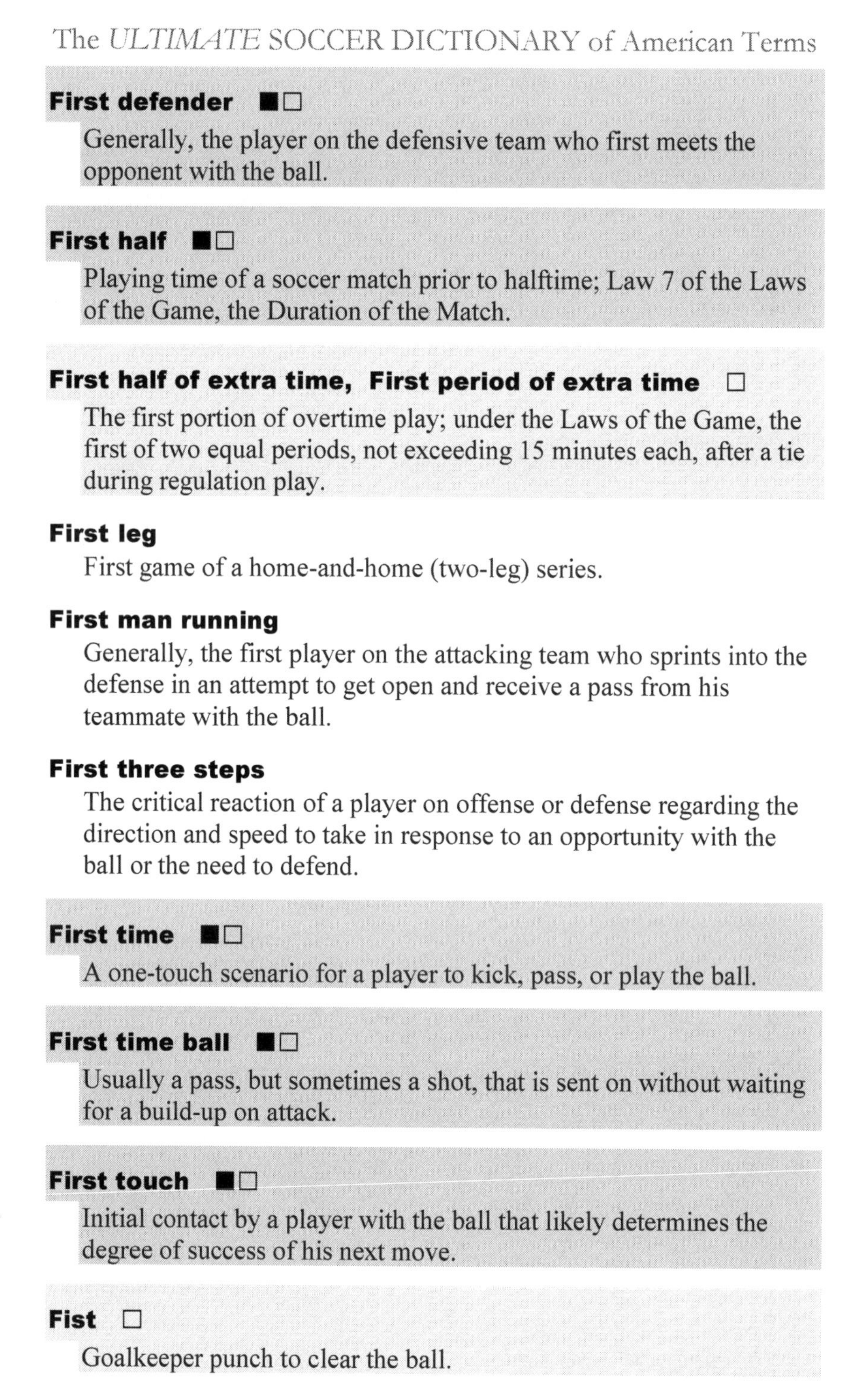

First defender ■□

Generally, the player on the defensive team who first meets the opponent with the ball.

First half ■□

Playing time of a soccer match prior to halftime; Law 7 of the Laws of the Game, the Duration of the Match.

First half of extra time, First period of extra time □

The first portion of overtime play; under the Laws of the Game, the first of two equal periods, not exceeding 15 minutes each, after a tie during regulation play.

First leg

First game of a home-and-home (two-leg) series.

First man running

Generally, the first player on the attacking team who sprints into the defense in an attempt to get open and receive a pass from his teammate with the ball.

First three steps

The critical reaction of a player on offense or defense regarding the direction and speed to take in response to an opportunity with the ball or the need to defend.

First time ■□

A one-touch scenario for a player to kick, pass, or play the ball.

First time ball ■□

Usually a pass, but sometimes a shot, that is sent on without waiting for a build-up on attack.

First touch ■□

Initial contact by a player with the ball that likely determines the degree of success of his next move.

Fist □

Goalkeeper punch to clear the ball.

Fit ■□

Match fit; physically able to perform for the entire duration of a game.

Fitness ◘ □

(1) A player's level of ability to run and perform;
(2) One of U. S. Soccer's four components ("4 pillars") of the game (Fitness, Psychological, Tactics, and Technique).

Fitness test □

(1) Annual examination of referees' ability to perform physical duties;
(2) Examination of a player's physical status.

Fixture date(s)

A day or block of days established by a soccer administrative body to be reserved for other games outside of a competition schedule. See also: International Fixture Date.

FK *(Abbrev.)*

Free Kick.

Flag (1); Assistant referee's flag; Linesman's flag ■□

Device used by assistant referees to indicate a foul, offside, or that the ball has gone out of play; Law 6 of the Laws of the Game, The Assistant Referees.

Flag (2) ■□

Corner flag; corner post.

Flag is up

Phrase used to denote that the assistant referee has raised his flag to identify to the referee that offside should be called.

Flag stays down

What looks like a possible offside is not identified as such by the assistant referee by keeping his flag at his side.

Flagposts

Law 1 of the Laws of the Game; posts with a rounded top, a minimum of 5 feet tall, with a flag attached at the top, are required at each corner of the field.

Flagposts, optional

Law 1 of the Laws of the Game; posts may be placed 1 yard or more outside the touchline to mark the halfway line.

Flair

Demonstrating craftiness with the ball.

Flanks

The right or left sides of the field closest to the touch lines, either on the attacking or defending ends of the field.

Flat □

Uninspired play.

Flat (back line)

All defenders in a row from sideline to sideline.

Flat back four

A defensive system which has the back defenders starting in a position which intentionally has them in a straight line from touchline to touchline.

Flat ball □

A kick which imparts no spin on the ball.

Flat front

All forwards in a row from sideline to sideline.

Flat pass

Pass which is perpendicular to the sideline; square pass.

Flat throw-in ■□

A straight, hard, long throw-in with little or no arc.

Flat-footed ■□

Standing with the full soles of both feet in contact with the ground; not "on your toes" (i.e., not on the balls of your feet); Implies an inability to react quickly to a change of direction by an opponent.

Flats

Training shoes with no cleats and a rubber or composition sole; "tennis shoes."

Flavor of a match; Tenor of a match

Overall attributes that could be applied to the conduct of a match, such as fast or slow, or physical or tactical.

Flexibility ■□

(1) Muscle and tendon elasticity;
(2) Ability to make changes rapidly and smoothly.

Flexion

To bend a body part at a joint as a result of contraction of a muscle.

Flick header □

A head ball characterized by a subtle or glancing touch designed to only slightly alter the flight of the ball.

Flick, Flick on

A minimal kick to a ball, or header, characterized by a subtle or glancing touch designed to only slightly alter the path of the ball.

Flight, Flight of the ball ■□

The airborne path of a soccer ball.

Flip throw, Flip throw-in

A summersault with the ball where a throw-in is accomplished by holding the ball to the ground, bringing the legs over so that the feet land just outside the touchline, and then slinging the ball into the middle of the field.

Flip, flips, Flip-flops

Sandals.

Flipper, Flipper kick, Flipper juggle

A movement of the lower leg which brings the foot up and outside the area of the body by bending and twisting at the knee to kick the ball with the outside of the foot.

Floater ▫ ▫

A lofted ball with little pace and too much height, such that multiple attacking and defending players usually have sufficient time to get to the point where it will come down.

Floating off; Peeling off

Losing a defender.

Floating, Floated ball

A pass or result of a kick where the arc of the ball is higher above the ground than usual and its pace is often soft.

Flood, Flooding, Flooding an area □

To send a large number of attacking players into a small space.

Floor, On the floor

The playing surface; to keep the ball in contact with the ground.

Flop, Flopping ◘ □

To fake having been fouled by falling or diving to the ground, often in the Penalty Area to illegally try to draw a Penalty Kick; Dive.

Flow, Flow of the match, Flow of the game □

The speed at which a match is being played.

Flow of play, Free flow of play

The usual, ongoing, performance of a match; not a re-start.

Flubbed, Flubbed a chance

Misplayed a ball, particular an opportunity to shoot and score.

Fluid

Smooth, easy movement by a player, usually while dribbling the ball.

Fluid intake ■□

Maintaining proper hydration.

Flying kick □

Leaving one's feet to make any type of kick.

Flying volley

Leaving one's feet to make a volley kick, usually a side volley.

Focal point

Offensive target player; central striker.

Focus; Stay focused ■□

Trying to maintain mental discipline on the game, particularly under fatigue.

Folding goals

Goals with articulated joints that allow them to be compressed for easier transport.

Follow – ▶ ■□

▶ ***On-field Oral Communication:*** A reminder that attackers must continue to follow-up shots on goal in order to play rebounds or loose balls. This includes the original shooter.

Follow-through ■□

(1) Completion of leg swing during a kick;
(2) Completion of arm swing during a throw-in;
(3) Completion of a run once it has been started.

Follow-up

Continuing to run at goal after a shot to possibly collect a rebound.

Foot care, Footcare

The need to keep the feet healthy and free from injury and disease in order to play soccer.

Foot save □

Goalkeeper stops a shot using one of his feet.

Foot skills ■□

All soccer techniques involving contacting the ball with the feet.

Foot trap ■□

Receiving the ball with the sole of the foot.

Footbag

Small sphere less than the size of an orange made of leather or a similar material, filled with sand or a similar material, used to juggle; the act or game of juggling a footbag. See: Hacky-Sack®.

Football ■□

Soccer (the sport); or, the soccer ball itself.

Football Club

An administrative organization which fields soccer teams in organized competitions; FC.

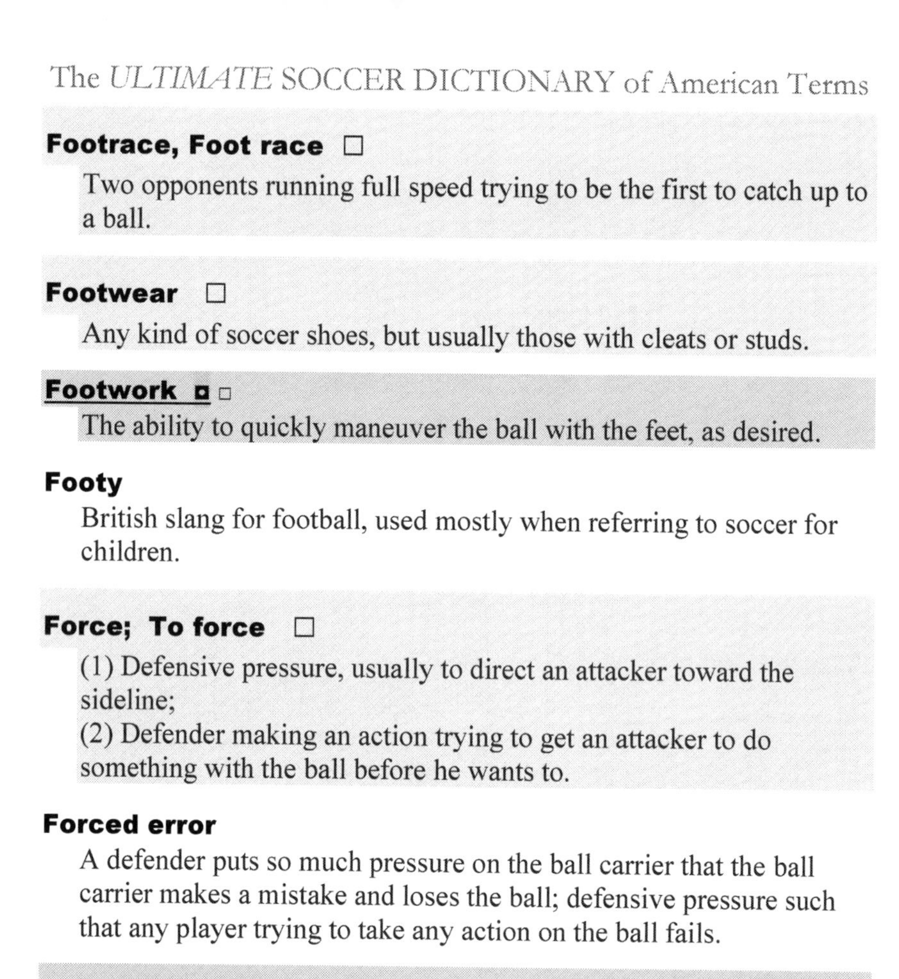

Footrace, Foot race □

Two opponents running full speed trying to be the first to catch up to a ball.

Footwear □

Any kind of soccer shoes, but usually those with cleats or studs.

Footwork ■□

The ability to quickly maneuver the ball with the feet, as desired.

Footy

British slang for football, used mostly when referring to soccer for children.

Force; To force □

(1) Defensive pressure, usually to direct an attacker toward the sideline;
(2) Defender making an action trying to get an attacker to do something with the ball before he wants to.

Forced error

A defender puts so much pressure on the ball carrier that the ball carrier makes a mistake and loses the ball; defensive pressure such that any player trying to take any action on the ball fails.

Forced pass ■□

An attempt to squeeze the ball between defenders which has little chance of successfully reaching a teammate.

Forcing the issue

A team in an attacking mode, dynamically taking the attack to the opponent.

Forfeit ■□

A 1-0 match result by administrative rule where one team fails to meet its obligation to play or to complete a game, usually due to an insufficient number of players.

Format (1)

Design of a competition; example, single-elimination tournament with seeded brackets.

Format (2), Format of a practice, Format of a program

Design of a training session or an entire training program of study.

Formation ◘ □
Placement of players, designating the number of back defenders, midfielders and strikers, e.g., 4-3-3 from the goal out; the goalkeeper is assumed; always adds up to 10 for full-sides play.
See: Alignment. See also: Appendix 2B, Appendix 2C.

Fortunate bounce
A player gets lucky when the ball deflects or caroms off a defender such that it is easily received and controlled.

Forward (1), Forwards *(plural)* ◘ □
Player or players positioned to lead the attack; strikers.
See: Appendix 2: Player Positions.

Forward (2)
To advance upfield; to move into the attack.

Forward line □
All of the strikers, as a group.

Forward passes □
Passes directed toward the attacking goal, usually parallel to the sidelines; contrast with back passes, diagonal passes, or square passes.

Forward runs □
Runs toward the attacking goal made by players who do not have the ball.

Foul ◘ □
Generally recognized as any illegal body contact made with an opponent in violation of the provisions of Law 12, "Fouls and Misconduct," as contained in the Laws of the Game; any violation of the rules.

Foul throw
Any violation of Law 15 of the Laws of the Game, The Throw-in, which results in the ball being given to the other team for a throw-in.

Fouled □
General term for player on the receiving end of the body-contact fouls contained in Law 12 of the Laws of the Game, "Fouls and Misconduct."

Fouls and Misconduct ☐

Law 12 of the Laws of the Game; specific major and minor offenses which, when performed, result in direct and indirect free kicks for the other team.

Fourth Official

Law 5 of the Laws of the Game; when appointed, an individual who assists in such duties as identification of substitutions and the amount of added time.

Fourth substitution, Fourth substitute

Modification to Law 3 of the Laws of the Game, "The Players," providing for an additional substitution, above and beyond the basic three allowed, which may only be made during extra time.

Fragmented play

Inconsistency on the part of a team to complete passes, maintain possession, or sustain an attack.

Frame ☐

The physical goal itself, including the uprights and the crossbar, usually referring to those parts that face the interior of the field.

Frame rattled

A shot that is so hard that, when it rebounds off the upright or crossbar, the goal actually shakes.

Framework

The uprights and crossbar of the goal.

Frantic

The actions of defenders when a ball is bouncing around uncontrollably in front of the goal.

Free ■☐

Open for a pass; not covered.

Free ("You're free") – ► ☐

► ***On-field Oral Communication:*** Tells teammate that there is no defender nearby and that they can work with the ball.

Free flowing

Match play which exhibits a lot of running and passing with few tackles or collisions.

Free Kick, Free Kicks ◘ □

Law 13 of the Laws of the Game; certain types of re-starts defined as "direct" or "indirect." A direct free kick may result in a goal without having to touch another player. An indirect free kick may result in a goal only after having been touched by at least one additional player other than the original kicker.

Free oneself

To get away from a marking defender in order to be available to receive a pass.

Free play

A pick-up game with no coaching, often among players of different ages.

Free shooting □

Players, on their own initiative and without direction of a coach, taking shots on goal, with or without a goalkeeper present.

Free-kick specialist

A player who has demonstrated a unique ability to bend or swerve a dead-ball restart kick from within approximately 25-yards of the goal such that he has a significant chance of scoring; the player on a team designated to try to score on a direct free kick.

Free-kick taker

A player designated to take free kicks under certain circumstances.

Freestyle juggling □

Juggling a soccer ball to keep it up in the air using any body parts; contrast with using feet only or "programmed" juggling.

Freshman team

Developmental squad; in college, a squad of incoming first-year players.

Freshmen on the team

USSF term referring to first-year players with the top-level squad.

Friendly ◘ □

A full game between two teams which is not part of a competition.

Frog

To jump with the ball while keeping it stuck firmly between both feet.

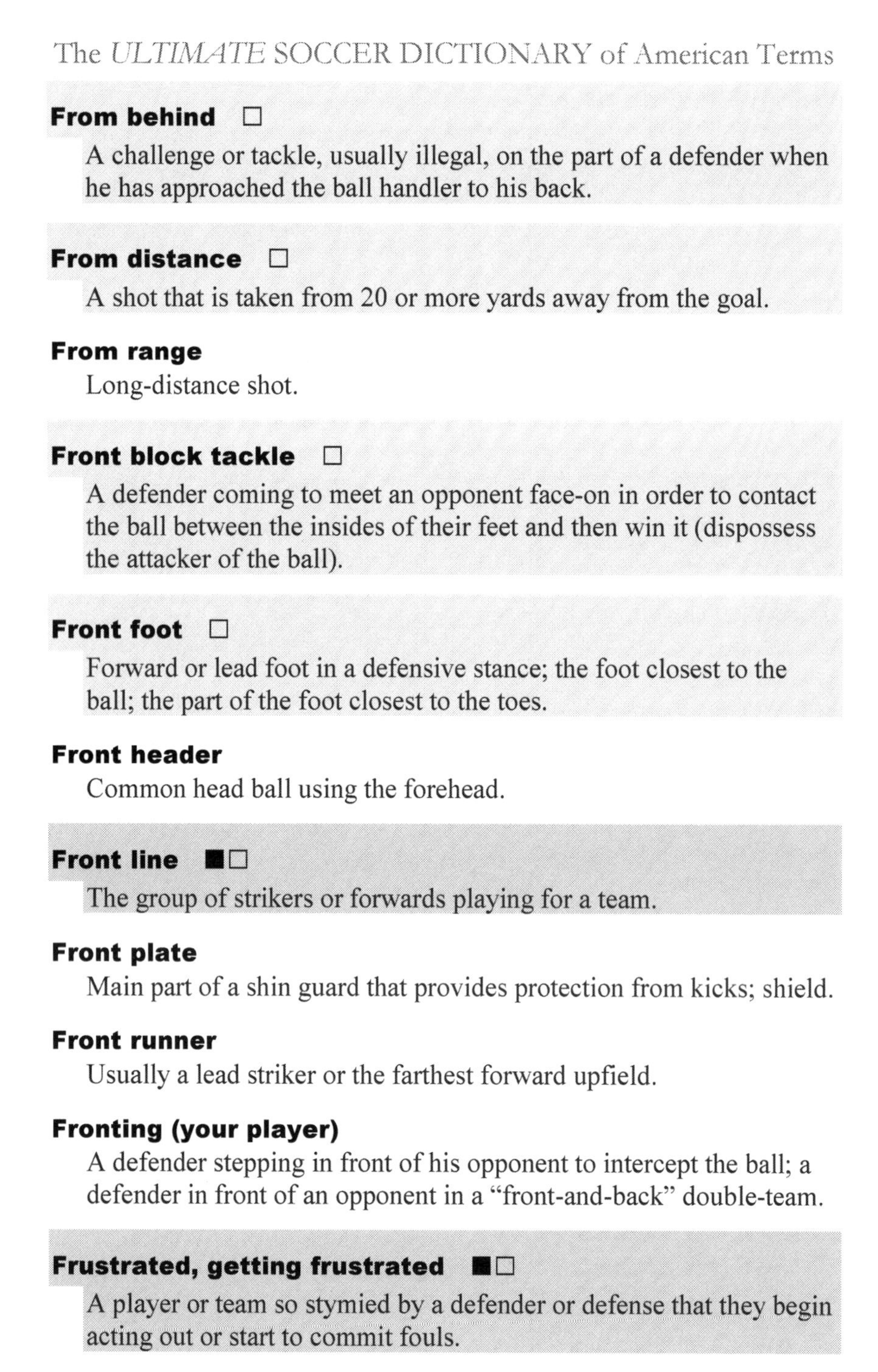

From behind ☐

A challenge or tackle, usually illegal, on the part of a defender when he has approached the ball handler to his back.

From distance ☐

A shot that is taken from 20 or more yards away from the goal.

From range

Long-distance shot.

Front block tackle ☐

A defender coming to meet an opponent face-on in order to contact the ball between the insides of their feet and then win it (dispossess the attacker of the ball).

Front foot ☐

Forward or lead foot in a defensive stance; the foot closest to the ball; the part of the foot closest to the toes.

Front header

Common head ball using the forehead.

Front line ■☐

The group of strikers or forwards playing for a team.

Front plate

Main part of a shin guard that provides protection from kicks; shield.

Front runner

Usually a lead striker or the farthest forward upfield.

Fronting (your player)

A defender stepping in front of his opponent to intercept the ball; a defender in front of an opponent in a "front-and-back" double-team.

Frustrated, getting frustrated ■☐

A player or team so stymied by a defender or defense that they begin acting out or start to commit fouls.

FT *(Abbrev.)*

Full Time; shorthand for fulltime.

Full fitness

A player's ability to run and perform for an entire match and extra time.

Full sides □

Eleven players on both teams participating in a match.

Full strength; Back to full strength □

Returning to having 11 players on the field after someone comes back on after having been treated for an injury.

Full time □

The end of the regulation time period of a game; the conclusion of 90-minutes plus stoppage time.

Full volley □

Kicking the ball in the air without it having touched the ground.

Fullback ◘ □

General term for player playing a mostly-defensive position closest to his own goal; back defender. Back. See: Appendix 2: Player Positions.

Full-time whistle

Final whistle blown by the referee to end a game.

Fumble ■□

Goalkeeper misplays the ball and drops it while trying to make a save.

Fun games; Soccer fun games ◘ □

Competitions using soccer balls intended to provide youth with an atmosphere of enjoyment and whimsy while learning skills and teamwork.
See: Soccer Fun Games http://coachingamericansoccer.com/youth-soccer-instructional-coaching-manual/soccer-fun-games/

Functional training □

Practice training or training under match conditions which stress skills that are position-specific.

Fundamentals ◘ □

The basic skills of soccer.

Funnel ☐

To concentrate players in attack as they get closer to the goal.

Fútbol

Spanish for football; soccer. (Portuguese: Futebol)

Futsal

FIFA-recognized indoor soccer.

Futsal goals

Small goals for use with indoor soccer, specifically for FIFA-recognized play.

FWWC *(Abbrev.)*

FIFA Women's World Cup.

G *(Abbrev.)*
Goalkeeper; shorthand for the goalkeeper position.

GA *(Abbrev.)*
Goals Allowed; Goals Against.

Gaffe
A blunder on the part of the goalkeeper resulting in a goal.

Gambling
Sending great numbers into the attack at the expense of possibly not having enough defenders if a counter-attack occurs, usually as a result of little time remaining and being down at least one goal.

Game ■□
Soccer match; practice activity.

Game clock ■□
The official timekeeping device of a match.

Game contract
Formal agreement, usually a document, that two teams or the teams of two institutions will meet to play a match at a certain location, date and time.

Game fit □
A player's ability to run and perform for the entire time of a match; match fit; physically and mentally prepared to play.

Game flow □
See: Flow of the Game.

Game jersey □
A player's shirt (worn during match play) that must otherwise conform to recognized administrative standards; Law 4 of the Laws of the Game.

Game Plan □
A formal or semi-formal overall strategic approach to attack and defend a specific opponent, often based on scouting.

Game report

The referee's written summary of the events of a match, usually including the goals scored and any record of misconduct, which is then submitted to the organizing authority; Referee's report.

Game shorts ☐

A player's pants (worn during match play) that must otherwise conform to recognized administrative standards; Law 4 of the Laws of the Game.

Game situation ☐

To create in practice a scenario that would be encountered in a match.

Game socks ☐

A player's hose (worn during match play), that must otherwise conform to recognized administrative standards; Law 4 of the Laws of the Game.

Game summary

Final statistics of a match, showing the teams that played, the result, who scored, time scored, assists, shots, corner kicks, cautions, ejections and other pertinent information.

Game video, Video of game, Game film

Visual record of a match for personal use or analysis.

Gamesmanship ☐

Possibly poor behavior on the part of a player or coach intending to cause frustration or misconduct by an opponent; sometimes, potential comments directed at referees to try to influence a call; sometimes, modifications to a schedule or field to try to influence the outcome of a game.

Gap, Gaps ■☐

(1) Space between defenders which could be exploited by the team on offense;
(2) Space between the lines of a formation, e.g. - between the backs and the midfielders or between the midfielders and the forwards.
(3) Space left in the back of a defense due to a defender who has just overlapped in attack.

Garbage time

The time remaining before the end of a match, where the outcome of the match has been decided and is highly unlikely to change, available to substitute players who normally would not get any playing time.

Garbage, Garbage goal ■□

A player following up a rebound and scoring a lucky goal after a shot has been taken by a teammate which resulted in the ball deflecting off a defender or the goal itself; trash.

Garters

Elastic or cloth ties used to hold soccer socks up to a position just below the knee.

Gassed □

A player who is noticeably tired, not performing skills well, and not able to run or recover position.

Gathered in

Ball is caught or otherwise collected by the goalkeeper.

Gave it up □

Lost the ball; dispossessed.

GD *(Abbrev.)*

Goal Differential; the total number of Goals For minus the total number of Goals Allowed for a defined number of games.

Gear ■□

(1) Clothing and equipment worn or used by players and coaches.
(2) Fan gear - clothing worn by supporters of a team.

General passing ■□

The act of one player kicking the ball successfully to a teammate. There are many types of specific passes, the first one introduced usually being the inside-of-the-foot pass.

General receiving ■□

The act of one player successfully collecting or trapping a ball that has come to him. The most common way to receive a ball is a pass from a teammate.

Generate, Generated

Creation of an opportunity to score.

Genuine chance

A pass or set-up that creates a high possibility of scoring a goal.

German Soccer

Traditional form of play using strength, fitness and relentlessness.

Get a foot on □

Did not successfully complete a tackle, but deflected the ball; stretched out and was able to reach the ball with little effect.

Get a piece of the ball, Get a piece of the man □

To make contact with only a portion of the ball during a tackle; to make questionable, improper or illegal contact with the ball carrier during a tackle.

Get a point □

To obtain one point in the standings by salvaging a tie in a game.

Get a result

To win or tie a game.

Get away from defender or man □

To quickly sprint away from an opponent and keep running such that the defender doesn't follow or is left behind.

Get back – ► □

►***On-field Oral Communication:*** When the defense is in desperate need of help, this tells teammates to return and play defense immediately.

Get forward, Getting forward □

To move into the attack.

Get free, Get open ■□

To lose, or separate from, one's defender and move or run into space in order to be available to receive a pass.

Get in □

To play in a game, usually as a substitute.

Get involved, Getting involved ☐

An individual who makes active runs, usually into the attack; not ball watching.

Get out – ▶ ☐

▶ ***On-field Oral Communication:*** Goalkeeper or central back is telling the defenders to move upfield. See: Step, Step Out.

Get some minutes ☐

To play in a game, usually as a substitute.

Get there – ▶ ■☐

▶ ***On-field Oral Communication:*** Encouragement to get to the open spot on the field where the ball is arriving; encouragement to win a 50/50 ball.

Get three points ☐

To win a game and obtain the maximum number of points applied to the standings.

Get turned (1); Can't get turned ☐

The ability, or inability, to manipulate the ball so that one is facing the attacking goal, after having received the ball or being forced to have one's back to the goal.

Get turned (2) ☐

As a result of a fake, feint or move by an attacker, the defender is forced to face his own goal.

Get up – ▶

▶ ***On-field Oral Communication:*** Tells a teammate to immediately get back on their feet after having been knocked down or slipping to the ground in order to continue to immediately fight for the ball.

Get up for the game, Getting up ☐

Prepare mentally and psychologically to play at the optimum level during a match; psyched; psyched up.

Gets by ☐

Beats a defender.

Getting beaten ☐

A player in a defensive position who allows an attacker, who usually has the ball, to get around or behind him.

Getting behind the defenders ☐

Running into open space between the defenders and the attacking goal.

Getting into it ☐

Two players escalating the game challenges between them into something personal.

Getting into position ■☐

A player, particularly a goalkeeper, who properly recognizes and anticipates the flow of play and moves in advance to a spot that best benefits his team.

Getting loose ☐

Making a run that frees oneself from a defender.

Getting narrow, Playing too narrow

As a team, playing or staying too much in the middle of the field. (Can apply offensively or defensively.)

Getting some minutes ☐

A substitute receiving some playing time in a match, usually after the outcome of the match has been decided.

Getting too narrow ☐

As a team, playing or staying too much in the middle of the field in such a way as to significantly constrict the offense and reduce the chances of scoring due to causing defenders to be packed in front of the goal.

Getting turned ☐

Defender is forced to face his own goal by an offensive player.

Getting under it ☐

Unintentionally lofting a ball when kicking it, usually causing it to go high and over the crossbar on a shot.

GF *(Abbrev.)*
Goals For.

Ghost goal
A call that a goal was scored which did not actually occur.

Gift □
An easy, uncontested, goal, often scored as a result of a defensive error.

Give away, Giveaway, Given away □
Lost the ball to an opponent due to a misplay.

Give it – ► □
► ***On-field Oral Communication:*** Go ahead and pass the ball to the open teammate you see.

Give it away, Give the ball away □
A player or team making a bad pass or making no challenge such that the ball is easily obtained by the other team.

Give it up □
To lose the ball.

Give the ball to ■□
To pass to a teammate.

Give up a corner, Give up a throw-in ■□
To provide an out-of-bounds restart to the opponent.

Give-and-go ◘ □
A combination of two passes where a player passes to a teammate and then runs around a defender and immediately receives the ball back with a return pass; wall pass; one-two; 1 - 2.

Giveaway ■□
To lose the ball to the opponent, often due to a misplay.

Gives it away
Makes a poor pass or commits a dribbling error that easily allows an opponent to take possession of the ball.

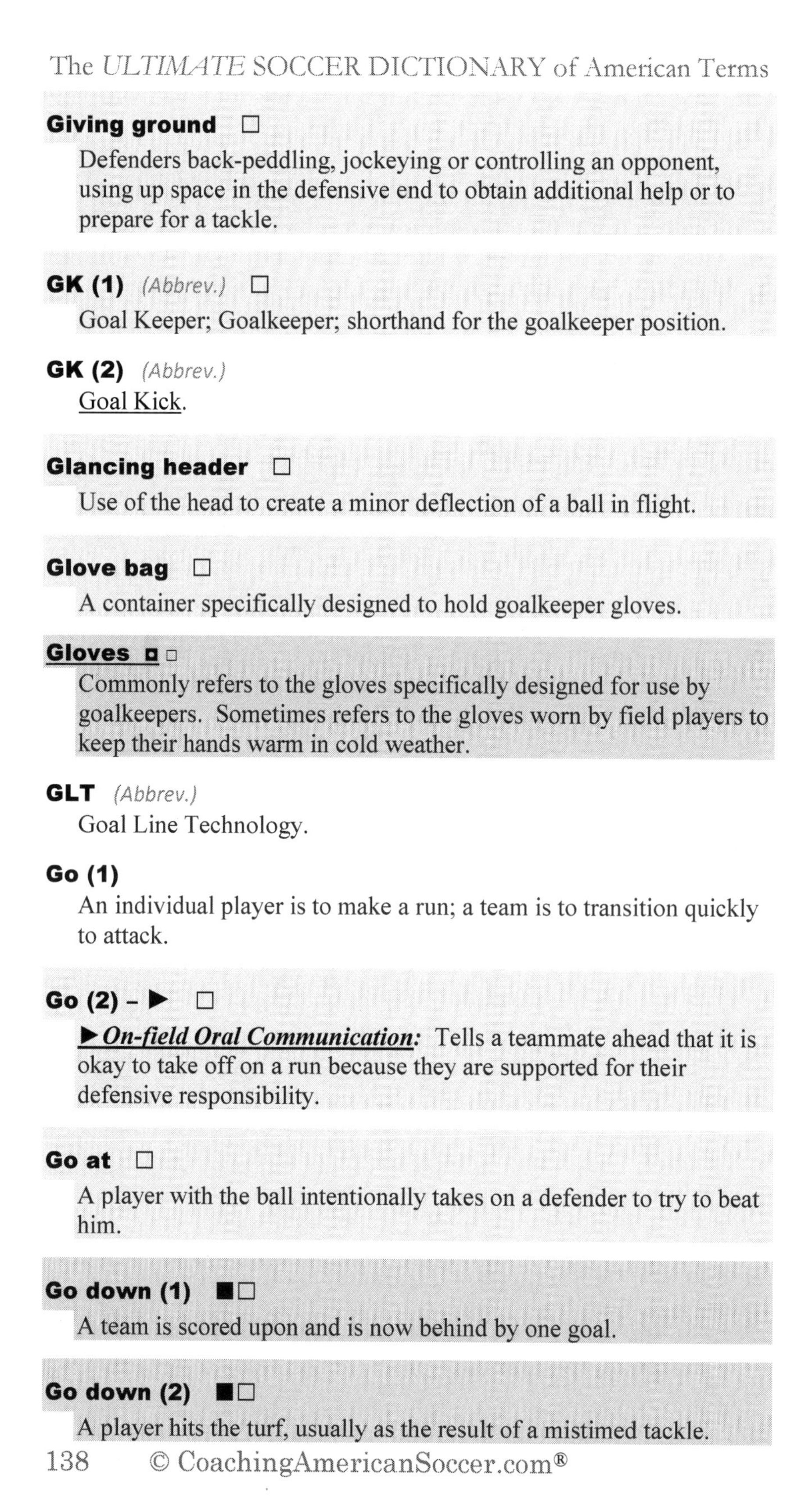

Giving ground ☐

Defenders back-peddling, jockeying or controlling an opponent, using up space in the defensive end to obtain additional help or to prepare for a tackle.

GK (1) *(Abbrev.)* ☐

Goal Keeper; Goalkeeper; shorthand for the goalkeeper position.

GK (2) *(Abbrev.)*

Goal Kick.

Glancing header ☐

Use of the head to create a minor deflection of a ball in flight.

Glove bag ☐

A container specifically designed to hold goalkeeper gloves.

Gloves ◘ ☐

Commonly refers to the gloves specifically designed for use by goalkeepers. Sometimes refers to the gloves worn by field players to keep their hands warm in cold weather.

GLT *(Abbrev.)*

Goal Line Technology.

Go (1)

An individual player is to make a run; a team is to transition quickly to attack.

Go (2) – ▶ ☐

▶ ***On-field Oral Communication:*** Tells a teammate ahead that it is okay to take off on a run because they are supported for their defensive responsibility.

Go at ☐

A player with the ball intentionally takes on a defender to try to beat him.

Go down (1) ■☐

A team is scored upon and is now behind by one goal.

Go down (2) ■☐

A player hits the turf, usually as the result of a mistimed tackle.

Go for goal □

Attacking player with the ball runs/dribbles directly to the goal to shoot; the overwhelming desire to score.

Go the right way □

The goalkeeper guesses correctly and makes a save on a penalty kick.

Go the wrong way □

The goalkeeper guesses incorrectly and fails to make a save on a penalty kick.

Go through midfield

To build an attack by utilizing the midfield players, usual with short passes on the ground.

Go through the back of the player □

To forcefully contact an opponent from behind when the opponent has position, usually resulting in a foul.

Go to ground □

(1) Slide;
(2) Perform a slide tackle;
(3) Slide when one shouldn't or doesn't have to.

Go up for ■□

Jumping for a head ball; goalkeeper jumping to catch or punch a ball.

Go-ahead goal ■□

A team scores to go up by one goal.

Goal (equipment) ◘ □

Law 1 of the Laws of the Game; consisting of two goalposts and a crossbar and centered on each goal-line, must have an inside dimension of eight-feet high and eight-yards across; material, dimensions and color stated in Law 1; The Goal.

Goal (to score) ◘ □

Law 10 of the Laws of the Game: "A goal is scored when the whole of the ball passes over the goal-line, between the goalposts and under the crossbar, provided no infringement of the Laws of the Game has been committed previously by the team scoring the goal."

Goal anchors

Any of a number of devices designed to hold goals in place, specifically for safety purposes, so that they won't tip over; e.g., weights, sand bags, spikes, stakes.

Goal Area (1) ◘ □

The Goal Area is the small ***rectangular box*** (6 yards x 20 yards), immediately in front of the goal – (i.e., ***within*** the larger Penalty Area). See: Appendix 3 – Field Diagram.

Remember: In the electronic versions, each "**Quick-Start**" term – ***hyperlinked*** and with the symbol ◘ – is linked to Appendix 1 (and ***linked back*** to its definition).

Goal Area (2)

• Law 1 of the Laws of the Game describes the Goal Area as a rectangle (at each end of the field) formed by the goal-line and lines drawn **six yards into the field** (from a point **six yards from each goal post**) and the parallel line connecting the two ends.
• In some instances, the Goal Area is used to determine ***where and how play will be restarted***. E.g., goal kicks may be taken from anywhere within the Goal Area (including the line). (This also applies for defenders' free kicks awarded within the Goal Area.)
• A.k.a.: "the 6-yard box".
See: Appendix 3 – Field Diagram.

Goal Average, G Ave., Goal Difference Average

The total number of Goals For minus the total number of Goals Allowed, divided by the number of games played, during a competition or certain timeframe.

Goal Box (= Goal Area)

• The term "Goal Box" is synonymous with "Goal Area". Whenever any reference is made to the "Goal Box", it means "Goal Area". All rules that apply to the "Goal Area" apply equivalently to the "Goal Box".
• Goal Area = Goal Box (just as: Penalty Area = Penalty Box)
See: Goal Area; Penalty Area (a.k.a. "Penalty Box").
See: Appendix 3 – Field Diagram.

Goal celebration □

An act of exuberance demonstrated by a player or team just after scoring a goal; celebration; an "unwritten rule" of soccer is to not engage in a celebration that demeans the opponent.

Goal Difference □

The total number of Goals For minus the total number of Goals Allowed, during a competition or certain number of games.

Goal Kick ◘ □

Law 16 of the Laws of the Game; a re-start awarded to the defending team when the whole of the ball passes over the goal-line, whether on the ground or in the air, when last touched by an attacking player (as long as a goal has not been scored in accordance with Law 10); kick is taken from within the Goal Area in accordance with the procedures identified in Law 16.

Goal kick defense

A designed pattern of play or coverage of players, used by a defending team, to try to disrupt the opponent or intercept the ball during an opponent's goal kick.

Goal kick offense

A designed pattern of play or placement of players, used by the offensive team, to try to successfully retain possession of a goal kick and keep the ball in play on attack.

Goal line, Goal-line ◘ □

One of the two end-lines of the field of play - see Goal-lines; A common-use term for only that portion of the goal-line between the two goal posts (although each goal-line actually extends the entire width of the field). Law 1 of the Laws of the Game.
See: Appendix 3 – Field Diagram.

Goal Line Technology

Computer-based system using five- to eight-cameras which can determine if a ball has completely passed between the uprights, under the crossbar and past the goal-line, intended to help the referee determine if a goal has been scored; GLT.

Goal-lines □

Law 1 of the Laws of the Game; the two shorter lines of the rectangular field of play; the full end lines of a soccer field from corner to corner, including the part of the line between the goal posts; must be the same width as the goalposts and crossbar of the goal; end lines. See: Appendix 3 – Field Diagram.

Goal mouth scramble

A number of players contesting for the ball, often including the goalkeeper, with no one in clear possession, usually in an area directly in front of the goal.

Goal mouth, Goalmouth ◘ □

The plane of the goal inside the uprights, under the crossbar, and above the goal-line.

Goal poacher, Goal poaching □

An attacker who always hangs around the top of the Penalty Area, harassing and stretching the defense, looking for misplays or errors which could lead to scoring easy goals.

Goal posts ◘ □

Law 1 of the Laws of the Game; vertical components of the goal; two upright posts equidistant from the ends of the goal-line.

Goal safety

Law 1 of the Laws of the Game; goals must be securely anchored to the ground, especially true for portable goals.

Goal sand bags

Heavy-duty non-porous sacks, filled with sand, designed to hold goals in place, specifically for safety purposes so that they won't tip over.

Goalie ◘ □

See: Goalkeeper.

Goalie box, Goalkeeper's box

The terms "Goalie Box" and "Goalkeeper's Box" are synonymous with "**Penalty Area**" (and "**Penalty Box**"). Whenever any reference is made to these terms, it means "Penalty Area". All rules that apply to the "Penalty Area" thus apply fully and identically.
See: Penalty Area.

Goalie gloves ■□

Specifically-designed handwear to help goalkeepers catch soccer balls; Oversized mitts usually incorporating some type of synthetic rubber or other material that aids in gripping the ball.

Goalie headgear ☐

A soft helmet designed to provide some protection to a goalkeeper's head in the event of a collision with an opponent or a goalpost.

Goalkeeper, Goal Keeper ◘ ☐

Player position specifically designated under Law 3 of the Laws of the Game; must wear contrasting jersey; has unique handling privileges within his own Penalty Area under Law 12.

Goalkeeper change

Law 3 of the Laws of the Game; the goalkeeper may be substituted according to the provisions for the match, or a player on the field may switch with the goalkeeper, either upon informing and receiving permission from the referee, during a stoppage in the match. Law 4 jersey color must be followed.

Goalkeeper jerseys ■☐

Often long-sleeve shirts with padded elbows.

Goalkeeper pants ☐

Usually full-leg pants with padded hips and knees.

Goalkeeper shorts ■☐

Usually shorts with padded hips.

Goalkeeper's "W" ◘ ☐

The "letter" formed by the thumbs and index fingers of both hands as the fingers are spread and the thumbs are touched together; the basic hand position used by a goalkeeper to catch a ball.

Goalkeeper's box, goalie box; Keeper's box (Penalty Area)

The terms "Goalkeeper's Box", "Keeper's box", and "Goalie Box" are synonymous with "**Penalty Area**" (and "**Penalty Box**"). Whenever any reference is made to these terms, it means "Penalty Area". All rules that apply to the "Penalty Area" thus apply fully and identically to each of these terms.

See: Penalty Area.

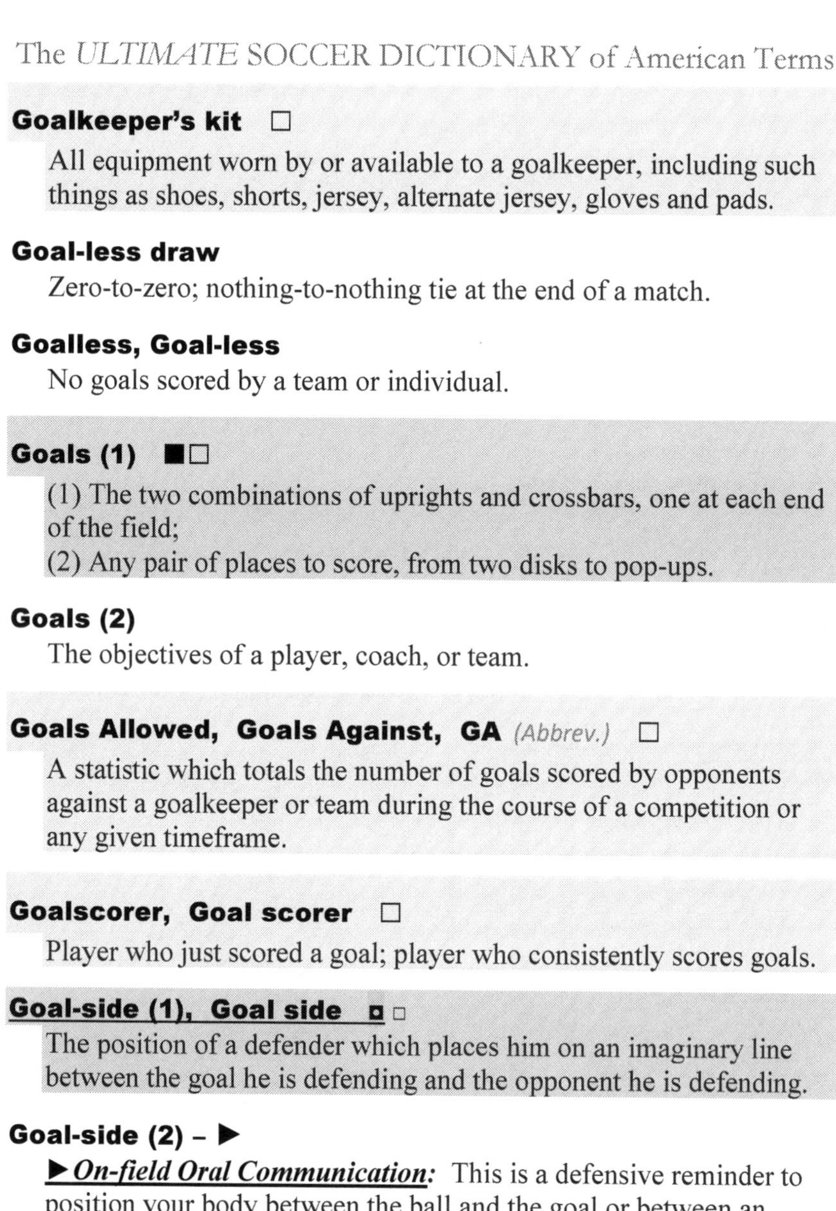

Goalkeeper's kit ☐

All equipment worn by or available to a goalkeeper, including such things as shoes, shorts, jersey, alternate jersey, gloves and pads.

Goal-less draw

Zero-to-zero; nothing-to-nothing tie at the end of a match.

Goalless, Goal-less

No goals scored by a team or individual.

Goals (1) ■☐

(1) The two combinations of uprights and crossbars, one at each end of the field;
(2) Any pair of places to score, from two disks to pop-ups.

Goals (2)

The objectives of a player, coach, or team.

Goals Allowed, Goals Against, GA *(Abbrev.)* ☐

A statistic which totals the number of goals scored by opponents against a goalkeeper or team during the course of a competition or any given timeframe.

Goalscorer, Goal scorer ☐

Player who just scored a goal; player who consistently scores goals.

Goal-side (1), Goal side ■☐

The position of a defender which places him on an imaginary line between the goal he is defending and the opponent he is defending.

Goal-side (2) – ▶

▶ ***On-field Oral Communication:*** This is a defensive reminder to position your body between the ball and the goal or between an opponent and the goal. (Recognize that there may be occasions where you may think you are properly aligned but are not and this lets you know.)

Goal-side position ■☐

A defender must be between the opponent and his own goal to effectively defend.

Goal-side of the ball ☐

A defender who is challenging an attacker who has the ball must be on an imaginary line drawn from the ball to the center of his own goal in order to properly defend.

Goes down easy ☐

A player hits the ground with minimal contact, usually in an attempt to draw a foul or particularly a penalty kick.

Goes off (Comes on) ☐

Player substitution; one player leaves the field so another player may enter.

Going early ☐

Offside; running into an offside position before the pass is made.

Going forward ☐

Making runs and taking the ball into the offensive third (as opposed to maintaining possession and passing the ball around at midfield or in the back).

Going in the book ☐

To have one's name recorded by the referee due to committing a yellow- or red-card offense.

Going in; Coming off ■☐

Substitution; one player leaves the field of play and one player enters.

Going inside ■☐

Making a run from near the sideline into the middle of the field.

Going on; Moving on ☐

Team advancing from a group stage to the second or knockout round of a tournament.

Going through ☐

Team advancing from a group stage to the second or knockout round of a tournament.

Gold Cup; CONCACAF Gold Cup

Regional competition for the men's national teams of the CONCACAF federation held every two years.

Golden ball □

Award to player designated most valuable player in a tournament.

Golden boot □

Award to player scoring the most goals in a tournament.

Golden glove □

Award to goalkeeper designated most valuable goalkeeper in a tournament.

Golden Goal

Where provided for by game or tournament rules, the first team to score in an overtime period wins and the game is immediately over.

Good ball ■□

A player has made an excellent pass to a teammate, which has created an opportunity for a scoring chance.

Good idea

Excellent choice on the part of a player, when given a number of options, to pass, shoot, or make a run.

Good run

Movement into open space that sets up the option of receiving a pass.

Good touch □

A well-played ball.

Got me – ►

►***On-field Oral Communication:*** I'm open for a pass.

Got your back – ► ■□

►***On-field Oral Communication:*** Defender is telling his teammate, who is ahead of him, that he is covered if he wants to take on the opponent with the ball.

GP *(Abbrev.)*

Games Played.

Grabbed
(1) Goalkeeper caught the ball with his hands;
(2) Player held an opponent.

Grabbing ☐
Defender intentionally holding on to an opponent's shirt or shorts.

Grade
(1) Referee designation of level of games which can be officiated, due to knowledge, performance, and assessments;
(2) Performance level of a referee, assessor or assignor;
(3) Player assessment.

Graphics software
A computer application, specifically designed for soccer, used to illustrate plays and movement.

Greasy
A slick surface due to rain.

Great ball
An excellent pass or service.

Grid
A confined area designated by discs or cones delimiting a space used for a practice drill.

Grip ☐
Quality of a goalie glove as determined by the goalkeeper's feeling of how well he can hold on to a ball.

Ground crossbar
Stabilizing metal rod running along the ground which connects the backstays of a goal.

Ground game ☐
The strategy and tactics used by a team when the ball is played on the turf, as opposed to in the air (aerial game).

Ground, Grounds ☐
The soccer field; pitch; stadium, stadium complex.

Group of Death
Teams in a division of a tournament deemed the hardest from which to advance because all of the teams are good.

Group play ☐

A selection of teams playing in a round-robin format where usually the top-two teams advance to a knock-out or single-elimination phase of a tournament.

Grudge match

Next meeting between two teams after a particularly contentious game.

GS *(Abbrev.)*

Goals Scored.

Guard ◘ ☐

Mark an opponent.

Guard stays

Material or devices (such as sleeves, “hook-and-loop” fasteners and tape), used to keep shinguards in position.

Guess, Guessing ☐

Goalkeeper diving one way or the other in an attempt to anticipate the direction of a penalty kick.

Guest player ☐

Player registered with another team who is permitted by organizing-committee rules, usually for a tournament, to participate with a different team.

Guided questions

Like a classroom teacher, interrogatories directed by coaches to players, designed to elicit a specific response in order to reinforce a soccer concept provided during instruction.

Hack, Hackers

Players who consistently foul with unnecessary contact, poorly-timed tackles, inappropriate play, or intentional kicks into opponents that are just short of fouls.

Hacking □

Consistently kicking an opponent's feet or legs without contacting the ball.

Hacky Sack® ■□

Registered trademark for a popular "footbag" (similar to a beanbag), often used to practice soccer juggling skills, for fun, or even during rehab.
[See photo (top right) of a popular style of Hacky Sack® footbag. Used with permission of the manufacturer: InterSport Corp. dba Wham-O.]

Half (1) ■□

One side of the two sides of the field of play; the offensive side or the defensive side of the field; each team's defensive side of the field.

Half (2) ■□

The first or second timed portion of a game.

Half volley, Half-volley □

A kick, usually using the instep, of an airborne ball just after it bounces.

Halfback, Halfbacks ■□

Midfielders; "middies;" players positioned between back defenders and strikers. See: Appendix 2: Player Positions.

Half-space, Halfspace, Half-spaces □

A coaching construct in which the field is divided into imaginary zones, with these main zones located horizontally between the wings and the center.

Halftime, Half-time interval ■□
Law 7 of the Laws of the Game; halftime interval may not exceed 15 minutes; duration based on competition rules and agreement of referee.

Halftime changes, Halftime adjustments
Substitutions or tactical modifications made by the coach at the half-time interval to try to correct deficiencies or improve the chances of scoring, as identified by the play observed in the first half of a match.

Halftime whistle ■□
The referee signals the end of the first half of a match.

Halfway Line
Law 1 of the Laws of the Game; joins the midpoints of the two touch lines of the rectangular field of play; the midline which divides the field into two equal halves; the "50."

Halves ■□
The two equal periods of play of a soccer game. (First half; second half.)

Hand / Arm fighting
Defender and/or attacker placing their hand and pushing on the other person's hand or arm in an attempt to gain an advantage in relative position, most usually while sprinting for the ball.

Hand checking
Defender placing his hand on the back of an attacker to help gauge distance and relative movement.

Hand signals
On-field, non-verbal, visual communication which identifies such things as the type of corner kick to be taken, or that a player is open for a pass.

Handling outside the area ■□
The goalkeeper contacting the ball illegally with his hands, outside of his Penalty Area in violation of Law 12, Fouls and Misconduct, of the Laws of the Game.

Hands, Handling, Handles the ball, Hand ball ◘ □

Violation of Law 12 of the Laws of the Game, "Fouls and Misconduct," which is the deliberate act of a player making contact with the ball with his hand or arm; resulting in a direct free kick.

Hands-Body-Feet □

Mnemonic device to help remember the contact fouls contained in Law 12 of the Laws of the Game.

Handshake ■□

Personal greeting among players to demonstrate sportsmanship, either before or after a match.

Harsh call

The referee gives a card when it is apparently undeserved; a foul which is over-penalized.

Has position, Having position, Have position

(1) To occupy a position on the field that provides the player with better opportunities to play the ball (compared to the opponent's opportunity); (2) To establish and occupy a spot on the field such that the opponent would have to make contact (e.g., illegally) to play the ball. [For example, assume an opponent wants to head a ball being crossed toward him. If he doesn't have good position, he might still attempt to head the ball, but to do so, he might end up ***(illegally)*** jumping onto the back of the player that has position.]

Hash mark

Optional Mark; field marking identified in Law 1 of the Laws of the Game placed at 90-degree angles outside of the end lines and side lines, 11-yards from each corner, to help the referee and assistant referees determine that defenders are the proper distance away from corner kicks.

Hat trick

Player scores three goals in a game.

Head trap □

Player receives a ball in the air and takes the pace off the ball by contacting it with his forehead and relaxing his neck so the ball drops toward his feet.

Head up – ▶

▶ ***On-field Oral Communication:*** Teammate is telling the ball carrier that his vision is down and he needs to look up and see the field.

Headband ■□

String, piece of cloth, or other soft device wrapped around the head, usually used to keep long hair away from the eyes.

Head-butt ■□

A player intentionally striking an opponent with the part of the head usually used in heading; violation of Law 12, Fouls and Misconduct, subject to ejection.

Header, Head ball, Heading the ball ■□

Player aggressively strikes a ball with his head to shoot, pass, or defend.

Headgear; Protective headgear ■□

A soft "helmet' worn mostly by goalkeepers to minimize the possible effects of collisions; a device worn around the skull to reduce the effects of possible concussion; padded headgear. Also comes in a "headband" variety.

Heading, Head the ball, Head ball, Header ■□

Intentionally contacting the ball with the head for any purpose.

Heads up – ▶ ■□

▶ ***On-field Oral Communication:*** Call made, typically during a practice session, to warn a player who is unaware that a ball may strike them.

Head-to-head contact □

Two players inadvertently hitting their skulls together, usually going for a header; may result in a split scalp or a concussion.

Head-to-head record

The cumulative results in wins, losses, and ties, of games played between the same two teams.

Health ■□

The physical well-being of a player; the well-being of a player as it relates to his status or ability to play.

Health and injury insurance
Medical coverage for players and coaches.

Heat exhaustion ■□
Heat-related illness due to exposure to high temperatures, often accompanied by fatigue, nausea, or vomiting, which requires stopping exercise, getting out of the heat, and replacement of fluids.

Heat stroke
An extremely serious elevated body temperature, often accompanied by the lack of the ability to sweat, which can cause systemic failures and needs immediate medical attention.

Heavy contact
Colliding with an opponent forcefully, often to the point of committing a foul.

Heavy first touch
Initial contact with the ball – trying to trap, receive, or collect it – that does not sufficiently take the pace off and causes the ball to get away from the player.

Heavy touch □
Any contact with the ball that is insufficiently soft and results in the ball rebounding too far away.

Heavy traffic
A lot of players (usually defenders) concentrated in a small area, through which a player with the ball is trying to navigate.

Heel – ► ■□
► ***On-field Oral Communication:*** Trailing teammate is telling the ball carrier that he is available for a back pass.

Heel pass □
A pass executed by kicking the ball with the heel of the foot; usually a back pass; back heel.

Height ■□
Measurement of how tall a player is; Distance of a ball above the ground at any point in time.

Height advantage □

A player or group of players taller than the opponent, usually representing a greater chance of success in heading.

Height disadvantage

A player or group of players shorter than the opponent, usually representing less of a chance of success in heading.

Helicopter parent

A mother or father constantly hovering around their child, sometimes hovering around the coach.

Help(!) – ▶ □

▶ ***On-field Oral Communication:*** Defender is making an urgent plea for assistance because there are too many attackers to cover.

Helping a player up ■□

An act of sportsmanship to assist a player who has landed on the ground back to a standing position; considered to be one of the "unwritten rules" of soccer.

Here – ▶ □

▶ ***On-field Oral Communication:*** You are open and calling for the ball. (Generally, a short-pass option to a specific spot. The teammate with the ball likely has an imminent challenge and needs to get rid of the ball quickly.)

Here we go – ▶

▶ ***On-field Oral Communication:*** Enthusiastic request to get the entire team to transition into attack, usually a fast break.

Here's your help – ▶ ■□

▶ ***On-field Oral Communication:*** You are open and available for a pass. (Generally, a short-pass option to a specific spot. Lets the teammate with the ball know that you are a passing option.)

Remember: Each "***On-field Oral Communication***" term has this symbol ▶ and in the electronic versions is ***hyperlinked*** to Appendix 4, where all of these terms are listed together. Each term is linked back to its definition.

Hermann Award, Hermann Trophy

Trophy presented annually to the top men's and women's college players in the United States by the Missouri Athletic Club (MAC).

Hesitation

A pause, faltering, or delay to act decisively, usually due to a split-second doubt in decision-making, which often results in a missed opportunity to score or block a goal, or in the loss of the ball.

Hesitation move □

A dribbling feint where the ballcarrier stops momentarily, in order to unbalance his defender, and then starts dribbling again.

Hexagonal

A World Cup qualifier competition with six teams.

HG *(Abbrev.)*

Hard Ground; soccer shoes with cleats designed to be used on hard ground.

High (1) ■□

A shot over the crossbar.

High (2)

Playing/player closest to the attacking goal.

High (3)

A shot that scores within the upper-third of the goal.

High ball ■□

Intentionally sending a ball arcing up and into the area in front of the attacking goal, not necessarily to a specific teammate, to see if something dangerous might occur.

High catches ■□

Goalkeeper has to jump, stretch and reach up in order to obtain possession.

High cross □

An airborne pass, usually taken from near the sideline, which lofts particularly up into the air.

High dive □

Goalkeeper projecting himself into the air to make a save generally at waist level or above.

High kick ◘ ☐

Common usage for a form of dangerous play (Law 12) where a foot is raised above the waist into an oncoming opponent.

High line

Back line staying far upfield or farther upfield than might be considered to be normal; Forward line staying closer to the attacking goal or farther upfield than might be normally expected.

High line – ►

►***On-field Oral Communication:*** Goalkeeper or defensive organizer tells his backs to switch to a defensive posture that has them stay as far upfield as possible.

High point, Highest point

Farthest spot up from the ground achievable by any given player to successfully make a jump header or for the goalkeeper to catch a ball.

High scoring

A match with a lot of goals.

High shot ■☐

A shot which goes over the crossbar.

High tempo

A team playing a match with fast action and speed.

High tipping

The act of the goalkeeper jumping high, up or to the left or right, in order to deflect or parry the ball over or just outside of the goal, when unable to catch it cleanly.

Higher

Forward play where a striker stays as close to the farthest back defender as possible and tries to force the defense to play closer to its own goal; farther upfield.

High-pressure defense

Defense noted for a high-energy level by the defenders, usually utilizing tight, man-to-man marking and a high line, in order to create errors and intercept the ball.

High-quality chance

A pass or set-up that creates a significant possibility of scoring a goal.

History of the Sport
The record of soccer from its origins to the present day.

Hit
A ball strike or shot.

Hit the deck
To land on the ground, usually due to being tripped.

Hit the post, Hit the crossbar ■□
A shot which bounces off of, or deflects from, the goal; "hit the woodwork."

Hit the wall □
A player or team suddenly loses fitness and the ability to run and perform skills, at a point in time during a match.

Hitch kick □
A ball skill whereby the non-kicking leg is thrust into the air in order to raise or alter the path of the kicking leg as it is thrust in the air to strike the ball immediately thereafter, before the first leg comes back to the ground.

Hitting the 30- to 40-yard bomb
A shot from great distance which scores.

Hitting the ground □
A field player is tripped or fouled in such a way as to land hard or awkwardly; a goalkeeper goes for a save and is undercut or otherwise lands badly.

HM *(Abbrev.)*
Holding Midfielder; shorthand for the holding midfielder position.

Hobbled
Limping or unable to run or perform skills at peak efficiency due to a foot injury.

Hobbling
A defender running behind an opponent with the ball nips at his heels or feet with the front of his shoes.

Hold (1), Holding the run □
Attacking player slows down or even stops in order to wait before going into a proper position to receive a cross.

Hold (2), Hold it – ► ☐

► ***On-field Oral Communication:*** Tells the ball carrier to continue to dribble or "carry" the ball until the teammate is comfortable that he can receive a pass (dribbler must be clear to do so).

Hold (3), Hold at the 18 – ►

► ***On-field Oral Communication:*** Keeper or defensive organizer asks defender(s) to stop backpedaling and stand their ground at the top of the penalty area.

Hold him/them there – ►

► ***On-field Oral Communication:*** Keeper or defensive organizer asks defender(s) to stop backpedaling and stand their ground.

Hold off a defender

Offensive player projecting an arm into the opponent in order to defeat a tackle, usually side-by-side on the run.

Hold on ☐

To retain possession and take whatever actions may be necessary near the end of a game to kill time in order to run out the clock.

Hold the ball ☐

To dribble the ball in order to maintain possession, wait for support, kill time, or allow for runs.

Hold up the ball ☐

Upon receiving a pass, a player intentionally screens or dribbles the ball into space in order to delay or wait until support can arrive.

Hold your spot ☐

To wait, stop, or not make a run, in order to not go into an offside position.

Holding a (yellow) card ☐

A player who may still be playing in a match after having received a Caution; A player who may be playing in a tournament who had received a Caution in a preceding game.

Holding a line ☐

Back defenders maintaining a unified position to try to keep opponents from advancing farther upfield or to try to force them offside.

Holding ground ☐

A defender or defenders stop backpedaling.

Holding midfielder

Position designation for a midfielder whose primary responsibility is to maintain possession of the ball as an attack is developed.

Holding on ☐

A team struggles to keep the ball away from the opponent long enough for a match to end with a favorable result.

Holding onto the ball ☐

An individual player maintaining possession of the ball while dribbling, usually while being challenged; a team maintaining possession of the ball by passing.

Holding the ball in the midfield ☐

A team tactic designed to maintain possession of the ball either as a desired type of attack is developed or simply to keep the ball away from the opponent.

Holding the high line

Tactic by the defensive backs, acting in concert, to try to stay as far upfield as possible in order to force offside.

Holding their line ☐

The back defenders of a team have taken a stand and are not retreating.

Holding up

A one-goal lead that looks like it will stand up until the final whistle.

Holding up play ☐

Intentionally delaying getting the ball back into play in order to waste time.

Holding, Holds an opponent

Violation of Law 12 of the Laws of the Game, Fouls and Misconduct, resulting in the award of a direct free kick.

Hole player

Secondary or set-back striker playing in the space (gap or hole) behind a lead striker.

Home ■□

Playing at one's own location; not playing "away" or at a neutral site.

Home field, Home ground

The field (pitch) or stadium where a team plays its home games.

Home kit

Uniform to be worn while playing at home or as the designated home team.

Home leg

The home game of a home-and-home (two-leg) series.

Home Team ▫□

Team playing at one's own grounds or as the "designated" home team on a common field.

Home-and-home

Two-game series, one game played at each team's location.

Home-field advantage

The benefits to be derived by a team as a result of being used to their own location, having their own fans present, or not having to travel.

Hoodie, Hoody

A hooded sweatshirt used in training or as fanwear.

Hook

An "inward" curve of the ball after it is struck, right-to-left when coming off the right foot, and left-to-right when coming off the left foot; often used to describe an unintended result.

Hook volley

See: Side volley.

Hooking run

An attacker, without the ball, runs toward his teammate who has the ball, in order to draw a defender, and then reverses direction and runs to the space created behind the defender.

Hooligans

"Fans," or "Supporters" of a team who engage in bad, violent, and/or illegal behavior.

Hop pass, Hopped pass

A ball sent past a defender around waist height which can bounce to a teammate or is used as a personal pass, usually performed with the upper toes of the foot.

Horizontal axis

The field from sideline to sideline, parallel to the goal-lines.

Horn

Noisemaking device used to signal the end of a time period (e.g., at the end of the first half).

Hospital ball, Hospital pass

A pass leading a teammate directly into a likely collision with an opponent.

Host

Home team; to provide facilities and services for a match.

Hostile environment

Generally, an away game where tensions, for whatever reason, are running high among the spectators supporting the home team.

House; House league

The recreational division of local youth soccer.

HT *(Abbrev.)*

Half Time; shorthand for halftime.

Huddle, Huddle up ☐

To gather in a group before or after a game or for coaching purposes.

Hug the post – ►

►***On-field Oral Communication:*** Goalkeeper is instructing a defender to take a position tight to the goalpost.

Hunger, Hungry

Demonstrated desire on the part of a player or team to move forward, attack, score, and/or control a match.

Hurdles

Training devices used to improve quickness, stamina, or jumping ability; generally not more than a foot off the ground (i.e., not track hurdles).

Hybrid system (1)

Formation established for a team by a coach who has melded components from two different "standard" formations.

Hybrid system (2)

Playing surface using an integrated combination of artificial and natural materials.

Hydration ■□

Maintaining the proper level of fluids within the body; ensuring that players drink enough.

Hydration break

(1) An intentional stoppage of practice or a match to allow players to hydrate by drinking water or sports drinks; cooling break; water break.
(2) A FIFA-authorized procedure where a referee may determine before the start of a match, based on a formula involving temperature, humidity, and direct sun, if a break for the intake of fluids will be used at the 30-minute mark or after, and at what stoppage of play, such as a throw-in.

I'm back – ▶ ■□

▶ ***On-field Oral Communication:*** Usually means: "You have help behind you for a back pass." Sometimes indicates: Returning to a position after a switch or overlapping run.

I'm Open – ▶

▶ ***On-field Oral Communication:*** Tells a teammate that you are not covered and therefore are available for a pass (usually used at lower levels when dribblers have their heads down). At higher levels, a decoy call intended to draw a defender in order to open up space.

I've got (#_) – ▶ ■□

▶ ***On-field Oral Communication:*** Tells teammates who you are marking. This is used to assist in organizing the defense.

I've got him/her – ▶

▶ ***On-field Oral Communication:*** Tells a teammate that you will cover the opponent that just went past them.

I've got two – ▶

▶ ***On-field Oral Communication:*** When a defender finds they are marking two players, this tells teammates that someone needs to come back and cover the opponent farthest from the goal of the two.

I've got your spot – ▶

▶ ***On-field Oral Communication:*** Tells a player that their position is covered if a natural switch has occurred (one during the normal course of play which was not announced with a call of "Switch.") Generally, this call is made after a player goes forward and the teammate is telling them that they have the position covered until the player gets back.

Ice ■□

Frozen water (or chemical cold packs) to be applied to the site of an injury; to apply ice to reduce swelling.

Icing □

To go up by two goals with little likelihood that the opponent has enough time left in the match to get more than one.

ID2, id²

"ID2" is a USSF program intended to identify talented players for advancement on the national level. US Club Soccer's ID2 National Identification and Development Program is an Olympic Development Program (ODP) approved by the United States Olympic Committee and the U.S. Soccer Federation.

IDFK *(Abbrev.)*

Indirect Free Kick.

IF *(Abbrev.)*

Inside Forward; shorthand for the inside forward position.

IFAB *(Abbrev.)*

The International Football Association Board; Composed of FIFA and four British countries, the organization that oversees and makes changes to the Laws of the Game; The IFAB.

IFK *(Abbrev.)*

Shorthand for Indirect Free Kick.

ImPACT

Immediate Post-concussion Assessment and Cognitive Testing. "The most-widely used and most scientifically validated computerized concussion evaluation system." https://www.impacttest.com/about/

Impact sub

A player known for coming in off the bench and having an immediate, positive effect on a match.

Impede, Impeding ☐

A player blocks or obstructs an opponent's path to the ball without the ball in playing distance; Violation of Law 12, Fouls and Misconduct, resulting in the award of an indirect free kick.

Impossible angle

Shooting from a position outside of the goalpost and extremely close to the end line (goal-line, bi-line) with seemingly little chance of scoring.

Improvisation

A dribbling move or a pass made by a player which is unexpected or unique. May not always have the desired outcome.

In

Behind the defenders.

In an offside position ■□

A striker who does not have two defenders even or between him and the goal he is attacking.

In bounds ■□

The ball is within the field of play and is playable.

In form

Fit, ready, skills up to par.

In front

One team has more goals than the other; in the lead.

In play □

The ball is within the field of play and is playable.

In the air

A ball that is airborne; a goalkeeper's ability to properly handle an airborne ball.

In the net, In the back of the net ◘ □

A goal has been scored; the ball is in the net.

In touch

Rugby term "touch" is outside the two sidelines (touchlines); out of bounds.

Incidental contact ■□

Player contact which is minor and not considered to rise to the level of a foul.

Incursion

Deep attack into opposition space.

Indirect free kick ◘ □

Law 13 of the Laws of the Game. A re-start which requires that the ball be touched by another player other than the kicker for a goal to be scored. If the ball goes into the opponent's goal without touching another player, a goal kick is awarded. If the ball goes into the team's own goal without touching another player, a corner kick is awarded.

Indirect free kick signal

Law 13 of the Laws of the Game. When an indirect free kick has been awarded, the referee is to raise one arm above his head.

Indirect Kick ■□

See: Indirect Free Kick.

Indoor ball

A soccer ball specifically designed to be used for indoor soccer played on a hard-court surface, like a basketball floor; often covered with felt or a similar material.

Indoor shoes □

Soccer footwear specifically designed for playing on inside surfaces.

Indoor soccer ■□

Soccer played on a court, such as wood or artificial turf, under a roof, using modified rules.

Infill

Very small pellets made from organic or synthetic material, such as cork or used tires (crumb rubber), placed within an artificial surface to absorb shock.

Inflate ■□

To put air into a ball.

Influence □

Movement designed to try to lure a defender away from where the ball is going.

Information sheet

Player questionnaire specifically designed to elicit personal data for soccer use. Usually includes such items as full name, address, birthday, and medical history.

Infraction, Infringement □

A violation of any part of the Laws of the Game.

Injury Time ■□

Part of the time added at the end of the first or second halves to compensate for the playing time lost while an injured player was accommodated during a match; Law 7 of the Laws of the Game.
See: Added Time, Stoppage Time.
Note: "Injury Time" is NOT the same as "Extra Time" ("Overtime").

Injury, Injuries, Injured ■□

Physical hurt or damage to the body; a team having to deal with players who are not 100% fit due to injury; justification for removal or substitution of players from the field.

Inner instep ■□

The upper-middle, inside part of the instep used to chip the ball. (See shaded areas in photo at right.)

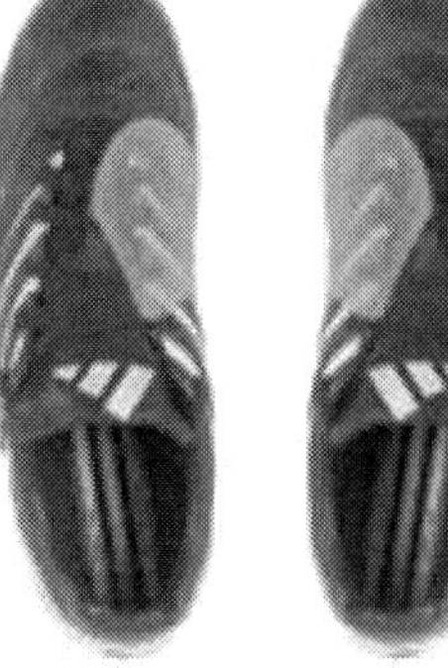

Inside

Toward the middle of the field.

Inside / Outside

Passing strategy combination intended to draw defenders toward the middle of the field and then the ball is sent toward the sideline.

Inside foot

The right foot of a player running forward and receiving a pass from the right; the left foot of a player running forward and receiving a pass from the left.

Inside Forwards *(plural)*, Inside Forward ■□

A pair of central strikers, designated as "left" and "right" (e.g., "left inside forward"), usually operating within a four- or five-forward system of play.

Inside of heel pass/shot

Use of the inside part of the heel of the foot to one-touch a pass or shot from behind the (other) foot. Also known as a "behind the back" pass or shot.

Inside of the foot ■□

The inward side of either foot, above the arch; That part of either foot that easily conforms to the shape of the ball. (See photo at right.)
See #11 Inside of the Foot
http://coachingamericansoccer.com/features/19-surfaces-of-the-soccer-shoe/

Inside of the foot pass ■□

Pass made by turning the foot and the leg outward at the hip and striking the ball with the inside of the foot, like a golf putter, so that the ball goes to a teammate.

Inside of the foot trap or receive ■□

Use of the inside of the foot to receive and take the pace off the ball.

Inside of the post

That portion of either upright of the goal that faces in or is otherwise perpendicular to the goal-line within the goal itself.

Inside of the side netting

That portion of either side of the net facing the interior of the goal; implies that, if a ball strikes it, a goal has been scored.

Inside the area ■□

The ball is within or, usually, a foul is committed within the Penalty Area.

Inside-outside

Dribbling move characterized by quickly moving the ball first with the inside of the foot and then with the outside of the same foot.

Inspection

The check by the referee prior to a match, of both the field and the players, for compliance with the Laws of the Game; check by the Assistant Referee of a substitute prior to being allowed to enter the field.

Instep ■□

The top of the foot, otherwise covered by the shoelaces of a tie shoe. See: #6 Full Instep http://coachingamericansoccer.com/features/19-surfaces-of-the-soccer-shoe/

Instep drive, Instep kick ■□

The main kick of soccer, using flexion generated from the hip and knee and then the force of the quadriceps extending the lower leg to strike the ball with the part of the foot covered by the shoelaces (the instep).

Instep trap or receive ■□

Use of the top of the foot to receive and take the pace off the ball.

Instinct

A natural or innate tendency to recognize and react to a situation that winds up being beneficial to the player or his team.

Instruction ■□

Coaching, teaching, demonstrating or otherwise presenting soccer information to players.

Instructional manual

A formal document providing the material for an instructional soccer program designed for youthful beginners.

Instructional soccer ■□

For the youngest, beginning players, a program that introduces the game of soccer and the ball and what to do with it. May include dribbling, goal scoring, juggling, passing, receiving, positions, shooting, and scrimmaging.

Instructor

Individual authorized to teach officiating to referees.

Insurance

Health and injury medical coverage; liability coverage.

Insurance goal

An extra goal or two in addition to the one-goal lead that might be expected to win a match. Scoring a goal that puts a team up by two or three scores, providing a margin for error.

Insurance kick

Putting the ball back into the net, if it has managed to bounce back into the field after a goal has been scored, in order to prove the goal.

In-swerve, In swerve

An airborne inswinger, bent, or banana kick of the ball, usually sent from near the sideline to the front of the goal, the flight of which hooks from right-to-left by a right-footed kick (from the left side of the field) or from left-to-right by a left-footed kick (from the right side of the field) usually performed as a corner kick or a cross.

In-swinger, Inswinger

A type of corner kick marked by the path of the ball in the air which starts into the field of play from the corner arc and then, due to spin imparted to the ball, curves back toward the goal.

Integrated Technology Balls

Soccer balls with electronics used in Goal Line Technology.

Intended for

The player to whom a pass was supposed to go before the ball was intercepted, deflected, or went out of bounds.

Intensity

High degree of concentration and performance.

Intentional ■□

Performing an act by choice, design, or decision; Intentional hand ball.

Intercept, Interception ■□

A defender cuts off and collects an opponent's pass.

Interchangeable, Interchangeable parts

Coaches having the ability to move players to different positions without loss of effectiveness.

Interchanging

Switching positions offensively during the course of play; offensive switching.

Interference with goalkeeper's release ■□

Usually a misguided attempt to keep the goalkeeper from releasing the ball from his hands; potential foul.

Interference; Outside interference □

Play is stopped due to things like a dog or fan on the field, or the ball striking an overhanging tree limb. Play is to be resumed with a drop ball.

Interfering with play □

Component of the Offside law, Law 11 of the Laws of the Game; player is to be penalized if he is both in an offside position and interfering with play.

Intermission ■□

Halftime.

Intermission whistle

The referee signals the end of the first half of a match.

International

(1) Any game between two national teams representing their country;
(2) A player who has played for his national team.

International fixture date

Dates on the calendar set aside by FIFA for matches between national teams. Clubs must release their players if called up to participate.

International Football Association Board

Composed of FIFA and four British countries, the organization that oversees and makes changes (amendments) to the Laws of the Game; IFAB; The IFAB.

International friendly

A game played between two national teams which is not part of a competition.

Interpassing

Close and quick passing among a group of teammates.

Interpretation

The conclusion of a referee as to whether or not a violation of the Laws of the Game has occurred.

Interval

Halftime.

Interval training □

A form of fitness training that involves alternating high-intensity exercises with low-intensity (recovery) exercises over a period of time.

Into space, Into the space, In the space ■□

Passing the ball into an area with no defenders, so that a teammate can run on to it.

Into touch

The ball is sent out of the field play over the touchline (sideline).

Inverted

A player or system orientation which is reversed from the usual.

Inverted pyramid, Inverted V

Two leading strikers with one trailing striker.

Isometrics

A form of strength training marked by applying force to an immovable object.

Italian Soccer

Traditionally a form of play emphasizing a strong, packed, defense with a counter-attack style of offense.

Jab

A goalkeeper's attempt to stab at or punch the ball in order to get it away from the goal.

Jacket

Windbreaker; zippered sweatshirt or warm-up top intended to retain heat or keep weather away from the body.

Jargon

Words and phrases specific to a particular topic – in this case, the game of soccer – including terminology that is peculiar and specific to soccer, as well as slang terms or technical terms.

Javelin throw

Long, overhand release by the goalkeeper. See: Baseball Throw.

Jersey ■□

Law 4 of the Laws of the Game, players must wear shirts; shirt.

Jersey colors

Law 4 of the Laws of the Game; players on a team must wear matching shirts; the two teams must wear different colors; all must be different than the referees; the goalkeeper must wear a shirt that is a different color from the other players and the referees.

Jersey numbers

Unique numbers printed or otherwise imparted onto team shirts, usually both the front and the back according to competition-organizer standards, which are otherwise used to identify players.

Jersey swap, Jersey exchange

Players exchanging game shirts with opponents after a match, as a courtesy to provide a souvenir or memento.

Jersey tugging ■□

A defender grabs and holds onto an opponent's shirt in an attempt to slow him up or turn his direction. Technically a form of "holding" which should be called as a foul, but at the upper levels is called if the attacker is seriously affected or if the defender fails to let go.

Jewelry

Adornments such as rings, necklaces and earrings which, if determined by the referee to be dangerous to the wearer or other participants in accordance with Law 4 of the Laws of the Game, must be removed. This may include electronic performance and tracking system (EPTS) devices.

Jock ■□

Clothing designed to support male genitalia; jock strap; athletic supporter.

Jockey – ►

► ***On-field Oral Communication:*** As a supporting defender, this tells a teammate to defend a dribbling opponent by slowly giving ground. By not tackling and attempting to take the ball, thereby avoiding the possibility of being beaten, this buys time so the defense can return, reorganize, balance and cover.

Jockeying

Movements by a defender intended to delay an opponent with the ball from advancing, allow time for more defenders to arrive, force the player toward the sideline, and/or create an opportunity to make a tackle.

Jog; Jogging ■□

An easy or slow run.

Jogging in place

An easy or slow running motion while staying in the same position.

Jostle, Jostling

To push against an opponent, usually in a crowd of people in front of the goal just before a free kick or corner kick.

JR *(Abbrev.)*

Junior; soccer shoes or cleats designed to be used by young or junior players.

Judgment

Decision by a player on what action to take; decision by a referee.

Juggle, Juggling ◘□

Generally, as a practice activity, to repeatedly strike the ball to keep it up in the air; may be done as an individual or in groups.

JUGS Soccer Machine™

Electric device designed to project soccer balls in a variety of directions with different pace and spin; often used in goalkeeper training.

Juke □

To fake or feint, causing an opponent to be set off balance.

Jump header ■□

A head ball performed in the air at the peak of a jump off the ground.

Jump rope ■□

Typically, a single rope for an individual to skip over for fitness and agility.

Jumping up; Getting up

Goalkeeper quickly standing up and recovering his position after having had to go down on the ground.

Jumps at an opponent, Jumping

Violation of Law 12 of the Laws of the Game, Fouls and Misconduct, resulting in the award of a direct free kick.

Junior varsity

In the United States, members of a secondary team below the main team; "B" team; JV.

Just behind

Pass intended for a running teammate that did not lead him enough.

Just over, Just over the top ■□

A shot which flies barely above the crossbar of the goal.

Just wide ■□

A shot which travels barely outside an upright of the goal.

Justice

After an incorrect or particularly bad call by the referee close to the goal, the resulting free kick (or penalty kick) does not result in a score.

Keep (i.e., "Keeper") – ►
►On-field Oral Communication: Goalkeeper is going to get the ball, leave the ball alone.

Keep it alive
Field player saves a ball from going out of bounds such that it can be played by a teammate.

Keep it in play
To sprint to the ball and keep it from going out of bounds.

Keep playing – ►
►On-field Oral Communication: The Referee did not blow the whistle, play on.

Keep your shape – ►
►On-field Oral Communication: The defensive organizer is reminding players to stay in, or return to, their positions.

Keep-away ■□
A practice drill, usually between two small-side teams, in which the object is to maintain possession and not allow the opposing team to get the ball.

Keeper (1) ■□
See: Goalkeeper.

Keeper (2) – ► ■□
►On-field Oral Communication: Used by the goalkeeper only, the goalkeeper is calling all defenders off in order to get the ball (or otherwise wants the ball).

Keeper's in Charge – ► □
►On-field Oral Communication: Goalkeeper announces that he has now taken control of the overall defense from the upfield defensive organizer.

Keeping everything in front □
Defenders maintain their goal-side positioning to ensure that neither the ball nor any opponents are behind them.

Keeping shape
The right players in the right place at the right time within a formation or system of play; can refer to attacking or defending.

Keeping the ball
An individual or a team maintaining possession of the ball.

Keeping the ball in front ■□
Given the inability to make a clean trap, a player is at least successful in blocking the ball forward with his body.

Kept in play, Keep it in play
Player saves the ball from going out of bounds.

KFPM *(Abbrev.)*
Kicks From the Penalty Mark.

Kick ■□
To strike with the foot.

Kick and Run
An old style of play involving long balls into the attack; unskilled play.

Kick save □
Foot save by a goalkeeper.

Kickball ■□
Soccer demonstrating little possession, skill, or technique with the ball.

Kicker
The person striking the ball with their foot.

Kick-in
A practice technique for putting the ball back into play after it goes out of bounds over a sideline, used in lieu of a throw-in.

Kicking around
Two small-sided teams playing an informal game.

Kicking the ball away
At a stoppage of play, intentionally kicking the ball astray, to keep play from restarting quickly by the opponent. Unsportsmanlike conduct which may be penalized with a Caution, yellow card.

Kicking, Kicks or attempts to kick an opponent
Violation of Law 12 of the Laws of the Game, Fouls and Misconduct, resulting in the award of a direct free kick.

Kickoff ■□
Law 8 of the Laws of the Game; a place kick taken at the center mark to start play, after a goal is scored, at the start of the second half, and to start each period of extra time.

Kick-off circle ■□
See: Center Circle.

Kickoff time ■□
The specific time designated for the actual start of a match.

Kicks, Kicks from the Penalty Mark
Penalty kick tiebreaker procedure.

KidSafe*Plus*®
Program providing background checks for adults working with children.

Kill the ball □
To trap or receive the ball so that it fails to move or "stops dead."

Kill the game
The use of passing and dribbling, and/or timewasting techniques just short of illegal activity, to maintain possession of the ball in order to run out the clock and win a match. Often involves taking the ball into a corner of the offensive end of the field.

Killer pass
A particularly well-struck and well-placed pass to an on-rushing striker, often resulting in a shot and a goal; generally a through ball.

Kinesio Tape
Elastic cotton strip with acrylic adhesive which, when applied to athletes when stretched, is intended to pull back to support the movement of muscles and joints; Physio tape.
[Pronunciation: kuh-NEES-ee-oh]

Kit
Originally, a player's game uniform, including jersey, shorts and socks; Now, generally refers to a player's full set of equipment, including shoes, shinguards, and everything else necessary for a practice or game.

Kit bag

Gym bag, game bag, duffle bag or other device designed to hold a player's equipment.

Knee pad ■□

Soft, protective device allowed to be worn by players to cover the patella, designed to try to prevent bruising or cuts; often recommended for growing girls.

Knit shoe uppers

The tops of next generation soccer cleats, with "compression-fit" features, designed to be extremely light-weight and to uniquely mold to the foot of the wearer.

Knock it around ■□

(1) To retain possession by multiple passes, usually in a match that has already been decided; or (2) A friendly pick-up game.

Knockdown

Goalkeeper deflects a shot into the ground.

Knocked away

A defender, unable to make a clean tackle, dispossesses an opponent of the ball by kicking it out of reach; kicked away; cleared.

Knocked off-stride □

To be legally contacted, shoulder to shoulder, in a way that disrupts a ball carrier's run.

Knocked out □

(1) The ball is kicked out of bounds; (2) A loss in a single-elimination phase of a tournament keeps the team from advancing.

Knocking balls down □

Due to the pace of a shot, the goalkeeper redirects the ball to the ground instead of trying to catch it directly.

Knock-out round □

The single-elimination phase of a tournament.

Knockout stages

The single-elimination portion of a tournament.

Knowing where the defense is

Situational awareness on the part of players in order to attack a defense's weakness or space which is undefended.

Knuckle ball

The wavering and unpredictable flight of a shot which resembles the flight of a specific type of pitch thrown in American baseball.

L *(Abbrev.)*
Lost; number of games/matches lost.

La Liga
The top Spanish professional league.

Laces ■□
String devices to help shoes conform to and stay on the foot; must be properly tied so as to not come untied during a match.

Laces kick ▫□
See: Instep Drive; Instep kick; term often used with young children who may not understand the word "instep."

Lack of focal point
A team which does not have a central striker or someone playing the role of a forward target.

Lack of shape
Defenders are not in the relative areas where they are expected to play in order to properly repel an ongoing attack or a quick counter-attack.

Lacking possession
During the course of a match, a team fails to control the ball for any length of time.

Lanes
Four running spaces, just outside the field of play, used by the Assistant Referees. These include the two portions of shoulders of the field, just outside the touchlines (sidelines), from the halfway line to the corner, and the two portions of the field just outside the goal lines, from one corner to the nearest goalpost.
See: Appendix 3A – Soccer Field Diagram.

Lanyard
Rope or cloth worn around the neck to hold a whistle.

Last defender
Closest field player to the goal available to resist an attacker, not including the goalkeeper.

Last man

The only defender left to beat by an attacker in order to score.

Late (1) ■□

Very little time left in a match, especially to try to score a tying goal.

Late (2) ■□

A player should have made a pass sooner; A player should have arrived at the end of a pass sooner.

Late goal

Goal scored very near the end of a match, generally within the last five minutes, to tie or win.

Late on

Usually less than 10-minutes remaining in a match.

Late runner

Attacking player coming into the offense well after the ball was initially sent; beyond the "3rd Attacker."

Late whistle □

Referee blows the whistle for a foul after a brief period of time when it might have been normally expected; sometimes associated with an "advantage" scenario.

Late, Late run, Late arriving

Forward not making a run fast enough to get to a pass; defender not making a tackle fast enough to get there before the ball is gone.

Late, Late tackle; Coming in late

Mistimed tackle that occurs just after the ball is gone, usually resulting in a foul.

Lateral movement

A team running and passing the ball from one sideline to the other to effectively use the space in attack; movement of a player to his left or right.

Lateral pass □

A pass made by a player to a teammate directly to his left or right such that the path of the ball is parallel to the halfway line or perpendicular to the sideline; square pass.

Law 1 ☐
(Laws of the Game) The Field of Play. Identifies the field markings and measurements and the size and types of goals.

Law 2 ☐
(Laws of the Game) The Ball. Identifies the size and construction of the ball.

Law 3 ☐
(Laws of the Game) The Players. Identifies the number of players on a team, the specific designation of a goalkeeper, and how substitutions are made.

Law 4 ☐
(Laws of the Game) The Players' Equipment. Identifies the specific apparel to be worn by players.

Law 5 ☐
(Laws of the Game) The Referee. Identifies the authority, powers and duties of the referee.

Law 6 ☐
(Laws of the Game) The Other Match Officials. Identifies the authority, powers, and duties of the assistant referees, a fourth official, two additional assistant referees, and a reserve assistant referee.

Law 7 ☐
(Laws of the Game) The Duration of the Match. Addresses the length of games, halftime, and how to account for time lost due to such things as injuries.

Law 8 ☐
(Laws of the Game) The Start and Restart of Play. Addresses the coin toss, selection of ends, the kick-off and dropped ball.

Law 9 ☐
(Laws of the Game) The Ball In and Out of Play. Addresses when the ball is in bounds or out of bounds.

Law 10 ☐
(Laws of the Game) Determining the Outcome of a Match. A goal is scored when the whole of the ball passes over the goal-line, between the goalposts and under the crossbar, provided that no infringement of the Laws of the Game has been committed previously by the team scoring the goal. Also, specifies extra time and the penalty-kick tiebreaker procedure.

Law 11 ☐

(Laws of the Game) Offside. At the moment the ball is passed, a potential receiver must be: (a) in an offside position, and (b) either interfering with play, interfering with an opponent, or gaining an advantage from being in that position.

Law 12 ☐

(Laws of the Game) Fouls and Misconduct. Identifies the offenses and the penalties to be imposed for violation of the rules. Also identifies those offenses which result in cautions (yellow card) and ejections (red card).

Law 13 ☐

(Laws of the Game) Free Kicks. Addresses the requirements for taking Indirect and Direct free kicks.

Law 14 ☐

(Laws of the Game) The Penalty Kick. Addresses the requirements for taking a Penalty Kick. "A penalty kick is awarded against a team which commits one of the ten offenses for which a direct free kick is awarded, inside its own penalty area and while the ball is in play."

Law 15 ☐

(Laws of the Game) The Throw-In. Addresses the procedure for putting the ball back into play after it has gone out of bounds over a sideline.

Law 16 ☐

(Laws of the Game) The Goal Kick. Identifies the procedure for placing the ball back into play after it has gone out of bounds over the end-line, having last been touched by an offensive player.

Law 17 ☐

(Laws of the Game) The Corner Kick. Identifies the procedure for placing the ball back into play after it has gone out of bounds over the end-line, having last been touched by a defensive player.

Law 18 (Euphemism)

Referees should apply the Laws of the Game using common sense.

Laws of the Game ▫ ☐

The 17 rules of soccer as controlled by the IFAB; new rule book issued annually by June for the upcoming competitive year (fall/spring); available on the IFAB's website; published in multiple languages by the IFAB. See Appendix 5: Laws of the Game (Overview)

Lay off, Lay the ball off

(1) To make a simple pass to an open teammate when confronted by a defender. (2) To pass the ball to a teammate at a trailing angle, usually after having received it with back to goal.

Laying it off, Lays it off, Laid off

Generally, passing a ball to an open teammate on attack instead of taking on a defender.

Layoff

A gap in time between being able to practice or play a game.

Lazy ball ☐

A pass struck with insufficient speed, power or pace which results in the ball being intercepted.

LB *(Abbrev.)*

Left Back; shorthand for the position of left fullback or left back defender.

LCB (1) *(Abbrev.)*

Left **Center Back**; shorthand for the position of **left center fullback** in a two-center-fullback alignment where one is positioned ***beside*** the other.

LCB (2) *(Abbrev.)*

Lead **Center Back**; shorthand for the position of **lead center fullback** in a two-center-fullback alignment where one is positioned ***in front of*** the other.

LCF (1) *(Abbrev.)*

Left **Center Fullback**; shorthand for the position of **left center fullback** in a two-center-fullback alignment where one is positioned ***beside*** the other.

LCF (2) *(Abbrev.)*

Lead **Center Fullback**; shorthand for the position of **lead center fullback** in a two-center-fullback alignment where one is positioned ***in front of*** the other.

LCF (3) *(Abbrev.)*

Lead **Center Forward**; shorthand for the position of ***lead*** **center striker** in a two-center-striker alignment where one is positioned ***in front of*** the other.

LDMF *(Abbrev.)*

Left **Defensive Midfielder**; shorthand for the position of ***left*** **defensive midfielder** in a two-defensive-midfielder alignment where one is positioned ***beside*** the other.

Lead (1), Lead pass ■□

To place a pass in the space in front of a teammate so that he can run onto it.

Lead (2) ■□

Ahead on goals.

Lead center back

Defender farther upfield in a two-center-fullback alignment where one is positioned in front of the other; LCB.

Lead center forward

Striker farther upfield in a two-center-striker alignment where one is positioned in front of the other; LCF.

Lead-pass into trouble

To place a pass into space for a teammate to run on to that is likely to cause a collision with an opponent.

League ■□

An organization of teams aggregated to create a competition structure.

Leaning, Leaning the other way □

Goalkeeper headed in the opposite direction to which the shot goes.

Leaning back

Failure to get the body properly positioned above the ball when shooting, causing the kicking leg to be on the upswing as the ball is contacted, resulting in a shot that goes over the crossbar.

Learning progressions □

A teaching technique designed to impart skills which build upon one another from the simple to the complex.

Leathered to his feet

A player who is highly skilled dribbling the ball and able to keep the ball extremely close.

Leave your man

A defender intentionally or unintentionally drops coverage of an opponent.

Leave, Leave it – ► ■□

► ***On-field Oral Communication:*** You are calling off a teammate to let him know that you are taking the ball.

Leave, Leaving

Coming off the field in order for a substitute player to enter.

Leaving a player open

An attacker is not defended, often in a re-start scenario.

Left ■□

That half of the human body, to the side of the midline, which contains most of the heart.

Left Back ■□

The position of left fullback or left back defender; LB.
See: Appendix 2: Player Positions.

Left Center Back

The position of left center fullback in a two-center-fullback alignment where one is positioned beside the other.
See: Appendix 2: Player Positions.

Left Center Forward

Striker on the left side in a two-center-striker alignment where one is positioned beside the other; LCB.
See: Appendix 2: Player Positions.

Left for

Player does not play the ball in order that it may be collected by a teammate; drop.

Left Forward ■□

The position of left forward. Player positioned to help lead the attack; a striker. Generally positioned toward the front of the attacking team, toward the left side. See: Appendix 2: Player Positions.

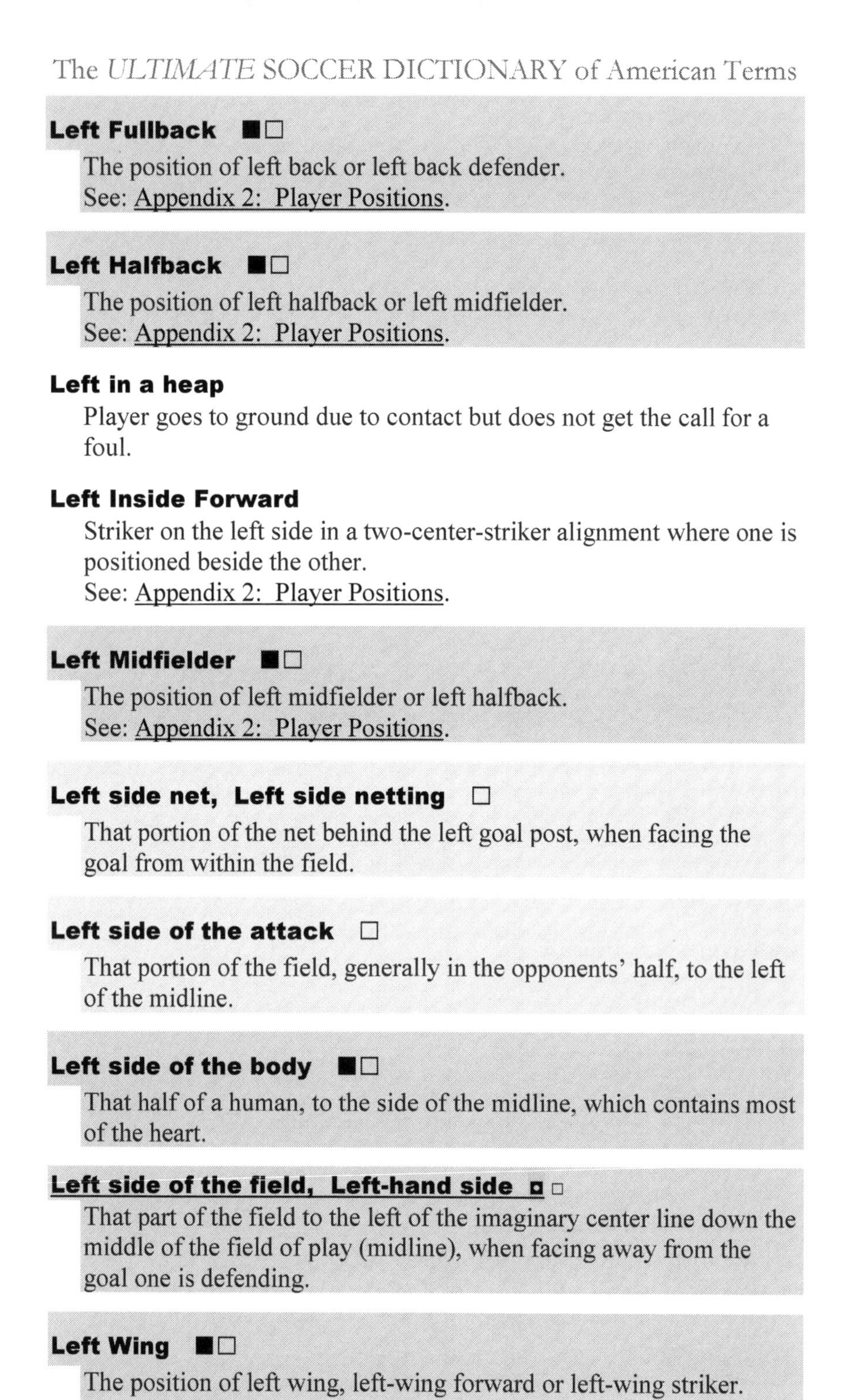

Left Fullback ■□

The position of left back or left back defender.
See: Appendix 2: Player Positions.

Left Halfback ■□

The position of left halfback or left midfielder.
See: Appendix 2: Player Positions.

Left in a heap

Player goes to ground due to contact but does not get the call for a foul.

Left Inside Forward

Striker on the left side in a two-center-striker alignment where one is positioned beside the other.
See: Appendix 2: Player Positions.

Left Midfielder ■□

The position of left midfielder or left halfback.
See: Appendix 2: Player Positions.

Left side net, Left side netting □

That portion of the net behind the left goal post, when facing the goal from within the field.

Left side of the attack □

That portion of the field, generally in the opponents' half, to the left of the midline.

Left side of the body ■□

That half of a human, to the side of the midline, which contains most of the heart.

Left side of the field, Left-hand side ◘ □

That part of the field to the left of the imaginary center line down the middle of the field of play (midline), when facing away from the goal one is defending.

Left Wing ■□

The position of left wing, left-wing forward or left-wing striker.
See: Appendix 2: Player Positions.

Left Wing Back
Either the position of left fullback or a hybrid position of left back and left midfielder. See: Appendix 2: Player Positions.

Left-footed ■□
Player who shows a natural preference or desire to use his left leg before using his right, when given a choice.

Left-hand side (left side) ■□
For the team facing the goal being attacked, the entire part of the field from end line to end line on the left side of the ***imaginary*** midline.

Left-Wing Striker
The position of left wing, left-wing forward or left-wing striker. See: Appendix 2: Player Positions.

Leg
(1) Lower limb body part; (2) A round of play in some multiple-game competitions and tournaments; e.g., a two-leg (home-and-home) series.

Leg 1
First game of a home-and-home series.

Leg 2
Second game of a home-and-home series.

Leg save
Stop made by the goalkeeper as a result of contacting the ball with his leg.

Leggings
Skin-tight article of clothing designed to provide warmth and protection for the legs during practices or games.

Leggy
Tired; legs feel "heavy."

Length (1)
Distance of a field marking; distance of the field along one sideline.

Length (2)
Distance of a shot or pass.

Length of Time
Amount of time in a game.

Lesson Plan

A detailed, written, description of the instruction to be imparted during a practice session.

Let down, Let (someone) down *(verb)* ■□

To fail to meet expectations; to disappoint. E.g., "Don't let your teammates down by failing to give your best effort."
Compare: Letdown *(noun)*; Let up *(verb)*.

Let it go, Let it ride, Let it roll – ► □

►***On-field Oral Communication:*** Let the ball roll over the end-line or side-line. This is used to let you know that your team will have possession of the ball after it goes out of play.

Let off

Let off the hook; a team does not suffer the consequences of a significant error because the opponent fails to capitalize on the mistake; the opponent does not score on what should have been a sure goal.

Let up *(verb)* ■□

To fail to give your best effort, intensity, or focus (e.g., due to being ahead in a game), even if only for a brief period of time (which may allow the opponent to score). Compare: Letdown *(noun)*.

Letdown *(noun)* ■□

(1) Typically, a mood of discouragement or disappointment, often resulting in a reduction in effort, intensity or focus, e.g., because of being scored upon.
(2) A reduction in effort for whatever reason, e.g., being ahead in a game.
Compare: Let up *(verb)*; Let down *(verb)*.

Lethal

An attacker who is particularly good at scoring goals, especially if the defense makes a mistake.

Letter of the Law

The Laws of the Game as specifically printed in the text; contrast with the Spirit and Intent of the Laws of the Game.

Level (1) ■□

Onside; forwards are in a position that is even with the back defenders; level with.

Level (2) ■□

Tied score; tied up after being down a goal.

Level (3)

Even with a team in the standings; having the same number of points.

LF *(Abbrev.)*

Left Forward; shorthand for the position of left forward.

LFB *(Abbrev.)*

Left Fullback; shorthand for the position of left fullback.

LHB *(Abbrev.)*

Left Halfback; shorthand for the position of left halfback or left midfielder.

LI *(Abbrev.)*

Left Inside; shorthand for the position of left inside forward.

Liability Release ■□

A signed, written, document (by players, parents or guardians) that acknowledges the dangers associated with participation in a sport and takes personal responsibility for their involvement.

Libero *(Italian for "free" or "unattached")*

Free-roaming defender, without a marking assignment, usually active behind the main group of back defenders; sweeper. [Pronunciation: LEE-beh-ro]

License

Certificate or diploma issued by the national soccer organization for successful completion of classwork, fieldwork and examination as a result of a course of study.

Lift over

To slide the instep under the ball and then scoop the ball up and over a defender.

Lift; Lifted

Generally, to scoop the ball over the goalkeeper's head in an attempt to score a goal.

Line (1) – ►

►On-field Oral Communication: Kick the ball upfield on a diagonal toward the sideline.

Line (2) ■□

Commonly refers to the touchline (sideline); any of the lines laid out on the field of play under Law 1 of the Laws of the Game.

Line of flight

Path of the ball in the air.

Line of offside

An imaginary line that runs through the body of the next-to-last defensive player, moves with him as he moves, and is used to determine if an offensive player is in an offside position. See also: Offside line.

Line of recovery

The shortest route to be taken by a defender in an attempt to get back to being goal-side of the ball.

Line of retreat

The route taken by a defender to remain goal-side of the ball while delaying the progress of an attacker.

Line of the ball; Path of the ball; Flight of the ball; Arc of the ball

The travel through the air of a lofted kick.

Linesmen, Linesman ■□

(1) Outdated term for Assistant Referees; see Law 6 of the Laws of the Game;
(2) Volunteer(s) who calls touchline outs.

Lineup, Line-up; Starting Lineup ■□

The group of players designated to be on the field at the start of a match.

Link up (with)

A teammate runs into position and receives a pass from the ballhandler.

Link, Link play

Passing connection between back defenders and midfielders or between midfielders and strikers.

LM *(Abbrev.)*

Left Midfielder; shorthand for the position of left halfback or left midfielder.

LMF *(Abbrev.)*
Left Midfielder; shorthand for the position of left halfback or left midfielder.

Loaf
To rest during the game (being lazy instead of being fully engaged and ready); to not play at full capability.

LOAF *(Abbrev.)*
Laws of Association Football; the Laws of the Game.

Lob ■□
A high chip pass or shot from a field player; a high, arcing throw-in; a high, arcing release from a goalkeeper.

Local rules
Changes to the Laws of the Game for a specific league or competition, usually based on age group.

Location
The place where a game or practice is held; the position of a player; the place on the body where a ball is contacted; the place on the field where the ball is to be sent; the place on the ball where it is struck.

Lock in
Double-teaming (or sometime triple-teaming) by defenders against a dribbler, usually pinning him against a sideline or in a corner, in order to create a turnover.

Lock on
Tight marking by a defender.

Locker room ■□
Team room for changing and storing clothes in lockers.

Loft
To kick a ball into the air; the height of a ball kicked into the air.

Lofted pass, Lofted drive ◘□
A pass sent in the air from one teammate to another which takes it over the heads of defenders; does not necessarily impart backspin to the ball like a "chip."

Logistics
All of the administrative actions required and necessary to get a team to a match, on time and properly equipped.

Logo

Badge or crest of the team or soccer organization, worn on a jersey.

LOMF *(Abbrev.)*

Left Offensive Midfielder; shorthand for the position of left offensive midfielder.

Lone striker

A formation or system of play which uses only one center forward.

Long (1) – ►

►On-field Oral Communication: Pass the ball far upfield to a teammate who is making a run.

Long (2), Too long

A pass which was struck too hard is going to go over (or went over) the end line.

Long ball, Long pass ■□

Generally, a pass beyond approximately 30 yards, usually in the air, which requires an instep kick.

Long corner

Type of corner kick that sends the ball directly from the corner kick arc, in the air, to the far side of the goal.

Long game

A team's use of long passes as a strategy.

Long run up, Long approach

Many steps taken before striking the ball on a penalty kick.

Long runs □

Covering a more than usual distance to get into the attack, often an overlap; covering a more than usual distance to get back on defense.

Long-ball □

A style or system of play marked by long passes and crosses.

Look at goal; Getting a look; Getting a good/great look

More than the usual time available to a striker to see a place to shoot before looking back at the ball to take the shot.

Look left – ► ☐

► ***On-field Oral Communication:*** A teammate from behind is telling the ball handler that there is an open teammate available for a pass on the left.

Look right – ► ☐

► ***On-field Oral Communication:*** A teammate from behind is telling the ball handler that there is an open teammate available for a pass on the right.

Look; Looks

The opportunities for a striker with the ball to quickly see the goal for a shot.

Looking

Any player with the ball glancing around to make a shot or a pass.

Looking for help ■☐

Player with the ball seeks a teammate to pass to who is open.

Looking for the ball ☐

A player who is open or making a run wants the ball carrier to pass to him.

Looking sharp

Showing particularly good skills; well dressed.

Looking to get behind

Attackers seeking to get players and the ball between the back defenders and the goal.

Loose ball ■☐

Ball not immediately under the control of any player. E.g., goalkeeper makes a stop on the ball, but the ball bounds away from him.

Loose mark

A defender not playing particular closely to the attacker to whom he is assigned, allowing for support to teammates or providing reaction time.

Loose midfield

Midfield players playing off the ball on defense or giving up the ball on attack.

Loosening up ■□

Stretching or warm up prior to entering a match.

Lose concentration

To make an error due to lack of focus on the ball or the actions of the opponent, often because of fatigue.

Lose ground on

Fall behind on points in the standings.

Lose the defender

To make a run that separates you from the defender who is marking you; get open.

Loses it

Player with the ball has it taken away by a defender, usually due to the inability to obtain or maintain control.

Lost footing

A player slips or has his foot lose proper grip with the ground, often due to a wet or muddy field, sometimes due to improper footwear.

Lost the ball □

Possession of the ball is obtained by the other team due to poor ball handling or an interception.

LOTG *(Abbrev.)*

Shorthand for "Laws of the Game"; published in multiple languages by the IFAB.

Lovely ball

A well-timed, well-placed, well-paced pass (service) to a teammate, usually resulting in a shot.

Low (1)

A pass, shot, cross or any moving ball generally below waist level.

Low (2)

A shot that scores in the bottom-third of the goal.

Low cross □

A crossing pass that is generally below waist-height.

Low dive □

Goalkeeper projecting himself into the air to make a save generally at waist level or below.

Low line, Lower line

A defensive back line which tends to stay closer to its own goal during the normal course of play.

Low shot ■□

A shot which stays low, often below waist-height, targeting the lower third of the goal.

Low tipping

The act of the goalkeeper diving close to the ground to deflect or parry the ball outside of the upright of the goal, when unable to catch it cleanly.

Lower 90

The bottom-right or bottom-left corner of the goal, just inside the goal post.

Lower left corner ■□

When facing the goal, the bottom left corner of the goal, at the ground just inside the goal post.

Lower right corner ■□

When facing the goal, the bottom right corner of the goal, at the ground just inside the goal post.

LW *(Abbrev.)*

Left Wing; shorthand for the position of left wing striker.

LWB *(Abbrev.)*

Left Wing Back; shorthand for the position of left wing back.

LWS *(Abbrev.)*

Left Wing Striker; shorthand for the position of left wing striker.

M *(Abbrev.)*
Midfielder; shorthand for the position of midfielder.

Made a meal of it
Acting or embellishing to make a foul appear worse than it was.

Magic sponge
Old expression for when a trainer would go to an injured player with a sponge and a bucket of water, wipe at the injury, and then the player would be better.

Maintain width of the field ■□
Players positioned outside who remember to operate closer to the sidelines, opening up attacking space for their entire team.

Maintaining width □
Players on the sides or flanks of an attack staying closer to each touchline in order to create space.

Major League Soccer (MLS)
First tier of men's professional soccer in the United States.

Major violation ■□
The commitment of a foul that would result in a direct free kick and/or yellow and red card offenses, from Law 12, "Fouls and Misconduct," of the Laws of the Game.

Majority of possession
The amount of time greater than 50% that a team is in control of the ball during a match.

Make a meal of it
To embellish the effects of minor contact to try to elicit the call of a foul.

Make a move ■□
Free oneself from an opponent; juke, deke, or feint while dribbling.

Make a run – ►
►***On-field Oral Communication:*** Tells a teammate that he needs to join the attack (and appears to be standing around).

Make a run, Making a run (1)

To sprint or move into open space to set up receipt of a possible pass.

Make a run, Making a run (2)

A team wins a number of games or gains points in the standings near the end of a competition or tournament.

Make-up call

The perception that a referee's decision to call a foul against an opponent was to "offset" a previous "bad call" awarded to the other team.

Making oneself bigger

Putting the arms out from one's side in order to create a larger defensive posture; runs afoul of the handling rule if the arm is struck by the ball.

Making the most (of one's chances)

The ability to get off shots that have a chance of scoring given a limited number of opportunities.

Making the most of it

Embellishment upon potentially illegal contact in an attempt to ensure that the referee calls a foul.

Man (i.e., "Man-on") – ►

►***On-field Oral Communication:*** A defender is arriving.

Man defense, Man-to-man defense, Man-to-man marking ■□

A system of defense based on individual defenders covering specific opponents every time the opposing team is on attack.

Man down, Man short □

Due to injury or ejection, a team has fewer than 11 players on the field.

Man in the Middle

The Referee.

Man of the match

Player of the game; most valuable player in a game.

Man on the floor, Man on the ground

A player is down on the ground, possibly injured.

Manager ■□
(International usage) coach; (American usage) team administrator.

Mannequin
A full-sized cut-out or silhouette of a player, used in practice, usually combined with other mannequins and positioned on the field to simulate a defensive wall. Dummy.

Remember: Each "***On-field Oral Communication***" term has this symbol ▶ and in the electronic versions is ***hyperlinked*** to Appendix 4, where all of these terms are listed together. Each term is ***linked back*** to its definition, which makes it easier to learn these terms.

Man-on – ▶ ■□
▶ ***On-field Oral Communication:*** An opponent who is probably outside your field of vision is about to challenge you for the ball.

Maradona
A type of dribbling move invented by and named for Argentine player Diego Maradona.

Mark, Marking ■□
A defender identifying, covering, getting goal-side, and staying with a specific individual opponent during an attack.

Mark (#_) – ▶ □
▶ ***On-field Oral Communication:*** When the defense is organizing, the defensive leader may assign who is responsible for each attacker by jersey number, especially if the defense has broken down. This tells a defender to stay with a particular attacker until directed otherwise.

Mark up – ▶ □
▶ ***On-field Oral Communication:*** When the defense is first organizing, the defensive leader tells the defender to more tightly cover the opponents within their zones.

Mark; Minute mark
The time of the game.

Marked □
Covered one-on-one by an opponent.

Marker
The defender covering an opponent.

Marking assignment
The person or space that a player is responsible for on defense.

Marking backs
The defense's backs, ahead of a sweeper, designated to cover opposing strikers.

Marking in the box
Specific defensive assignments within the Penalty Area, usually during free kicks.

Marking out of the game
Assigning one or more defenders to a specific opponent for one-on-one tight marking in order to deny that opponent the ball at all times.

Marking the Posts
On corner kicks (or some free kicks near the goal), a defensive player can be "assigned" to an upright (not to leave the post until the ball is cleared). The purpose is to try to "shrink" the size of the 8-yard goal to 6 yards, which is much less space for the goalkeeper to cover, and also to provide coverage if the goalkeeper comes out to collect the ball and misses.

Mastery ■□
The ability to perform a skill or technique upon demand.

Match ■□
A regulation game played between two teams.

Match analysis
Post-game evaluation of the play of the team, individual players and responses to situations. See also: Analysis.

Match conditions ■□
To practice in situations that replicate those of an actual game.

Match fit, Match sharp
The ability of a player to run and perform skills effectively during an entire game.

Match officials
The set of referees working a game.

Match preview
Scouting report.

Match report

(1) Post-game analysis.
(2) Referee's summary of a game.

Match results □

Written record of the date, time, teams, scorers, final score, and other pertinent data of a match.

Match stats, Match statistics □

The collection, tabulation and manipulation of data from a game, including such things as the number of shots and corner kicks for each team.

Matchups □

One-versus-one, defensive player against offensive player, in the context of each other's skill-set.

Maximum speed

Fastest running time by a player over a specified distance.

Maximum strength

Highest amount of weight which can be displaced for a certain exercise.

Measured ball, Measured pass

A pass that is well-timed, well-placed, and has exactly the right pace to meet the receiver at the most opportune time.

Measuring

Analyzing the strengths and weakness of an opponent or a team.

Medical Waiver Form, Medical Release ■□

Signed release to provide for medical care in the event of an emergency.

Medium corner

A corner kick directed to an area in front of the goal.

Meeting

The two teams in a match set to play, or who played, each other.

Meg

Short for "Nutmeg;" to kick the ball between a player's legs as a dribbling move to beat a defender.

Men's National Team

Top-level men's team representing the United States in international competition; United States Men's National Team; MNT; USMNT.

Men's Olympic Team

Age-restricted team, with exceptions, representing the United States in Olympic competition.

Mental fatigue

Overall exhaustion that causes a player to make slow or poor decisions.

Mental game □

The psychological aspect of a player's ability to get "up" for a match and play at peak efficiency.

Mentality

Player's state of mind or approach to a game or to the team.

Mentor program

Activity which pairs experienced referees with inexperienced referees in order to provide training.

Metrics

Data, statistics or analytics associated with a player, usually aggregated over more than one practice or game; the use of data and statistics to evaluate players.

MF *(Abbrev.)*

Midfielder; shorthand for the position of midfielder.

Micro goals

Very small goals used in practice, for indoor games, or for micro-soccer.

Micro-soccer

Format of a number of small-sided games, using small goals, and usually involving very young players.

Middies

Midfielders; slang for the players in the midfield position.

Middle, Middle of the Field, Middle Third □ □

The middle of the field, approximately 20-yards on either side of the halfway line toward each goal, typically used to identify transition play from defense-to-offense or offense-to-defense. (Not synonymous with "Center.")

Midfield ◘ □

(1) A "moving" area representing the space between a team's back defenders and strikers as the team proceeds up-and-back on the field; (2) The players on a team, as a group, playing the midfield positions.

Midfield Anchor □

Defensive (center) Midfielder.

Midfield gap

Space between midfielders and strikers which may appear due to fatigue on the part of midfielders; area which could be exploited by an opponent.

Midfield general

A Center Midfielder, often leading and coordinating team play.

Midfield line

The players on a team, as a group, playing the midfield positions.

Midfield play □

Successful soccer by the midfielders, particularly in the area approximately 20 yards on either side of the halfway line, in initiating and supporting the attack, in initiating the defense, and in maintaining possession of the ball.

Midfield stripe ■□

The Halfway Line of the markings of the field as described in Law 1 of the Laws of the Game.

Midfielders, Middies ◘ □

Players in positions between the back defenders and the strikers. See: Appendix 2: Player Positions.

Mid-goal area

The space in front of the goal roughly between 6- and 12-yards away from the posts.

Midline, Middle line

An imaginary line, running the length of the field from the center of one goal to the other, which divides the field into two equal halves, "vertically," right from left.

Midpoints

Law 1 of the Laws of the Game; the intersections of the touchlines and the halfway line, equidistant from the goal-lines.

Mids

Midfielders; slang for the players in the midfield position.

Milk, Milk it, Milking it

To exaggerate the effects of contact or a foul.

Mind games

Psychological attempts, usually verbal, to try to cause an opponent to lose concentration, thereby affecting his level of play.

Mine – ► ■□

►***On-field Oral Communication***: Call's off a teammate when both are going for the ball. Not usually a very good call; see "Leave" or "Leave It."

Mini air ball pump

A small, hand-held, device used to inflate soccer balls; requires an inflation needle.

Mini goals

Typically, smaller-than-regulation goals used on game fields which are less than full-sized; downsized goals used for very young players.

Minimal contact

Perception that a foul has been incorrectly called by the referee where little contact has been made by the tackler.

Minor violation ■□

The commitment of a foul that would result in an indirect free kick, from Law 12, "Fouls and Misconduct," of the Laws of the Game.

Minute ■□

The time of the game; often identified with an apostrophe. For example, a goal scored in the 40th minute (40') was scored between 39:00 and 39:59.

Minutes □

A player's amount of playing time in real matches; particularly important for non-starters.

Miscommunication ■□

Incorrect or non-existent discussion between players, often resulting in a goal being allowed or an opportunity for a goal being missed.

Misconduct ◘ □
Serious inappropriate behavior subject to penalization under Law 12 of the Laws of the Game, resulting in a Caution or an Ejection.

Miscue
Misplayed ball.

Misdirection □
Physical movement or verbal calling designed to cause a defender to move away from the ball or from the space to be used for a play.

Mishandled □
Goalkeeper does not make a clean catch, punch or save of a ball.

Miskick
To fail to contact the ball properly in the performance of a foot skill.

Mismatch
A situation where an offensive player has far greater skill than a defender; or where an entire team generally has far greater skill than its opponent.

Miss ■□
Errant shot.

Missile
A particularly hard and well-struck, straight shot.

Mistimed
An early or late attempt at the performance of a skill; usually a late tackle.

Mistimed tackle
A late tackle resulting in a foul.

Mistouch
Poor contact with the ball, usually while dribbling, that often results in the ball being taken by the opponent.

Mixer ◘ □
A group of offensive and defensive players congregated in front of the goal awaiting a cross or free kick.

Mixer! – ►

►*On-field Oral Communication*: Attacking teammate is telling the dribbler to immediately cross or pass the ball into the area in front of the goal.

MNT *(Abbrev.)*

Men's National Team; United States Men's National Team; USMNT.

Mob-ball

The gaggle of beginning youth players all trying to get to the ball at once.

Mobility

(1) The ability of the body or a joint to perform a wide range of motion.
(2) Rapid movement of a player to a different spot on the field, particularly in attack.

Modified padded headgear

Headgear that is designed more like a headband than a helmet, intended to try to reduce the possibility of concussion.

Molded cleats ■□

Gripping studs, made of rubberized or synthetic material, specifically formed as one unit with the sole of the shoe; non-replaceable; contrast with replaceable/screw-in cleats.

Momentum (1) ■□

Increasing progress toward scoring a goal, controlling a match, or dominating the other team.

Momentum (2) ■□

A player's force or speed in any given direction.

Morale ■□

Player or team psychological state based on injuries, won-loss record or other factors.

Morphing

The ability of a coach to transition smoothly from one activity (drill) to another without creating a break or loss of time between events.

Motivation

Desire to perform at a high level.

Motivation Plan

Those activities on the part of a coach designed to instill a desire in his players to perform at their highest level.

Motor skills □

Ability of the body to perform muscular activities.

Mouth guard ■□

Plastic or rubber device worn to protect the teeth and lower jaw.

Move Up, Move Out – ► □

► ***On-field Oral Communication:*** Goalkeeper or central back is telling the defenders to move upfield.

Move, Move People! – ►

► ***On-field Oral Communication:*** Teammate is telling their team that they are standing around or ball-watching.

Movement (1) □

The ability of a team to proceed forward and back on the field as an organized unit.

Movement (2) □

Effectively passing the ball around to maintain possession and to probe the opponent's defense.

Movement Off the Ball ▫□

The strategy and tactics of players who are not in possession of the ball, while on offense or defense, to maximize the effectiveness of their location on the field at any given time.

Moves □

Fakes, feints, dekes or jukes performed by a player with the ball in order to beat a defender or create space for a shot or pass.

Movies; Soccer movies

Films (DVDs) with soccer-related themes or story lines.

Moving

Changing location on the field, usually as a result of tactical or strategic decision-making.

Moving backward

Giving ground; backpedalling; retreating toward one's own goal.

Moving service around

Changing the location from which the last pass to someone in scoring position is sent.

Moving the ball (around) ■□

A team's ability to pass the ball quickly and accurately to various parts of the field in order to create space or probe a defense for weaknesses or to maintain possession.

Moving to open space ■□

A player makes a run to a vacant area of the field, e.g., during an attack.

Moving together □

Coordinated action by defenders.

Moving; Ball moving; Ball movement □

The wavering and unpredictable flight of a shot taken with no follow-through; resembles the flight of a specific type of pitch thrown in American baseball, the "Knuckle Ball."

MP *(Abbrev.)*

Matches Played.

Mug, Mugged, Mugging

An attacker with the ball has it unceremoniously stolen by a defender while providing little or no resistance.

Muscle memory

A conditioned response by a muscle or group of muscles due to repetitive training.

Muscular

Use of strong physical contact to take the ball away or to keep it for oneself.

MVP *(Abbrev.)*

Most Valuable Player.

My ball – ► ■□

►On-field Oral Communication: Call's off a teammate when both are going for the ball. Not usually a very good call. See: Leave; Leave it.

Nagging injury
Damage to the body which doesn't get a chance to fully heal due to continued playing.

NAIA *(Abbrev.)*
National Association of Intercollegiate Athletics.

Nn

Name, pick up #_ – ▶ ☐
▶ ***On-field Oral Communication:*** Goalkeeper or defensive organizer tells a teammate to mark a specific opponent. (E.g., "Rick, pick up #12.")

Name, take #_ – ▶
▶ ***On-field Oral Communication:*** The person organizing the defense tells a teammate, by name, which opponent to mark, by jersey number.

Name, take the far post – ▶
▶ ***On-field Oral Communication:*** Goalkeeper is directing one of his defenders to get to the far post before the attacking team takes a free kick.

Name, take the near post – ▶
▶ ***On-field Oral Communication:*** Goalkeeper is directing one of his defenders to get to the near post before the attacking team takes a free kick.

Name's ball – ▶
▶ ***On-field Oral Communication:*** Used in a situation where two teammates are both likely going for an un-possessed ball, you are calling the other teammate off, using your name. (There must be no hesitation on the part of the caller and the other teammate is obligated to back off.)

Name's in charge – ▶
▶ ***On-field Oral Communication:*** Goalkeeper announces that he has relinquished control of the overall defense to the upfield defensive organizer.

Narrow; Playing narrow
As a team, playing or staying too much in the middle of the field. (Can apply offensively or defensively, offensively not using the flanks, defensively leaving the flanks open.)

Narrowing the angle

Defender moving closer to the ball or forcing an attacker wide in order to reduce shooting or passing area. See: Angles.

NASL *(Abbrev.)*

North American Soccer League.
(1) Old, defunct, top professional league in the United States.
(2) Current, lower-tier professional league in the United States.

Nasty challenge

A particularly poor or mistimed tackle which has a high possibility of creating injury during a collision.

National Association, National Football Association

A country's governing body authorized by FIFA to represent and administer soccer. The national association for the United States is the United States Soccer Federation (USSF).

National Coaching Schools

Training classes and on-field coursework provided by the United States Soccer Federation which, upon the successful completion of testing, may result in licensing.

National Soccer Coaches Association of America

Former name of United Soccer Coaches, "…the world's largest soccer coaches' organization that serves members at every level of the game."

National State Associations

State organizations, grouped into Regions, recognized by the United States Soccer Federation.

National team ◘ □

A group of players, made up of natural-born or naturalized citizens, authorized by a country's soccer governing body to represent the country in international competition.

National Women's Soccer League

First tier of professional women's soccer in the United States; NWSL.

Nationality

Player's place of birth, citizenship, or eligibility for a country's national team.

Natural surface

Law 1 of the Laws of the Game; an all-grass field or pitch.

Natural, Natural goalscorer
A striker who is comfortable in front of the goal and consistently scores.

NCAA *(Abbrev.)*
National Collegiate Athletic Association.

Near Forward
Striker closest to the ball.

Near Fullback
Back defender closest to the ball.

Near Midfielder
Midfielder closest to the ball.

Near post (1) ■□
The upright of the goal closest to the ball.

Near post (2) – ► ■□
► On-field Oral Communication: Pass or shoot the ball to the part of the goal nearest you.

Near side □
Whichever side of the field, left or right of the imaginary midline, the ball happens to be in at any given moment. This constantly changes.

Near-post corner, Near corner
A corner kick directed to a teammate usually situated approximately two yards inside the closest goalpost to the kicker and six yards into the field as the kick is taken.

Neck bridges
A form of strengthening exercise marked by only having the toes and the forehead in contact with the ground.

Needle ■□
Device used with an air pump to be placed in a valve within a ball in order to inflate it; inflation needle.

Negative space □
Area behind an attack which can become available to an opponent, especially on a quick counter attack.

Negligible

Contact deemed insignificant or minimal which does not result in the call of a foul.

Nervous, Nerves ■□

A player affected by game pressure such that they exhibit poor ball skills.

Nervy

Anxious to get to the end of a game; taking chances.

Net ◘ □

Corded or mesh fabric, attached to the back of a goal, designed to capture a ball. See also: Nets.

Net clips, Net ties

Devices used to securely connect the net to the goal.

Net minder

Archaic for goalkeeper.

Net securing

Before a game, the act of properly attaching the nets to the back of the goals and to the ground with clips, ties, cord, ropes or pegs in order to ensure that no gaps appear which could allow a ball to pass through.

Nets □

Law 1 of the Laws of the Game; optional under Law 1, corded or mesh fabric designed to help the referees determine if a goal has been scored; can be any color; must be of small enough weave to trap a ball, with no gaps; must be securely attached to the goalposts and the crossbar of the goal and the ground behind the goal; must not interfere with the goalkeeper.

Neutral ground, Neutral venue, Neutral site □

Field of play that is not controlled by, or associated with, either of the participating teams.

Neutralizing

Efficiently defending a player or a team so that their attack is ineffective.

NFHS *(Abbrev.)*

National Federation of State High School Associations; governing body for high school soccer.

Nice

Any particularly well-performed skill or action on the part of a player.

Nice ball, Nice pass ■□

A particularly well-performed pass on the part of a player.

Nice idea

A good attempt, good try, or good decision on the part of a player, even if the result is not optimal.

Nice save, Nice stop ■□

A particularly well-performed save on the part of a goalkeeper.

Nicked away

A finger-tip or toe-tip deflection on the part of a goalkeeper that saves a goal from being scored; a toe-tip deflection of the ball as part of a tackle by a field player.

Niggling foul(s)

Repeated minor violations consistently made by a player or team.

Nil ◘ □

Zero; nothing; no goals scored.

Nil-Nil

A zero-to-zero game score during or at the conclusion of a match; Nothing to nothing: **0-0**.

NISOA *(Abbrev.)*

National Intercollegiate Soccer Officials Association.

NJCAA *(Abbrev.)*

National Junior College Athletic Association.

No – ►

►***On-field Oral Communication***: Tells a player not to make the pass that it looks like they are going to make because it is likely to be intercepted by someone they may not see.

No angle

Striker takes a shot from so close to the end line (goal-linc, bi-line) that it has essentially no chance of going into the goal.

No bounce – ►

► ***On-field Oral Communication:*** Player is calling to the teammate to intercept an aerial ball before, or immediately after, it can hit the ground, so a rebound doesn't go over anyone's head.

No cover

A defender has no one behind them in support.

No goal

An apparent score either didn't actually occur or is disallowed for some reason.

No Man's Land □

Area in front of the goal where a goalkeeper comes out from goal, may stop or hesitate, but is in a position where he may not be able to get to the ball or a forward may be able to chip the ball over his head and into the goal.

No shot – ►

► ***On-field Oral Communication:*** Keeper asks defender to tackle the opponent with the ball in order to keep him from shooting.

No turn – ►

► ***On-field Oral Communication:*** Asks the defending teammate to challenge the opponent with the ball, who is facing away from the goal, in such a way as to not let the opponent turn and face the goal.

No whistle (1)

The referee does not make a call when it appears that a call is expected.

No whistle (2) – ►

► ***On-field Oral Communication:*** The Referee did not blow the whistle so play on or keep playing.

Nobody – ► □

► ***On-field Oral Communication:*** Tells teammate that there is no defender nearby and that they can work with the ball.

Nobody there

A pass made to a non-existent teammate in anticipation of a run that did not occur.

Nod the ball down

To use the head to, generally softly, redirect the ball to the ground, often while on the run.

Nod, Nodded, Nodded in, Nodded away
Header, as a deflection which is not necessarily overly forceful, as a pass, shot, or a clearance.

Noise
Very loud chanting, cheering, jeering or cacophony from the crowd which disrupts oral communications.

Non-call □
Referee does not blow his whistle for what appeared to be a foul.

Non-dominant foot, Non-dominant leg
The opposite appendage from the natural preference for the use of one extremity over the other, such as being right-handed or left-handed.

Non-kicking foot
The foot in contact with the ground which allows the kicking foot and leg to swing freely; plant foot.

Non-verbal communication ■□
Hand or visual signals used between teammates to request certain actions. For example, tapping on one's chest or head to request where a throw-in should be made. See the following CAS article: ***On-Field Non-Verbal Communications in Soccer*** at website: http://coachingamericansoccer.com/tactics-and-teamwork/on-field-non-verbal-communications-in-soccer/

Non-verbal cue □
A visual observation taking many forms, such as a defensive teammate indicating someone to be covered or a goalkeeper "leaning the wrong way," indicating to which side of the goal a striker should shoot. See also: Non-verbal communication.

North American Soccer League
Defunct top professional league in the United States and Canada; NASL; Currently, a second-tier professional league.

Nose for the goal
A striker who consistently gets himself in position for goal-scoring opportunities.

Not afraid; Unafraid ■□
Willingness to sacrifice one's body for the cause.

Not fit ■□

A player who is physically unable to perform at his peak level.

Not picked up □

Offensive player running free without a defender on him.

Not quitting □

Staying with the play when it could have been easy to stop.

Nothing over – ▶

▶ ***On-field Oral Communication:*** Don't allow the opponent to make a chip or create a bounce of the ball that would go over a defender's head.

NPL *(Abbrev.)*

National Premier League; U. S. Club Soccer National Premier League program.

NSA, NSAs *(Abbrev.)*

National State Associations, under the United States Soccer Federation.

NSCAA *(Abbrev.)*

Now United Soccer Coaches; the initials of the former National Soccer Coaches Association of America.

NSCAA Certificates and Diplomas

Awards for successful completion of the soccer courses offered by the former National Soccer Coaches Association of America, now the United Soccer Coaches organization.

Nth minute ■□

Time of the game. Example, the interval from 8:00 to 8:59 is the 9th minute, because the interval from 0:00 to 0:59 is the 1st minute.

Number 10 player (true…)

Historically, the jersey number assigned to an inside forward. More recently, the jersey number assigned to the best midfielder, playmaker, or striker on a team. Jersey number assigned in honor of Pele.

Number 9 player (true…)

Historically, the jersey number assigned to a center forward. More commonly, the jersey number assigned a forward playmaker or center striker.

Number of Players ■□

By competition rules, how many participants, including a goalkeeper, who may be on the field at one time (typically 11 players per team); by league rules, how many participants may be registered with a team; Law 3 of the Laws of the Game.

Number of Subs, Number of Substitutes, Number of Substitutes Allowed

By competition rules, the number of substitutes that may be used in a match.

Numbers (1) – ►

► ***On-field Oral Communication:*** A player is telling his teammates to move forward into the attack, or to "build numbers."

Numbers (2) □

One team has a numerical advantage over the other. This occurs in the attacking third of the field.

Numbers down

In context, on offense having fewer players in attack than the defense has to defend; on defense having fewer players to defend than the opponent has coming on attack.

Numbers in the box

Getting numerous attackers into the opponent's Penalty Area during an attack.

Numbers up

Advantage in players on attack versus the defenders; sending players forward.

Numerical advantage □

The team on attack, usually in the attacking third, has more players heading for the goal than the team on defense has defenders.

Nutmeg ◘ □

To kick the ball between a player's legs as a dribbling move to beat a defender.

Nutmeg Pass

Player is able to pass the ball to a teammate by sending the ball between the legs of a defender.

Nutrition ■□

Eating the right kinds of foods to stay healthy and be able to physically perform at an optimal level.

NWSL *(Abbrev.)*

National Women's Soccer League; First tier of professional women's soccer in the United States.

NYSCA *(Abbrev.)*

National Youth Sports Coaches Association.

O *(Abbrev.)*
Shorthand for Offense.

OB *(Abbrev.)*
Outside Back; a player playing a wing fullback position.

Obstruction, obstructing ◘ □
Older terminology for impeding the progress of an opponent; see "Impedes."

ODP *(Abbrev.)*
Olympic Development Program.

OFB *(Abbrev.)*
Outside Fullback; a player playing a wing back defender position.

OFC *(Abbrev.)*
Oceania Football Confederation; FIFA-recognized confederation of nations in the Pacific and South Pacific.

Off ■□
Offside.

Off his line, Off the line □
The goalkeeper has moved away from the goal, out into the field of play, possibly exposing more of the goal to a shot, especially over his head.

Off season ■□
The period of time between organized two competitions.

Off target □
A shot which misses the goal entirely and has no chance of going in.

Off the ball incident, Off the ball foul □
A foul, foul play, or unsporting conduct made at distance from the ball and the referee.

Off the ball run
Any run made by a player on the attacking team who is not in possession of the ball.

Off the bench ■□
Substitute coming into the game.

Off the crossbar ■□
A rebound or deflection of a shot from the crossbar of the goal.

Off the mark □
A missed shot.

Off the post ■□
A rebound or deflection of a shot from one of the goalposts.

Off their game
Team or player, which has demonstrated the capability of playing better, is not playing well.

Offense (1) ■□
Attack; attacking; plan of attack; type of attack.

Offense (2)
A violation of the Laws of the Game; infraction.

Offensive, insulting or abusive language
Verbal behavior which is deemed to be rude, hurtful or disrespectful and is subject to a red card ejection; violation of Law 12 of the Laws of the Game.

Offensive Midfielders
Players in the midfield position which are expected to play in a more-attacking mode.

Offensive Player ■□
Any player participating in an attack, not just a player identified in a forward or striker position.

Offensive pressure ■□
Constant probing, challenging, shooting, and moving the ball around while on attack.

Offensive switch □
An offensive player runs into the space occupied by a teammate and the teammate runs into the space vacated, effectively exchanging positions; may be "vertical" or "horizontal."

Offensive transition

Rapid change from defense to offense as soon as the ball is obtained from the opponent.

Off-frame

A missed shot.

Official FIFA Ball, Official FIFA size and weight □

Approved soccer ball which meets the standards set by FIFA and Law 2 of the Laws of the Game.

Official Game Clock ■□

Usually the watch managed by the Referee; In NCAA rules, a scoreboard clock or clock managed on the sidelines; any clock established as official by the competition organizers.

Officials ■□

Referee, Assistant Referees, Additional Assistant Referees, Reserve Assistant Referee, and Fourth Official; Match Officials; Competition organizers.

Officials' Lanes

Four running spaces, just outside the field of play, used by the Assistant Referees. These include the two portions of shoulders of the field, just outside the touchlines (sidelines), from the halfway line to the corner, and the two portions of the field just outside the goal lines, from one corner to the nearest goalpost.
See: Appendix 3A – Soccer Field Diagram.

Offside ■□

Law 11 of the Laws of the Game; a player shall be called for an offside penalty if, at the moment the ball is passed to him by a teammate, he is in an offside position ***and***, in the opinion of the referee, he is interfering with play, interfering with an opponent, or gained an advantage from being in that position. See: Offside position.

Offside line

An ***imaginary*** line which, assuming the presence of a goalkeeper at the goal-line, runs through the body of the last defender playing in the field closest to the goal and parallel to the goal-line. During the normal run of play, this imaginary line ***moves*** up-and-back on the field of play with the defender and switches defenders as these players move ahead of or behind one another.

Offside Offense, Offside Infraction

A violation of Law 11 of the Laws of the Game.

Offside position ◘ □

Law 11 of the Laws of the Game; a player is in an offside position if he is in the opponents' half of the field of play and he is nearer to his opponents' goal-line than both the ball and the second-to-last opponent. This is only the first requirement of two parts to be called for an offside violation. See: Offside and Two-Question Test.

Offside trap ◘ □

Defensive maneuver where all of the defensive backs step upfield, just before an opponent passes the ball forward to a teammate, causing the teammate to be caught in an offside position at the moment the ball was passed.

Offsides

An ***incorrect*** usage of the term "Offside." The correct spelling has no "s" at the end: The correct terminology is: "Offside."

Off-target □

A missed shot.

Off-the-ball ■□

Play or movement of a player, players, or an entire team when not in possession of the ball.

Off-the-ball movement □

Changes in place or direction of a player when not in possession of the ball.

OG *(Abbrev.)*

Own Goal.

Olympic goal

To score directly from a corner kick; a Direct Corner goal; "Olympic" meaning "heroic," does not refer to the "Olympics" or the "Olympic Games."

Olympic soccer, Olympic tournament

Those matches conducted during the Olympic Games.

Olympic Team

Men or women selected to represent the United States in Olympic competition. Age-restricted, with exceptions, for men. No age restrictions for women. Men are restricted to U-23 (but up to three players who do not meet this age limit are allowed).

OM *(Abbrev.)*
Offensive Midfielder; the position of Offensive Midfielder; depending on usage - Outside Midfielder.

OMF *(Abbrev.)*
Offensive Midfielder; the position of Offensive Midfielder; depending on usage - Outside Midfielder.

On a (yellow) card
A player still participating in an ongoing match who had received a Caution earlier in the contest; a player participating in a tournament game who received a Caution in a previous match.

On attack □
The team with the ball, going for goal, trying to score; on offense.

On defense ■□
The team without the ball, working to keep the opponent from scoring, is trying to get the ball back.

On form
Exhibiting properly performed skill or technique for the occasion.

On frame
A shot which, with no intervention by a goalkeeper or defender, would go into the goal; on goal.

On goal; Shot on goal ◘ □
A shot which, with no intervention by a goalkeeper or defender, would go into the goal; on frame.

On his line
The goalkeeper is in a position such that his feet are in contact with, or are just ahead of, his goal-line between the uprights.

On net
On goal; on target; on frame; a shot that would go into the goal if not otherwise stopped.

On offense ■□
The team with the ball, going for goal, trying to score; on attack.

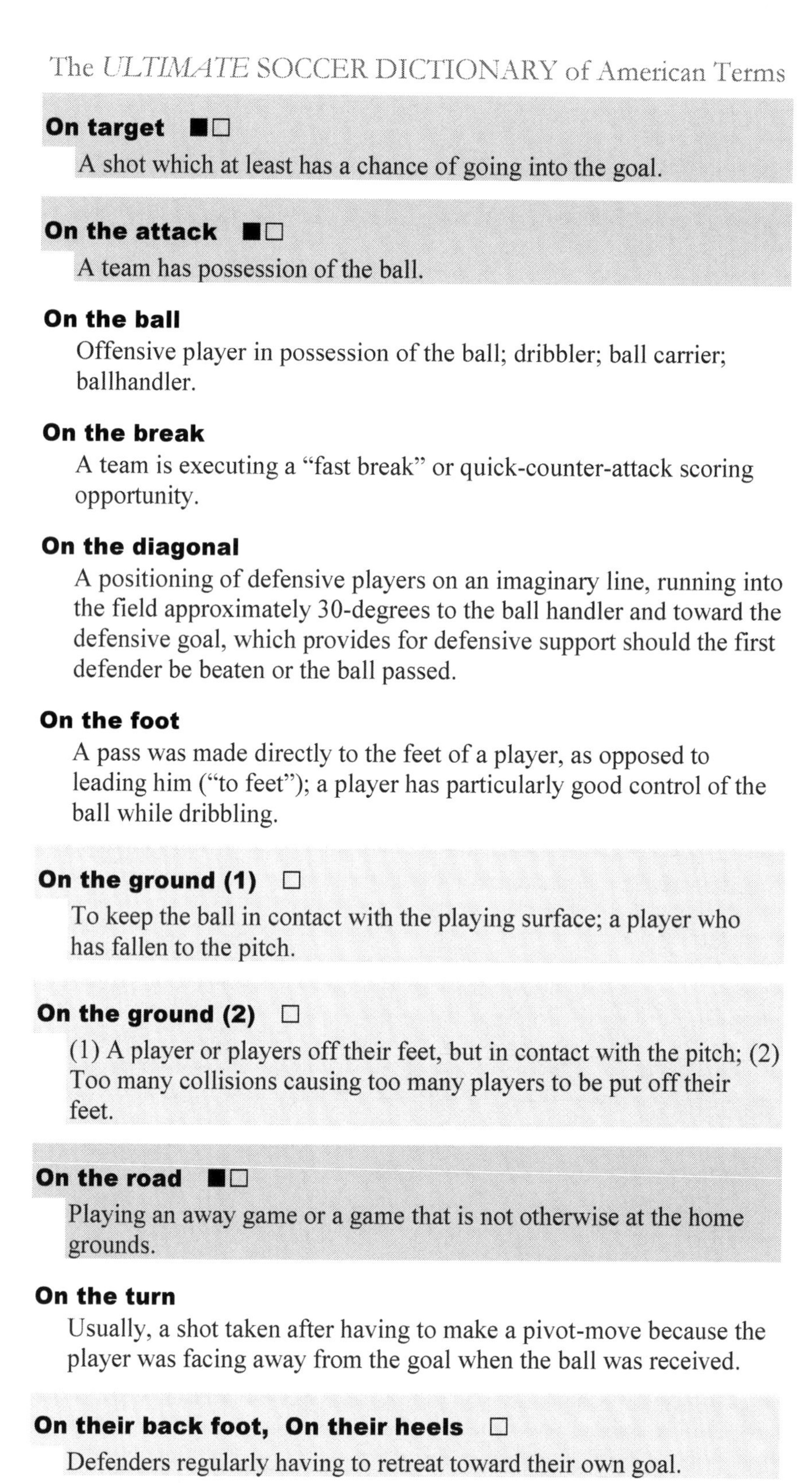

On target ■□

A shot which at least has a chance of going into the goal.

On the attack ■□

A team has possession of the ball.

On the ball

Offensive player in possession of the ball; dribbler; ball carrier; ballhandler.

On the break

A team is executing a "fast break" or quick-counter-attack scoring opportunity.

On the diagonal

A positioning of defensive players on an imaginary line, running into the field approximately 30-degrees to the ball handler and toward the defensive goal, which provides for defensive support should the first defender be beaten or the ball passed.

On the foot

A pass was made directly to the feet of a player, as opposed to leading him ("to feet"); a player has particularly good control of the ball while dribbling.

On the ground (1) □

To keep the ball in contact with the playing surface; a player who has fallen to the pitch.

On the ground (2) □

(1) A player or players off their feet, but in contact with the pitch; (2) Too many collisions causing too many players to be put off their feet.

On the road ■□

Playing an away game or a game that is not otherwise at the home grounds.

On the turn

Usually, a shot taken after having to make a pivot-move because the player was facing away from the goal when the ball was received.

On their back foot, On their heels □

Defenders regularly having to retreat toward their own goal.

On your back – ► □

► ***On-field Oral Communication:*** An opponent is coming up fast from behind to challenge you for the ball. A more urgent version of "Man on."

On-ball □

Offensive player in possession of the ball.

One more (1) (i.e., "Again") – ►

► ***On-field Oral Communication:*** Take another shot, pass or run, just as immediately before. ("Again" is better.)

One more (2) (i.e., "Don't play the ball.") – ►

► ***On-field Oral Communication:*** A request to a teammate ***to not play the ball***, but to let a pass proceed to the next player. Contextual - See: Dummy (5).

One point for a tie □

A system for establishing the relative positions of teams in a group whereby points are awarded for wins and ties and then accumulated and compared; usually involves one point for a tie and no points for a loss; alternative is usually three points for a win; part of a Point System for standings.

One side to the other □

A team playing the ball from touchline-to-touchline in order to create space for the attack.

One touch ◘ □

A player passes or shoots with only a single contact to the ball, as opposed to controlling it first.

One touch too many □

Player should have passed or shot one step earlier.

One up ■□

One goal ahead of the opponent.

One-man system

A single referee with no assistant referees or only club linesmen.

One-on-one ■□

The offensive player with the ball takes on a single defender; one defender against the ball carrier.

One-time, One-timer ■□

Generally, a shot performed without settling or otherwise controlling the ball first.

One-Two (1) – ▶

▶ ***On-field Oral Communication:*** Teammate is asking to perform a give-and-go passing combination.

One-Two (2)

Wall pass; Give-and-Go; 1 - 2.

On-field Oral Communication ■□

Verbal (i.e., spoken) communication between teammates during a match in order to direct activity. (See all entries marked with "▶") See: Appendix 4: On-Field Oral Communication.

Onside ■□

A player who is not in an offside position is said to be "onside;" in accordance with Law 11 of the Laws of the Game, a player who has at least two defenders between him and the goal (or is level with either, or both) at the moment his teammate passes the ball to him is "onside." See: Offside position.

Onside run □

A player making a run for a pass who is not offside at the moment his teammate passes the ball to him.

Open ■□

Player is unmarked or has freed himself from a defender and is available to receive a pass.

Open game

A match which usually exhibits equal play by both teams, ranging all over the field; a match which is not dominated by one team or the other.

Open goal ■□

Due to the run of play, the goalkeeper and defenders are away from the goal, leaving it unattended.

Open League

An organization of advanced teams which allows participation by both amateur and professional players.

Open net ■□

Goalkeeper is way out of position or is sprawled on the ground, leaving the goal undefended; open goal.

Open space ■□

A part of the field which is not occupied by a defender.

Open up – ►

► ***On-field Oral Communication:*** Move wide; create space; run to open space.

Open up the body/hips

To turn the frame of the body in such a way that it is roughly perpendicular or 90-degrees to the incoming path or flight of the ball; to turn the body similarly to create the proper flight to be placed on the ball.

Open up the game

To play less defensively; to attack using all options, generally faster with quick counter-attacks, long balls, and switching fields often.

Open; or, I'm Open; or, (Name) is Open – ► ■□

► ***On-field Oral Communication:*** You are open or a teammate is open and available for a pass. (Generally, a mid-range or long-pass option into space.)

Opening goal

The first goal scored in a game.

Opening leg

The first game of a home-and-home (two-leg) series.

Opening the angle

A striker with the ball makes a move that causes the goalkeeper to change his position such that more of the goal is exposed; striker turns toward the middle of the field before shooting.

Opening the field □

Switching the ball; spreading out; creating space.

Opens the body up

To turn at the hips so that the frame of the body is roughly perpendicular to the path of an incoming ball, or to create a similar position before striking the ball.

Opens the foot up

To turn the leg at the hips in order to use the inside of the foot.

Opponent ■□

The individual or team representing the adversary in a match.

Opportunities, making the most of

Either a team or a player getting a shot on goal, or actually scoring.

Opportunity □

A chance to shoot and score.

Opposite field □

The other side of the field from the location of the ball; the left side if the ball is on the right; the right side if the ball is on the left.

Opposite number

The other goalkeeper; opponent playing the same position; attacker – defender.

Opposite side

The other side of the field from the location of the ball; the left side if the ball is on the right; the right side if the ball is on the left.

Optimistic

Player takes a shot which has little chance of scoring and he knows it.

Optional Mark

Law 1 of the Laws of the Game; marks may be made just outside the field of play at right angles to the goal-lines and touch lines 10 yards from each corner arc; helps referee and assistant referees ensure that defenders are the proper distance away from a corner kick. (Since the arc has a one-yard radius, the mark is 11-yards from the corner.) Sometimes referred to as the "hash mark."

Options ■□

Choices of potential recipients to whom a player may pass the ball.

Options away from the ball ☐

Choices of places to which a player may run who does not have the ball.

Oral communication: ▶ ◘ ☐

Verbal (i.e., spoken) communication between teammates during a match in order to direct activity. (E.g., see all entries marked with this symbol: ▶.) Also, see: Appendix 4 – On-field Oral Communication.

Organization

(1) In proper position to defend and attack;
(2) The group responsible for a team, league or competition.

Organize

To prepare a proper defense, with defenders in the best positions.

Organizer

The player responsible for directing defenders to their optimal locations.

Origin of the Sport

Evidence exists of ancient games in Asia, the Roman Empire, and Central America using the feet, a "ball" and "goals." The modern game dates to the "schoolboys" of England and the formalization of rules into Association Football in 1863.

Oscar

Derogatory term directed to a player who has acted out the impact of a foul; play acting.

Other Match Officials

Law 6 of the Laws of the Game. As appointed, two assistant referees, a fourth official, two additional assistant referees and a reserve assistant referee.

Our end ■☐

A team's defensive half of the field of play.

Our goal ■☐

The goal the team is defending.

Out ◘ ☐

The ball has gone beyond the lines of the perimeter of the field of play; a player is unavailable.

Out of bounds ■□

The whole of the ball has passed outside of the field of play and is not playable.

Out of play

The whole of the ball has passed outside of the field of play and is not playable; the ball is "dead" due to a stoppage.

Out of position; Caught out of position □

(1) A player is not where he is expected to be given the system of play and formation of the team;
(2) The goalkeeper is not in the best place to try to make a save.

Out of shape ■□

Not physically fit to play up to standard.

Out wide □

(1) A player near the sideline;
(2) To send the ball toward the sideline.

Outdoor shoes ■□

Footwear, "cleats," worn by soccer players playing the game outdoors on natural or artificial turf.

Outer instep ■□

The upper-middle, outside part of the instep.
(See shaded areas in photo at right.)

Outfielder, Outfield player

A player who plays in the field; a player other than the goalkeeper.

Outlet □

A player set up to receive a pass to start an attack right after a goalkeeper save or the ball is taken away by the defense.

Outlet pass □

The goalkeeper or a defender kicks or otherwise sends the ball to a teammate who has run toward the sideline and upfield, after the ball has been stopped or saved near the goal; often used to start a fast break or quick counter-attack.

Outside ■□

Toward the sideline.

Outside Agent, Outside interference

A person or thing not associated with the game that influences the match, such as a dog or a fan running onto the field.

Outside backs, Outside fullbacks; Wing backs

Back defenders playing closest to either touchline.

Outside foot □

The left foot of a player running forward and receiving a pass from the right; the right foot of a player running forward and receiving a pass from the left.

Outside midfielder

A player in a midfield position closest to the sideline.

Outside of the foot ◘□

The lateral side of the foot closest to the sole, used mostly in dribbling and juggling. See: #10, "Outside of the Foot"

http://coachingamericansoccer.com/features/19-surfaces-of-the-soccer-shoe/

Outside of the foot pass ■□

A pass to a teammate executed with either foot, using the upper-middle, outside part of the instep (i.e., the "outer instep"). (See photo at: Outer instep.)

Outside of the post

That portion of either upright of the goal that faces or is otherwise perpendicular to the corner flag, outside of the goal itself.

Outside of the side netting

That portion of either side of the net facing away from the interior of the goal; implies that, if a ball strikes it, a goal has not been scored.

Outside the area, Outside the Penalty Area ■□

Near, but not within, the larger, 44- x 18-yard box extending from the goal; in context, a point from which a long shot has been taken or a point where a foul has been called which does not result in a Penalty Kick. See: Penalty Area.

Out-swerve; Out Swerve

See: Out-swinger.

Out-swinger, Outswinger

A type of corner kick marked by the path of the ball in the air which starts into the field of play from the corner arc and then, due to spin imparted to the ball, curves toward the field of play, away from the goal.

Over (1) – ►

►On-field Oral Communication: Called by the goalkeeper (or a teammate) when the ball is going to go over the top of the goal: Do not attempt to play the ball.

Over (2) ■□

The ball has passed fully beyond the end line (goal-line), without going into the goal.

Over the back □

A player charges illegally in the air from behind, contacting a player who has position, while attempting to go for a head ball in front of them.

Over the ball

A player's position in relation to the ball such that the most of the player's body is vertically above the ball.

Over the top (1) □

A shot that goes above the crossbar.

Over the top (2) □

A "long-ball" type of attack that sends lofted passes over the heads of defenders.

Over-coaching

Too much talking and not enough letting the players learn the game by playing.

Over-committing □

Defender runs to meet the ball handler too fast such that the ball handler can easily move around the defender.

Over-complicated

Trying to make too many passes, too many dribbling moves or too many actions of any type where a simple pass, or one move and then a shot might do; usually results in the loss of the ball.

Overhead back heel

To kick the ball, that has arrived from the front, from behind with the heel of the foot such that the ball returns from back and over the head. (Usually considered to be a "trick" and rarely seen in a game.)

Overhead throw ☐

A form of goalkeeper release; baseball throw; javelin throw.

Overhead volley

A ball skill whereby the non-kicking leg is thrust high into the air in order to raise the path of the kicking leg as it is thrust higher into the air to strike the ball immediately thereafter, above the original level of the head, with the player landing on his shoulders. Also known as a scissors kick or a bicycle kick.

Overhit, Overstruck

A ball which has been kicked too hard.

Overhitting

Kicking the ball too hard such that a teammate can't get to a pass.

Over-inflated ☐

A ball which has had too much air forced into it to meet the proper pressure standard.

Overlap, Overlapping run ◘ ☐

Defensive back runs beyond his midfielder or striker, without a switch of positions, to go into the attack; similarly, midfielder running past his striker.

Overlap – ► ☐

►***On-field Oral Communication:*** Make an overlapping run. Tells a defender or midfielder that the situation is acceptable for them to go beyond the midfielder or attacker, respectively, in front of them without a switch.

Overload, Overloading an area

Sending a large number of players into the same space at the same time, in an attempt to gain superior numbers or to draw defenders.

Overmatched

Opponent is too strong, too talented and too well coached to be competitive against.

Overspin

See: Topspin.

Overtake

To catch up to and pass by an opponent.

Over-the-ball tackle

Defender attempting to make a tackle raises his leg above the level of the ball and contacts the opponent's leg.

Overtime ◘ □

Competition rules state the amount of time and other conditions to extend play beyond regulation time if the game ends in a tie (draw). Usually two 15-minute periods in international matches.
A.k.a.: Extra Time.

Overtouch

Taking too many touches or trying to make too many moves with a ball instead of doing something simple like passing to an open teammate or shooting immediately; usually results in the loss of the ball.

Over-training

A player is subjected to so much exercise that the body can not sufficiently recover before the next round of exercise; often results in susceptibility to illness.

Own goal ◘ □

A defender inadvertently sends the ball into his defensive goal, giving a score to the opponent.

Oxygen debt

A deficiency or lack of oxygen, typically resulting from vigorous physical exercise.

P, (P) *(Abbrev.)*
Shorthand showing that a goal had been scored on a penalty kick.

P, Pts. *(Abbrev.)*
Points.

Pace ◘ □
The speed of the ball.

Pace of the game □
Team speed while in possession of the ball, ranging from slow, as demonstrated by multiple back passes and moving the ball from side-to-side among the back defenders, to fast, with energetic runs and passes being sent forward.

Pack
The pack; a large group of players, from both teams, congregated in front of the goal.

Pack it in
When a team puts most of its players in the defensive third of the field or at the top of the penalty area and makes it very difficult for the other team to score. The defensive team will then generally attempt to score on a fast break.

Pack the goal
To put a large number of defenders directly in front of the goal.

Packed defense
When a team intentionally puts most of its players in the defensive third of the field or at the top of the penalty area and makes it very difficult for the other team to score. The defensive team will then generally attempt to score on a fast break.

Padded head gear, Protective headgear
A soft "helmet" worn mostly by goalkeepers to minimize the possible effects of collisions; a device worn around the skull to reduce the effects of possible concussion; padded headgear.

Paint
Liquid used for field marking.

Paint marker
Device used to hold cans of paint to aid in field marking.

Pair of goals

Two goals scored by the same player; brace.

Panels

Portions of fabric or other material sewn together to make up a ball.

Panicked

A player has over-reacted to a ball or a situation, sometimes creating danger on defense or resulting in a goal.

Paradinha

Action where a player taking a penalty kick starts his run up and then slows suddenly, to throw off the goalkeeper or make him move, and then kicks the ball. [Portuguese; pahr-ah-JEEN-yah]. Generally, feinting before taking a penalty kick ***is*** allowed (unless the referee rules that the feinting action was "unsporting behavior"). A full stop during the run up is a violation of Law 14.

Parallel pass

A pass which is made close to, and follows the direction of, the sideline marking.

Park the bus

A packed defense for an extended portion of time during a match.

Parry, Parried

The goalkeeper redirected a shot so that it didn't score, usually by pushing it outside the upright or over the crossbar.

Partial block

Goalkeeper or defender only deflects the ball instead of cleanly sending it away from attackers.

Partial rainbow

A ball skill whereby a player pulls the ball up behind his calf using the instep or inside of one foot and then uses the heel of the other foot to kick it forward beside his waist.

Partner, Partnered

The other teammate in a center-back defensive pair.

Partnership

Both of the teammates in a center-back defensive pair.

Pass, Passing ◘ □

Intentionally kicking the ball to a teammate in order to advance the ball around the field or get the ball beyond an opponent.

Pass to feet □

Passer sends the ball directly to the feet of his teammate.

Pass to space □

Passer sends the ball to an area out in front of his teammate so that his teammate can run to it.

Passes attempted

Statistic used to accumulate how many times a player tries to pass to teammates.

Passes completed

Statistic used to accumulate how many times a player successfully passes to teammates.

Passes forward

Statistic used to accumulate how many times a player attempts passes directed toward the defenders' end of the field.

Passes into attacking third

Statistic used to accumulate how many times a player attempts passes directed into the opponent's defensive third of the field.

Passing accuracy

Number of passes completed divided by the number of passes attempted statistic.

Passing angle

The degree from straight ahead that a ball must be kicked in order for it to not be intercepted by a defender.

Passing it around ■□

A team using multiple passes in order to either maintain possession or probe a defense.

Passing lane □

Space between two defenders which can be exploited to get the ball to a teammate.

Passing range

The distance to which a player is able to successfully complete a pass.

Passing style

General team approach toward the majority use of short passing, back passes, long passing, through balls, or fast breaks.

Passive offside

Player in an offside position is not called for an infraction because he is not interfering with play or gaining an advantage.

Patience ■□

Maintaining possession of, or "holding onto," the ball and not trying to force it into well-defended space; waiting and probing on attack.

Patient run

Slowing down to not go offside.

Payback

Beating an opponent after losing to them in an earlier match.

PDL *(Abbrev.)*

Premier Development League.

PDP *(Abbrev.)*

Player Development Program.

Peeling off

To quickly move away from the close proximity of a defender.

Pen. *(Abbrev.)*

Abbreviation for Penalty Kick.

Penal foul

A foul which results in the award of a direct free kick.

Penalize, Penalized, Penalization

To punish an infraction of the Laws of the Game.

Penalties (1) ■□

Law 12 of the Laws of the Game; fouls and misconduct resulting in the award of direct and indirect free kicks.

Penalties (2) ■□

Common usage for the multiple penalty kicks used to determine the winner of a match. See: Penalty kicks.

Penalty (1) ■□

The consequence of a violation of the Laws of the Game.

Penalty (2) ■□

Shorthand for the award of a Penalty Kick.

Penalty Arc □

Law 1 of the Laws of the Game; that portion of a circle with a radius of ten yards marked on the field outside the penalty area from the Penalty Mark; "D"; bubble.

Penalty Area ◘ □

(a) The ***larger rectangular area*** (18 yards x 44 yards) at each end of the field. A.k.a.: "Penalty box," or "the box." The Penalty Area contains the Penalty Mark, which is where all Penalty Kicks are taken.
(b) The Penalty Area has an important impact on the game, affecting penalties and numerous other actions. A few examples include: (1) Within this area, the goalkeeper may legally handle the ball; (2) Penalty kicks are taken from the Penalty Mark; (3) During goal kicks and defensive free kicks (direct ***or*** indirect), opposing players must remain ***outside*** the Penalty Area, and the ball is ***not in play*** until it has left the Area.
(c) Law 1 of the Laws of the Game describes the Penalty Area as a rectangle (at each end of the field), formed by the goal-line and lines drawn **18 yards into the field** (from a point **18 yards from each goal post**) and the parallel line connecting the two ends. See: Appendix 3 – Field Diagram.

> Remember: Each "**Quick-Start**" term has the symbol ◘ and in the electronic versions is underlined and ***linked*** to Appendix 1. It shows all "Quick-Start" terms together, ***linked back*** to each term.

Penalty Box ■□

(1) The Penalty Area.
(2) See also: various uses of the term: the box.

Penalty Kick ◘ □

Law 14 of the Laws of the Game; awarded if, in the normal course of play, a defender within his own Penalty Area, commits kicking, tripping, jumping, charging, striking, pushing, tackling, holding or spitting against an opponent, or handles the ball.

Penalty Kick Procedure

Law 14 of the Laws of the Game; ball on penalty mark; kicker identified; goalkeeper must remain on goal-line, facing the kicker, and between the goalposts until the ball has been kicked; all other players must be inside the field of play, outside the penalty area, behind the penalty mark, and outside the penalty arc.

Penalty kick shoot-out □

Penalty kick tie-breaker procedure.

Penalty kick technique

Decisions by a penalty-kick taker on the angle and speed of approach to the ball; use of stutter steps or a feint; use of power or placement or both; where to kick the ball; where to look; and what type of kick to utilize.

Penalty Kicks, Penalty-kick tiebreaker □

Process for determining the winner of a match, usually alternating five players from each team; Law 10 of the Laws of the Game.

Penalty Mark, Penalty Spot

Law 1 of the Laws of the Game; a marking on the field 12-yards directly into the field from the center of the goal from which a penalty kick is taken.

Penalty marker

Vanishing spray; temporary paint applied by the referee to the field to mark the ten-yard distance from the ball before a free kick is taken. May also be used to mark the location of the ball.

Penalty Shootout □

Penalty Kick tiebreaker procedure.

Penalty shot ■□

Penalty Kick.

Penalty Taker, Penalty kick taker, Penalty kick specialist

The player designated to take a Penalty Kick.

Pendulum ball

Soccer ball with an attached hook that allows it to be connected to a rope for use with a pendulum training device.

Pendulum trainer

A tall, "T"-shaped pole from which a tethered ball may be hung, with an adjustable-length rope, mostly used to teach and practice proper heading.

Pendulum training

Use of a device for holding a freely-moving ball hung from a rope, used mostly to teach heading.

Penetrating run

An offensive player sprints into space between back defenders.

Penetration □

The amount of movement of an attack into defensive space in proximity of the opponent's goal.

Perception

Visual ability to see and properly comprehend what is happening around you.

Performance □

Successful execution and implementation of skills, tactics, and fitness.

Perimeter, Perimeter lines

The combination of the two end lines (goal-lines) and the two sidelines (Touch Lines) that define the outer playing area of a field.

Period ■□

The first or the second of the two halves of a game.

Periods ■□

The two halves of a match; the first and second half; the first and second periods.

Periods of play

Law 7 of the Laws of the Game; two equal halves of 45 minutes each, unless agreed upon by the teams and the referee to be less, based on competition rules.

Peripheral vision

That part of eyesight that detects objects and movement outside of the direct gaze.

Permanent goals

Goals, posts and crossbars, fixed in place on a field, such as set in concrete; non-portable; can't be moved.

Persistent Infringement

Persistent Infringement of the Laws of the Game; Cautionable, yellow card offense; Violation of Law 12 of the Laws of the Game.

Personal pass

Ball-handler is both the passer and the receiver, in effect passing the ball to himself, usually around an opponent.

Personal trainer

An individual hired to provide one-on-one skills and fitness instruction or coaching to a player.

Personality player

Individual on a team that sets them apart from their teammates due to their skill, attractiveness, looks, cordiality, friendliness or exceptionally good behavior; a "star" on a team.

Personality traits

Behaviors demonstrated by an individual that may apply positively or negatively to their performance on the field.

Phantom foul

A penalty awarded by the referee for a foul that did not really occur.

Phantom goal

A goal awarded by the referee where the path of the ball did not fully meet the criteria of having passed fully over the goal-line, between the uprights and under the crossbar.

Phase, Phase of the game

Characterization of the team being in attack, transition, or defense.

Philosophy

A coach's approach to the conduct of his program, team, and individual players.

Physical ■□

Shorthand for strong play and endurance.

Physical challenge □

A hard or harsh tackle with significant contact.

Physical therapy

The treatment of injury to restore movement and function.

Physical, get a

To obtain a medical review to certify the ability to participate in sports.

Physio tape

Elastic cotton strip with acrylic adhesive which, when applied to athletes when stretched, is intended to pull back to support the movement of muscles and joints; Kinesio Tape.

Pick (1) ☐

Scraping off a defender to free oneself by using a teammate (or sometimes an opponent) to block the defender's path. Mostly used on free kicks. Same as a pick in basketball.

Pick (2), Pick off ☐

Intercept a pass; interception of the ball.

Pick up (1), Pick-up, Pickup

A technique used to get the ball off the ground to start juggling.

Pick up (2), Picked up ☐

To take a man; to cover an opponent on defense.

Picking the ball out of the net

A team has been scored upon; the ball is retrieved to be set up for the ensuing kickoff.

Pick-up game ☐

Players meeting in an informal, unstructured setting to play soccer for fun.

Piece; Get a piece; Get a piece of

To make brief contact with the ball or an opponent.

Piercing run

An offensive player sprints into space between back defenders.

Pinafore

Origin of the words for a sleeveless overvest: pinnie; pinny. Training vest; training bib.

Pinballing

Soccer ball bouncing around, deflecting, and rebounding uncontrolled among players in front of the goal.

Pinched-In Diamond

A four-midfielder formation in a diamond shape but with the outside midfielders playing closer to the middle of the field.

Pinnie

Scrimmage vest, from the word "pinafore."

Pinny

Short for "pinafore," a scrimmage vest.

Pitch ◘ □

The field of play; soccer field; Law 1 of the Laws of the Game.

Pivot □

To plant the ball of one foot to the ground in order to use it as an axis to spin around and change direction.

Pivot turn

A 180-degree change in the direction a player is facing by spinning around the ball of one foot on the ground while pushing off with the other foot.

Pivot-turn-and fire/shoot/snap shot

Player with his back to the goal uses a pivot turn to shoot.

PK, PKs *(Abbrev.)* □

Penalty Kick(s).

Place (1)

The position of a team in the standings of a group competition.

Place (2)

To set the ball down firmly, so that it is not moving, in advance of taking a free kick.

Place kick

Any dead ball start or restart to a game within the field of play.

Placed shot

A soccer shot where the shooter has taken pace off the ball in order to direct it carefully to a particular spot on goal.

Placement

The specific location that a player has chosen to put the ball on the field prior to taking a free kick; the location on goal to which a shooter is aiming.

Placing players

The decision on the part of a coach of how to best utilize the talents of the team by putting players in certain positions.

Plant foot ■□

The foot in contact with the ground which allows the kicking foot and leg to swing freely; non-kicking foot.

Play ■□

(1) To participate in the game of soccer;
(2) A designed action for movement of the ball, usually set up by the award of a free kick; set piece.

Play acting ■□

Faking having been fouled; diving; flopping; exaggerating the effects of a foul or falsely claiming to have been injured.

Play for a corner

Attacking player attempts to influence a defender to last touch the ball over the defender's goal-line in order to intentionally obtain the award of a corner kick.

Play for a throw-in

Player attempts to influence an opponent to last touch the ball over the sideline in order to intentionally obtain the award of a throw-in.

Play it back □

To make a back pass.

Play it long □

To send a lofted ball deep down the field, usually over defenders' heads.

Play it wide □

To pass the ball toward the sideline, touchline, flank or wing.

Play long

To regularly pass lofted balls deep down the field.

Play maker □

Someone who is inordinately skilled or successful at setting up or scoring goals; target man.

Play on ■□

(1) To continue to play when a foul was expected to be called, but wasn't;
(2) Application of the advantage rule.

Play or "Play On" – ▶ ■□

▶ ***On-field Oral Communication:*** Keep playing, don't hesitate because the referee is not going to blow his whistle or call a foul.

Play short

To play with fewer than the maximum number of players allowed on the field, usually due to a red-card ejection, but sometimes due to injury or absence.

Play the advantage □

The referee applies the "advantage clause" and does not call a particular foul.

Play the ball, not the man □

Coaching phrase usually used to remind defenders going in for a tackle to concentrate on getting the ball and avoiding a foul.

Play to the flag

Attacking team passes or otherwise sends the ball into the corner of the field, usually to set up a cross.

Play to the whistle ■□

To not anticipate a referee's call; to continue to play until the referee actually blows his whistle.

Play wide

To regularly keep the ball near the sidelines.

Playability □

The state of a field or pitch, based on damage or the impact of weather or other conditions, that may determine whether or not a match can be played on it or not.

Played

A player made contact with the ball while it was in play or part of a restart.

Player contract □

(1) A written agreement between a player and an organization, mostly involving compensation; (2) A written agreement between a player and a coach, mostly involving behavior.

Player dropping back

Midfielder or forward joining the defense or any defender retreating toward his own goal.

Player notebook □

Collection of documents or paper handouts, provided by the coach, maintained by a player, usually involving team rules and team tactics.

Player pass

Document confirming registration, usually with a USSF affiliate.

Player questionnaire ■□

Document requesting player personal information and soccer experience, often used for tryouts.

Players ◘ □

Law 3 of the Laws of the Game; teams consist of not more than eleven players; a match may not start or continue with a team of fewer than seven players; participants in the game of soccer.

Players rested/resting

Players not on the roster or available to play as substitutes.

Playing a man down, Playing a man short, Playing with 10 □

To play with 10 players allowed on the field, usually due to a red-card ejection, but sometimes due to injury or absence.

Playing distance; Within playing distance

Used in a number of the Laws of the Game, but not specifically defined, this is generally interpreted as approximately three feet from the ball.

Playing down, Playing short

To play with fewer than the maximum number of players allowed on the field, usually due to a red-card ejection, but sometimes due to injury or absence.

Playing for a penalty

Attacking team or player directing the ball into the Penalty Area, not necessarily in an attempt to get a shot off, but rather to try to draw a foul which would result in a penalty kick.

Playing it back ☐

To pass the ball from forwards to midfield, from midfield to back defenders, or from back defenders to the goalkeeper.

Playing it in

Passing the ball from near the sideline to the middle of the field, usually in front of the goal.

Playing it out of the back

Usually a long pass sent forward from the defensive third of the field.

Playing narrow

Consistently attacking up the middle of the field; not generating or utilizing space on the wings.

Playing out of position ☐

A player who is used to playing almost exclusively in one position is asked to play in another position, often causing him to be unfamiliar or uncomfortable with the actions expected of him.

Playing short

To play with fewer than the maximum number of players allowed on the field, usually due to a red-card ejection, but sometimes due to injury or absence.

Playing the ball wide ☐

Kicking or otherwise sending the ball toward the sideline in order to create space or to attack from the outside.

Playing the break

Taking advantage of an opportunity to initiate a quick counter-attack.

Playing the man ☐

Defender going in for a tackle or to head the ball with little or no regard for contacting an opponent who has position.

Playing tight

Tight-mark defending.

Playing too narrow

As a team, playing or staying too much in the middle of the field. (Can apply offensively or defensively, offensively not using the flanks, defensively leaving the flanks open.)

Playing up (1)

A younger player playing with older players.

Playing up (2)

A team of a certain age-group of players competing against a next-older age group.

Playmaker ☐

Generally an offensive midfielder who is particularly good at setting up the attack or passing to players in a good position to score.

Playoff ☐

An after-season game used to determine a champion.

Plays in a dangerous manner

Law 12 of the Laws of the Game; generally kicking too high, heading too low, or failing to get up from the turf, when engaged with an opponent; results in an indirect free kick.

Plyometrics

A fitness regimen intended to increase explosive power, particularly for jumping.

PNT *(Abbrev.)*

Paralympic National Team; the U.S. Paralympic National Soccer Team.

Poach ☐

To hang around the opponents' back defenders in search of a misplayed ball.

Poacher

Forward who hangs around near the goal looking for the opportunity to snatch up a loose ball to shoot.

Poaching

Forwards who always seem to get into the penalty area and wind up with the ball.

Point of attack □

Location of the ball and general concentration of offensive players as a team heads for the opponents' goal, generally described as right, middle, or left.

Point system (for scoring) □

Players are awarded two points for a goal and one point for an assist.

Point system (for standings) □

Teams are awarded three points for a win and one point for a tie.

Point-blank, Point-blank range, Point blank range ■□

Shot at goal from within roughly two yards of the goal-line.

Poke tackle, Poked away

Taking the ball away from an opponent by extending the leg and generally contacting the ball with the toe-end of the shoe.

Pole-ax

To attack, strike or fell an opponent with an unexpected blow.

Policy, Policies, Policy Sheet ■□

Document provided to players by the coach or organization regarding behavioral expectations and possibly listing the consequences of noncompliance.

Pool □

(1) Group of players potentially available for selection to a team or higher-level instruction; club pool, state pool, regional pool.
(2) A group of teams available for random seeding in a tournament.

Pop-it

A personal pass; to kick the ball past an opponent and run on to it.

Pop-up goals, Pop-ups

Small, hinged or spring-loaded goals, often with nets attached, for use in practice or for small-sided games without goalkeepers.

Portable goals

Any number of small- to full-sized soccer goals which can be moved from one place to another; soccer goals which are not fixed or permanently set in the ground.

Position (1) ◘ □
Player's designation, duties, and responsibilities within a formation or system of play.

Position (2) ◘ □
The location of a player at any particular moment on the field.

Position (3) □
The location of a team in the standings of a group competition.

Position names ■□
The terms assigned to designate the location and duties of players. See: Appendix 2 – Player Positions.

Position of free kick
Law 13 of the Laws of the Game. Upon infringement of the Laws of the Game, the resulting free kick is to be taken from the spot where the infringement occurred.

Position shorthand, Position acronyms, Position initialisms
A letter or group of letters used to simplify the terms for the location and duties of players. For example, "G" or "GK" is used to represent the Goalkeeper. See: Appendix 2 – Player Positions.

Positions ◘ □
The assignment of players to particular areas of the field in order to facilitate tactics and strategy; commonly goalkeeper, back defenders, midfielders, and strikers.
See: Appendix 2 – Player Positions.

Position-specific training
Coaching directed to impart the technique, strategy and tactics to be applied by players related to their particular locations and responsibilities on the field.

Possession (1) ◘ □
(1) An individual in control of the ball;
(2) A team, through dribbling and passing, controls the ball for a period of time;
(3) The goalkeeper has the ball in his hands.

Possession (2) □
A statistic representing the percentage of time during a match that one team controlled the ball versus the other team; Time of Possession divided by the Length of the Game; example: A team that

controlled the ball for 55 out of 90 minutes of play would have had 61% possession.

Possession pass

A pass intended to retain possession of the ball for the team; usually a back-pass or square-pass to a clearly-open teammate, not necessarily intended to further any specific type of attack.

Possession-style soccer

A strategic emphasis on the part of a team to make a lot of short, quick passes to keep the ball away from the opponent. Attackers are then expected to make runs to receive an entry pass to score.

Post ◘ □

One of the uprights (goalposts) of a soccer goal.

Post line

An imaginary line extending directly out into the field from either goalpost, parallel to the sidelines, generally used in goalkeeper training.

Post or Post up – ►

► ***On-field Oral Communication:*** Attacker to run toward teammate coming upfield with the ball, stopping before the passing distance between the two becomes too short. Ball may be received and then passed back or flicked and turned.

Post-concussion assessment

Baseline capture of demographic and neurological data just after a concussion for use in comparing future progress.

Post-game analysis

After a match, the critical review of team and individual play in order to make improvements for the future.

Power

The physical faculty of applying strength or force.

Power shot □

A hard shot taken 18 or more yards away from the goal.

Practice ■□

(1) A training session;
(2) Instruction, repetition or exercise of a skill.

Practice games ■□

Small-sided activities during practice; scrimmages, full-sided games against an opponent; controlled scrimmages; exhibitions; pre-season matches.

Practice plan

Written agenda prepared in advance and used by a coach to conduct a training session; lesson plan.

Practice planners

Standardized forms or computer software available to coaches to fill out with the desired activities for a training session.

Practice vests

Scrimmage vests, pinnies; colored outer garments that can be pulled over existing clothing, used to visually designate members or a side, team or group.

Practice video; Video of practice; Film of practice

Visual record of a training session used to analyze players of the team.

Precision football

A style of play marked by crisp, short passes, ball possession and calculated, strategic thrusts at goal; contrast with “kick-and-run.”

Predictable; Too predictable □

A player or a team that does the same thing each time they get the ball; easy to defend.

Preliminaries

Activities just prior to the start of a match; Law 8 of the Laws of the Game. See: Coin Toss.

Preliminary

A game, often an exhibition, played before an official match.

Pre-match inspection

The referees check the equipment of each player in order to ensure that it conforms to Law 4 of the Laws of the Game, “The Players’ Equipment.”

Preparation □

Both as players and as a team, the act of getting ready strategically and tactically for the next match.

Pre-season ■□

Training, practice sessions and scrimmages, or exhibitions before the start of actual competition.

Pre-season schedule ■□

List of dates, times, and locations for scrimmages or exhibition matches against teams, prior to the start of the regular season.

Press □

Trying to force the level of play by running at opponents in an attempt to create errors. Often occurs near the end of regulation time.

Pressed the attack

Sending more players forward, usually near the end of a game, in order to try to score a tying or winning goal.

Pressing, Pressing the attack

Bringing more players forward into the attack in an attempt to get a tying or go-ahead goal; often leaves the team vulnerable in the back, especially to quick counter-attacks.

Pressure (1) ◘ □

To apply pressure to the attacking opponent, especially the player with the ball, by tightly marking, not giving ground, or going for the ball, in order to try to force a mistake which results in a takeaway.

Pressure (2) ■□

The measurement of air inflation in a ball.

Pressure (3) ("Man on") – ►

►***On-field Oral Communication:*** Man on; a defender is arriving. See: Man-on.

Pressure (4) ("Defense") – ►

►***On-field Oral Communication:*** In the defensive end, player is telling teammate, who is taking on an opponent with the ball, that he either has support or can no longer give ground and must force the opponent to stop or make a move; in the offensive end, player is telling a teammate to take on the opponent with the ball in order to try to force an error.

Pressure high

To apply immediate defensive pressure when the opponent gets the ball in their own defensive third of the field.

Pressure skills

The ability to perform techniques with the ball while under extreme duress.

Pressure training

A drill requiring rapid repetition of a skill during a short period of time.

Pressure; Under pressure

A team is constantly having every move challenged all over the field and is having difficulty getting the ball out of their own end.

Pressure-Cover-Balance

General philosophy of defensive strategy.

Preventive officiating

A concept and application that referees take an active role in order to forestall problems which may occur during a match.

Prime scoring area

The space in front of the goal roughly between six- and 18-yards away from the far post when the ball is delivered from the opposite side.

Pro ■□

Professional; A player who is paid to play the game.

Probable

A previously injured or unavailable player may be able to start or play in the next match.

Probe, Probing

Offensive thrusts into a defense to try to find a weakness that can be exploited.

Problem parent ■□

Mother, father or guardian of a youth player who does not conform to standards of conduct for the team, monopolizes the coach's time, seeks more favorable treatment for their son or daughter in comparison with other players, or otherwise presents inappropriate difficulties for the staff.

Procedures to Determine the Winner of a Match

Goals, extra time, and kicks from the penalty mark are approved methods in Law 10 of the Laws of the Game. Competition rules may include "away goals."

Professional attitude □

Taking on the proper demeanor and approach to training and the game of that of a player who is paid to play.

Professional coach

A coach who is paid to coach the game; not a volunteer.

Professional foul

A last defender intentionally trips, kicks, charges or otherwise brings down an attacker who has broken free and is about to go one-on-one with the goalkeeper and has a high chance of scoring; tactical foul made outside the Penalty Area; Cautionable offense.

Professional, Professional player, Pro

A player who is paid to play the game.

Program ■□

Sequence of instruction provided over a season or an extended length of time.

Progression; Learning progression □

Moving from fundamental, basic components to more advanced skills; For example: moving from the alphabet to writing an essay, or from dribbling to goal scoring.

Progressions; Passing progressions □

Generally a player with the ball would look for a long-ball, fast break option; then intermediate; then short; and then back options to pass.

Promotion

Advancement from a lower division to a higher division in a league as a result of a team's record after the end of a competition season.

Proper inflation, Properly inflated ■□

A ball that meets the regulation air pressure for its size and weight; Law 2 of the Laws of the Game.

Prospect ■□

A player under evaluation who has the potential to be offered a position on the team.

Protected species

Goalkeepers; goalkeepers tend to receive additional calls from referees for fouls due to contact from opponents because of the danger they are in from onrushing players.

Protection □

Local rule allowing pubescent girls or women to tightly hold their arms over their chest and contact the ball. (Movement of the arms toward the ball would constitute handling.)

Protective gear ■□

Any number of products allowed by the Laws of the Game used to cover body parts to reduce the chance of injury; always shinguards, sometimes elbow, knee, ankle or hip pads; cups for male goalkeepers; rarely, headgear.

Protective headgear ■□

Product usually made of soft padding, plastic and hook-and-loop fasteners designed to soften contact associated with the skull from heading the ball or with other players.

Provisional Roster

Names of players in a pool from which a final list of selections will be made for participation in a tournament.

Provocation

A verbal or physical action directed at an opponent in an attempt to incite anger or a response that violates the Laws of the Game.

Psyched out

To mentally become so discouraged or overwhelmed prior to, or during, a match as to not be able to perform effectively.

Psyched, Psyched up

To make oneself mentally prepared for high performance in a match.

Psychological

One of the four components ("4 pillars") of the game as taught by U.S. Soccer (Fitness, Psychological, Tactics, and Technique).

Psychology □

Mental aspects of the game of soccer regarding such things as motivation and desire.

Pull

To hook the ball.

Pull a second

To get another yellow card in the same game, resulting in an ejection.

Pull the goalie □

To send the goalkeeper into the attack in a desperate attempt to score; substitute for the goalkeeper.

Pull the trigger ■□

To shoot, usually at the right time, sometimes too early or too late.

Pull up – ►

►On-field Oral Communication: An offensive player is requesting that his midfield or defensive teammates move upfield to close a gap in support.

Pullback □

A basic ball move or feint where the sole of the foot is used to drag the ball backward.

Pull-back corner

A corner kick directed to the nearest point of the Penalty Area, 18-yards into the field.

Pulled down

Player was grabbed by an opponent and brought to the ground.

Punch, Punching, Punch out, Punch-out □

The use of the fist or fists by the goalkeeper to knock the ball away from the goal.

Punish, Punishing the/an error

Scoring a goal as the result of a miscue on the part of the defense.

Punished

Team is scored upon due to a failed attempt at an offside trap.

Punt □

To kick the ball upfield by the goalkeeper releasing the ball to his foot directly from his hands.

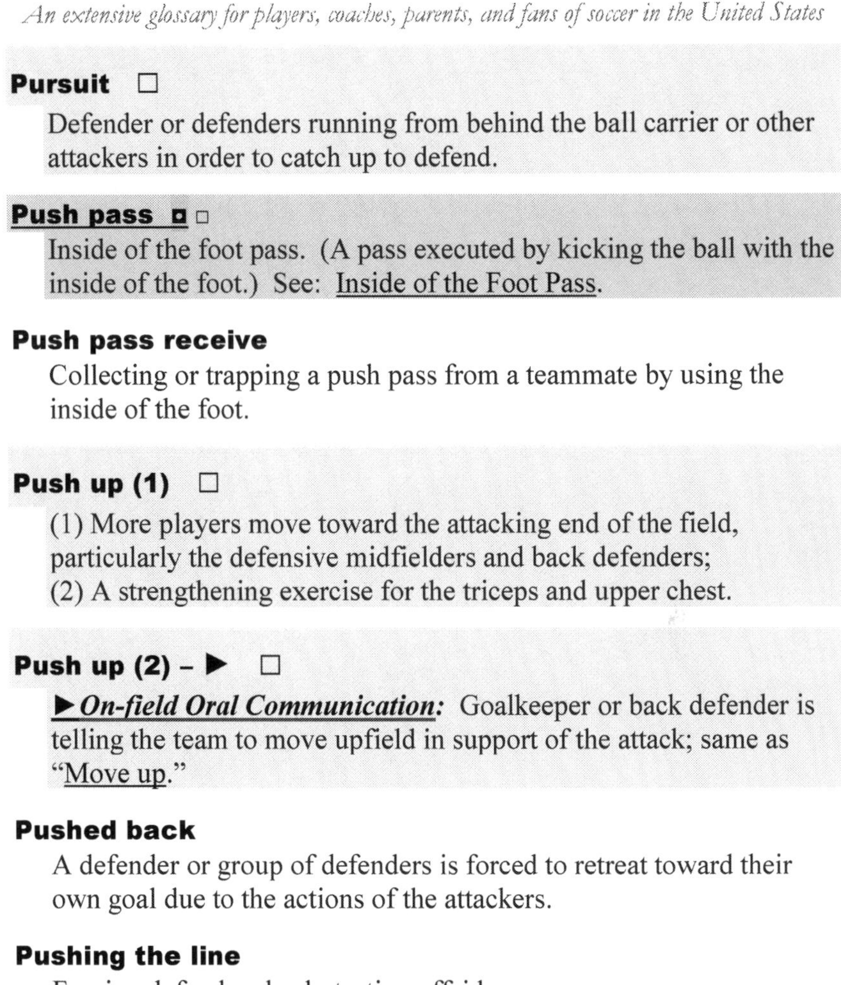

Pursuit □

Defender or defenders running from behind the ball carrier or other attackers in order to catch up to defend.

Push pass ◘ □

Inside of the foot pass. (A pass executed by kicking the ball with the inside of the foot.) See: Inside of the Foot Pass.

Push pass receive

Collecting or trapping a push pass from a teammate by using the inside of the foot.

Push up (1) □

(1) More players move toward the attacking end of the field, particularly the defensive midfielders and back defenders;
(2) A strengthening exercise for the triceps and upper chest.

Push up (2) – ► □

►On-field Oral Communication: Goalkeeper or back defender is telling the team to move upfield in support of the attack; same as "Move up."

Pushed back

A defender or group of defenders is forced to retreat toward their own goal due to the actions of the attackers.

Pushing the line

Forcing defenders back; testing offside.

Pushing, Pushes an opponent ■□

Violation of Law 12 of the Laws of the Game, Fouls and Misconduct, resulting in the award of a direct free kick.

Put away, Put it away

To complete the act of scoring by getting the ball into the goal.

Put it down

To place the ball on the ground for a free kick so that it is stationary.

Putting the ball back into play ■□

Any of those actions which re-start play after the ball has been dead due to such things as a foul being called or it going out of bounds.

Putting the ball out of play; Intentionally putting the ball out of play □

To kick the ball out of bounds on purpose so that an injured player may be attended; Sportsmanship upon injury; courtesy; showing the courtesy (when the referee does not see to stop play); One of the "unwritten rules" of soccer which demonstrates sportsmanship.

Pyramid

Part of a formation or system of play with one leading striker and two trailing strikers nearby.

Qualify, Qualifying ☐

To advance from a group stage in a tournament competition.

Qualifying Draw

An administrative procedure to determine which teams are placed into which groups for a tournament.

Qualifying Matches, Qualifier

The games between teams in a group stage, the results of which determine which teams will advance in a tournament.

Qualifying round

The entire slate of all games played by teams in the groups of a group stage in a tournament.

Quality chance, Quality chances ☐

The creation of shots that have a legitimate opportunity to go into the goal and score.

Quality possession

Control of the ball by a team for a length of time which results in masterful probing of the opponent's defense, usually resulting in a good shot and possibly a goal.

Quality win

A victory over a stronger or superior opponent; a well-played game resulting in a win.

Quarter circle

The Corner Arc.

Quarter finals, Quarterfinals ■☐

The round with eight teams in a single-elimination tournament.

Quick counter ☐

A fast counter attack; fast break.

Quick free kick, Quick kick □

Taking a free kick immediately after the ball is set, not usually waiting to establish a play or even for defenders to move back the required 10 yards.

Quick passing, Quick inter-passing □

Short passes successfully completed among a number of teammates at a high rate of speed.

Quick play □

A fast restart.

Quickness ■□

Fast movement or reactions.

Quiet the crowd

To score an away goal that makes a game close, ties the score, or takes a lead.

Quitting, Quit; To quit ■□

A player inappropriately stops going for the ball or stops doing what they are supposed to do; a player no longer puts out an appropriate effort.

Race juggling
A practice activity where players compete for who is the fastest over a certain distance while keeping the ball in the air.

Ragged □
Uneven or poor play.

Rain gear
Foul weather jackets, pants or coats made available to players and coaches.

Rainbow ◘ □
A ball skill whereby a player pulls the ball up behind his calf using the instep or inside of one foot and then uses the heel of the other foot to kick it forward over his head, creating a path of the ball from back to front that looks like the arc of a rainbow.

Rake, raked
To have an opponent's cleats dragged down the leg or the shoe.

Rankings □
Comparison of relative team strengths (e.g., FIFA World Rankings of national teams).

Rash challenge
An attempt at a tackle which should not have been made because it was doomed to failure, resulting in a dangerous collision, a foul, and a possible caution or ejection.

Raspberry
A surface scrape of the skin which is not very deep but may cover a wide area, usually red and purple in color.

Rattled (1) ■□
The goalkeeper, defenders, or a team are being constantly bombarded with shots and have lost their composure or confidence.

Rattled (2), Rattled the frame □
The post or crossbar literally shakes after being hit with a particularly hard shot.

RB *(Abbrev.)*
Right Back; the position of Right Fullback; right-side defender.

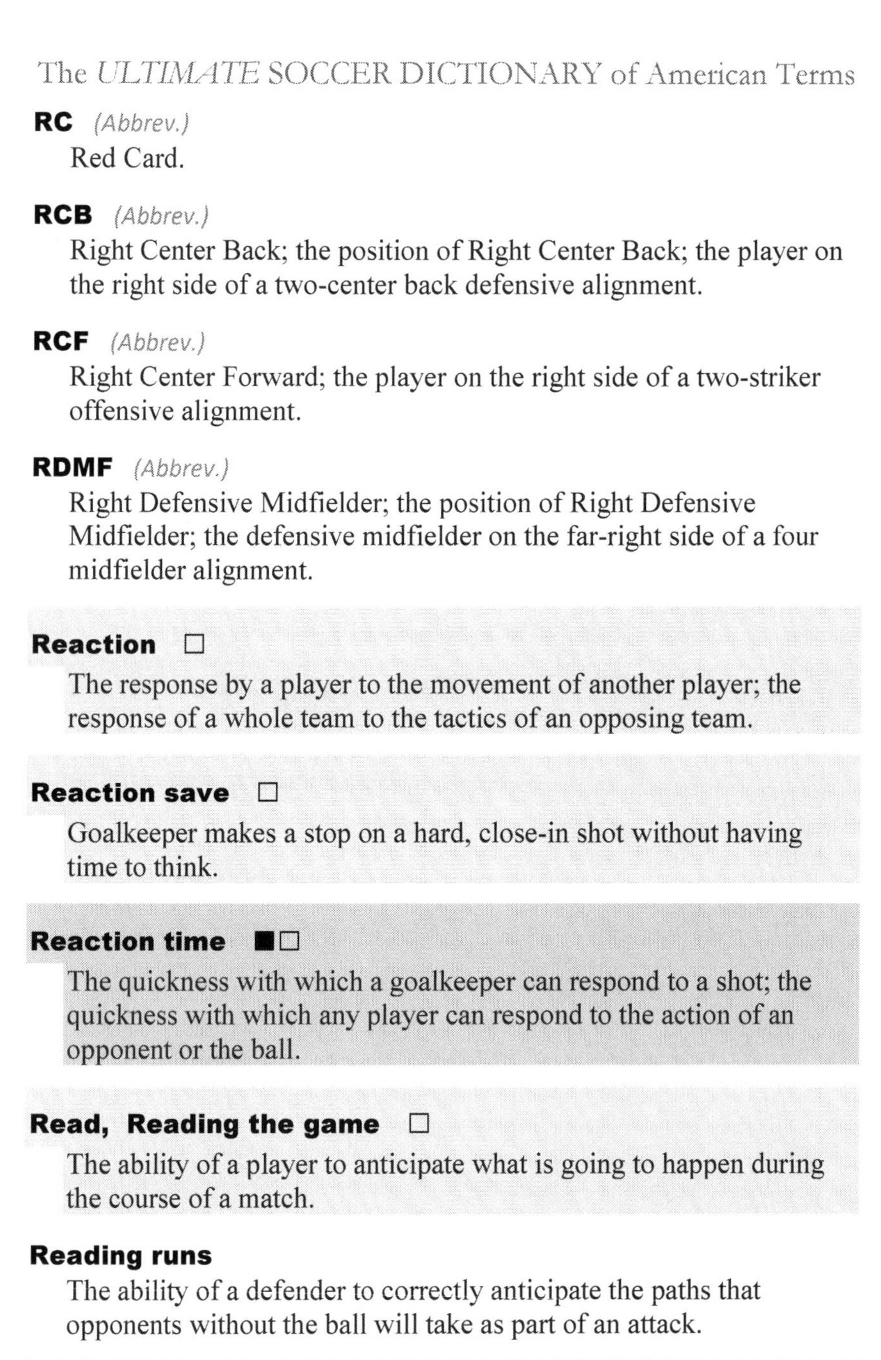

RC *(Abbrev.)*
Red Card.

RCB *(Abbrev.)*
Right Center Back; the position of Right Center Back; the player on the right side of a two-center back defensive alignment.

RCF *(Abbrev.)*
Right Center Forward; the player on the right side of a two-striker offensive alignment.

RDMF *(Abbrev.)*
Right Defensive Midfielder; the position of Right Defensive Midfielder; the defensive midfielder on the far-right side of a four midfielder alignment.

Reaction □
The response by a player to the movement of another player; the response of a whole team to the tactics of an opposing team.

Reaction save □
Goalkeeper makes a stop on a hard, close-in shot without having time to think.

Reaction time ■□
The quickness with which a goalkeeper can respond to a shot; the quickness with which any player can respond to the action of an opponent or the ball.

Read, Reading the game □
The ability of a player to anticipate what is going to happen during the course of a match.

Reading runs
The ability of a defender to correctly anticipate the paths that opponents without the ball will take as part of an attack.

Ready ■□
A player or team is prepared for a match or for an activity during a match.

Ready position ■□
The basic stance of a goalkeeper.

Real corner

A traditional corner kick from the corner arc to the front of the goal. Contrast with "short corner," "near-post corner," "skip-header corner."

Real pressure

Hard pressure and even contact by a defender as an offensive player is trying to work with the ball; contrast with "false pressure" perceived by the player with the ball, but not necessarily happening.

Rebound ◘ □

The ball bouncing off a field player, the goalkeeper, the goal, or even the referee, and returning in the direction from which it was kicked.

Rebounders

Elastic netting that is stretched over a goal and used to return shots to players.

Rec ■□

See: Recreational soccer.

Receiver

The player getting a pass from a teammate.

Receiving □

To take possession of the ball, usually as the result of a pass; controlling; trapping.

Recirculate the ball

Switching, changing fields, or swinging the ball on attack after a probe of the defense is thwarted, but the ball is not lost.

Reckless challenge

A defender going in for a tackle knowing that it has a high probability of being illegal and dangerous.

Reckless play, Reckless □

Any form of player contact, usually illegal, which may result in serious injury to an opponent and which should not have been undertaken in the first place.

Recoil

The drawing back of a body part upon contact with the ball in order to take the pace off.

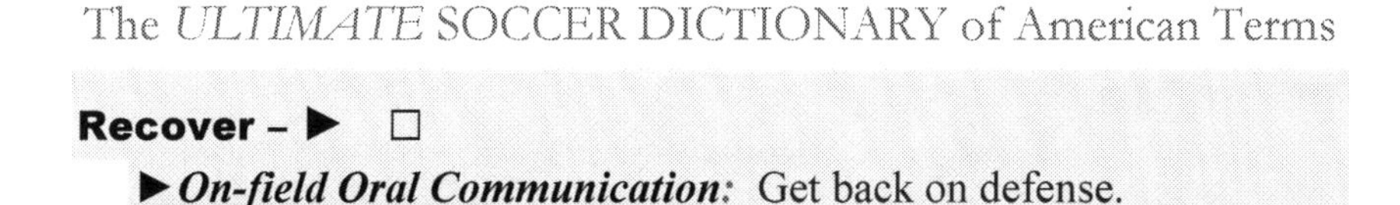

Recover – ► □

►*On-field Oral Communication:* Get back on defense.

Recovery run

The sprint of a defender to get back into the defense after having been beaten.

Recovery, recovers □

(1) During a game, the ability to get back on defense after the ball changes possession;
(2) During a game, the ability to regain normal breathing and fitness to continue play at the highest possible level;
(3) Between games, the ability to regain full fitness for the next match;
(4) Regaining fitness after an injury.

Recreational, Recreational soccer ◘ □

A level of soccer designed to be more for fun and exercise than for competition or based on the ability of players.

Recruiting □

To actively search for new players to join a team.

Recycled run

Player who makes a run and is not rewarded with a pass immediately makes another run; Forward comes out of the area after a corner kick or cross is lost, then recovered, and returns.

Red card ◘ □

Law 12 of the Laws of the Game; Colored piece of plastic shown to a player who has committed violations of the Law for which he is being sent off the field. See: Sent off.

Red card offenses ■□

Law 12 of the Laws of the Game, "Fouls and Misconduct," includes the following Sending-off violations: serious foul play, violent conduct, spitting at a person, denying a goal-scoring opportunity by deliberate handling of the ball, denying a goal-scoring opportunity by a person with a foul punishable by a free kick or penalty kick, offensive language or gestures, or receiving a second caution in the same game.

Redirect ■□

To intentionally change or modify the path or flight of the ball.

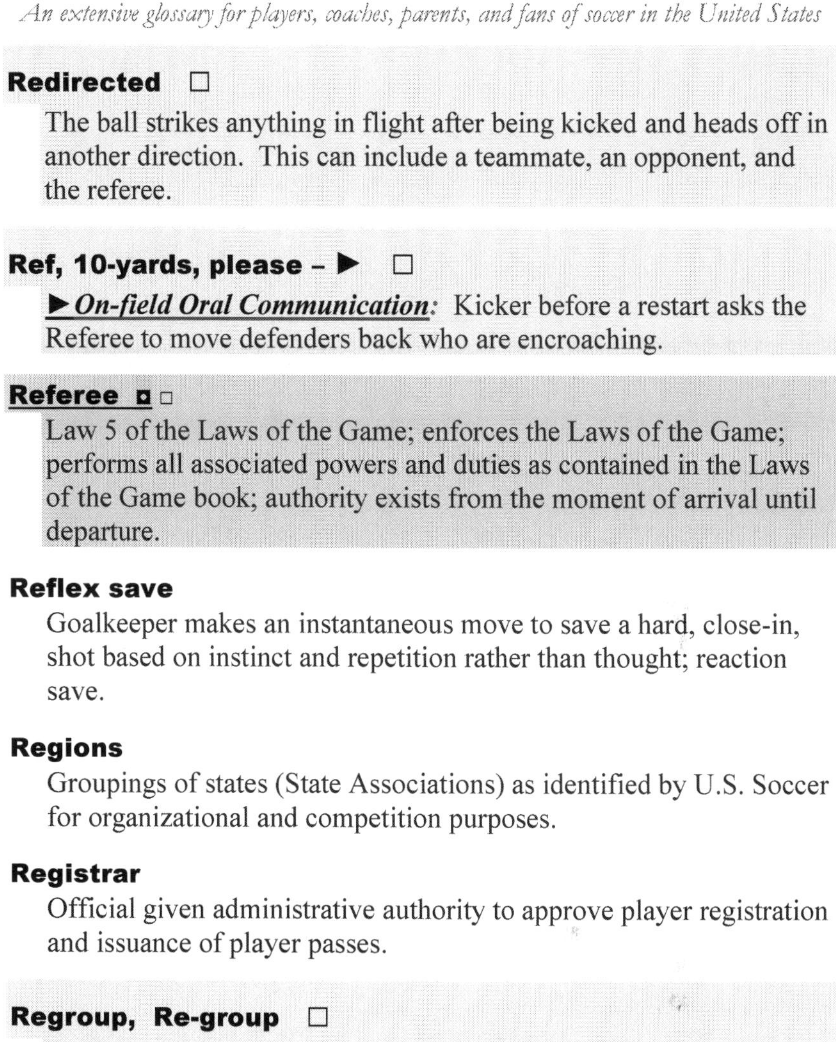

Redirected □

The ball strikes anything in flight after being kicked and heads off in another direction. This can include a teammate, an opponent, and the referee.

Ref, 10-yards, please – ▶ □

▶ ***On-field Oral Communication:*** Kicker before a restart asks the Referee to move defenders back who are encroaching.

Referee ◘ □

Law 5 of the Laws of the Game; enforces the Laws of the Game; performs all associated powers and duties as contained in the Laws of the Game book; authority exists from the moment of arrival until departure.

Reflex save

Goalkeeper makes an instantaneous move to save a hard, close-in, shot based on instinct and repetition rather than thought; reaction save.

Regions

Groupings of states (State Associations) as identified by U.S. Soccer for organizational and competition purposes.

Registrar

Official given administrative authority to approve player registration and issuance of player passes.

Regroup, Re-group □

Players and team try to regain their composure after being scored upon or after being put under great pressure or duress from the opponent.

Regular season □

Schedule of games among teams, established before the start of a competition, the results of which often determine seedings for a tournament or playoff.

Regulation (1) ■□

The full length of time for a basic game; implies that a game is tied at the end which, based on competition rules, may require extra time.

Regulation (2)

An administrative rule or requirement directed by a controlling organization or competition committee.

Regulation Game ☐

The completion of two equal halves of a match, in conformance with Law 7 of the Laws of the Game.

Regulation pitch, Regulation field, Regulation surface ☐

A full-sized playing field that meets the requirements of Law 1 of the Laws of the Game.

Regulation time ☐

The full 90 minutes of a match.

Rehab, rehabilitation ☐

A plan and action to restore a player to a normal, healthy condition after suffering an injury.

Rehydrate

To sufficiently replace fluids in the body after loss due to exercise, usually from sweating.

Reinforcements

Players who were out injured, out for national team duty, or otherwise not available, return to their home club.

Relative positions

The relation of any given position on the field to the rest of the positions, with regard to distance and responsibilities.

Relax – ► ☐

►On-field Oral Communication: Tells a teammate about to receive a ball that there is no pressure on him.

Relaxing, Caught relaxing ☐

A team mentally or physically not keeping up with the game and getting scored on.

Release (1) ☐

After obtaining possession of the ball, the goalkeeper throws it to a teammate; The goalkeeper tells defenders that they can go upfield after an opposition re-start.

Release (2)

Defenders go upfield after an opposition re-start.

Relegation

For leagues having multiple divisions, there is a procedure for losing teams to be moved from higher divisions to lower divisions after a competition has been completed. Winning teams move up as "promotion" or "advancement."

Reorganize

To return to positions in the base formation after being disrupted by the run of play.

Repetition, Repetitions ■□

Practicing a skill properly over-and-over until it becomes ingrained; Number of times an exercise is repeated.

Replica jersey

Shirt made available for commercial sale which looks like one worn by a particular player, team, or national team.

Repossessed

To get the ball back immediately after being dispossessed.

Re-possession □

Violation of Law 12 of the Laws of the Game, Fouls and Misconduct, resulting in the award of an indirect free kick; goalkeeper inside his own penalty area touches the ball again with his hands after he has released it from his possession and before it has touched another player.

Reps ■□

Repetitions; to repeat an exercise or drill. See: Repetition.

Reserve, Reserves, Reserve player □

Pool of available players to use as substitutes.

Reserve Assistant Referee

Discussed in Law 6 of the Laws of the Game, a reserve assistant referee is available only to replace an assistant referee or fourth official who is unable to continue performing their duties during a match.

Reserve team

Group of players potentially available for selection to a higher-level team within the same organization, but who play organized games.

Re-Set

Provisions of the rules of a tournament that allow the number of yellow cards accumulated by a player to go back to zero prior to the semi-finals; amnesty.

Re-sets the ball

Player getting ready to initiate a free kick picks up the ball and moves it slightly after having set it originally.

Resistance (1) ☐

Defensive ability to withstand attack.

Resistance (2)

Form of strength training.

Responsibility (1)

Duties of a player in a system of play.

Responsibility (2) ☐

Marking assignment; the opponent to be covered by a player while on defense.

Rest

Players' recovery time before the next match.

Restart, Re-start

Any of a number of procedures for putting the ball back into play after a stoppage, including throw-ins, corner kicks, goal kicks and free kicks; commonly refers to free kicks.

Restraining Line (1)

The farthest a forward can push up to the next-to-last defender without going into an offside position; offside line; imaginary line of offside.

Restraining Line (2)

The position of the next-to-last defender, established by the onfield defensive coordinator, creating the imaginary line for offside, usually during free kick situations.

Restricted play

Conditions placed on players during a drill or scrimmage, example: 2-touch; conditional play.

Restrictions

Any number of conditions placed on players during a drill or scrimmage; examples, 1-touch, 2-touch, man-to-man defense, ball only on the ground.

Resubstitution

The ability to return a player to a game who has already been substituted; determined by competition rules. Identified as "Return Substitutions" in Law 3 of the Laws of the Game.

Result ☐

Final score of a game.

Retaliation ☐

Striking an opponent after having (or perceived to have) been fouled by him; subject to sanctions of Law 12 of the Laws of the Game.

Return

As an individual or a group, to get back into a defensive position after having gone on attack; player coming back to a team after having been unavailable due to an injury.

Return match

Second game of a home-and-home series.

Return pass, Return ball ☐

A pass which is made right back to the player from whom an initial pass was received.

Return Substitutions

The ability to send a player back into a game who has already been substituted; determined by competition rules. Contained in Law 3 of the Laws of the Game.

Revenge, Revenge game

Motivation to defeat an opponent who one lost to in a previous match.

Reverse field ☐

To switch (pass) the ball to the other side of the field; As a dribbler, to perform a 180-degree turn and head in the opposite direction.

Reverse pass

Player with ball advances forward looking like he will make the obvious pass to a player in front of him, but instead makes a more-than-90-degree-angle pass to a trailing or on-rushing teammate.

Reward

Getting a goal after a lot of effort; getting a pass back after making a pass.

RF *(Abbrev.)*

Right Forward; the position of Right Forward; right-side striker.

RFB *(Abbrev.)*

Right Fullback; the position of Right Fullback; right-side defender.

RHB *(Abbrev.)*

Right Halfback; the position of Right Halfback; right midfielder.

Rhythm

Consistency with which a player or a team defends or attacks during a match.

RI *(Abbrev.)*

Right Inside; the position of Right Inside; right inside forward; right inside striker.

RICE ◘ □

Rest-Ice-Compression-Elevation; Acronym to be used for the immediate treatment of an injury.

Ricochet □

Rebound or deflection of a shot off the uprights or crossbar.

Right ■□

That half of the human body, to the side of the midline, which does not contain most of the heart.

Right Back ■□

Right Fullback; the position of Right Fullback; right-side defender. See: Appendix 2: Player Positions.

Right center back

The right-side central defender of a two-center-back alignment.

Right center forward

The right-side central striker of a two-center-striker alignment.

Right Forward ■□

Player positioned to help lead the attack; a striker. Generally positioned toward the front of the attacking team, toward the right side. See: Appendix 2: Player Positions.

Right Fullback ■□

The position of Right Fullback; right-side defender. See: Appendix 2: Player Positions.

Right Halfback ■□

The position of Right Halfback; right midfielder. See: Appendix 2: Player Positions.

Right Inside Forward ■□

The position of Right Inside; right inside forward; right inside striker. See: Appendix 2: Player Positions.

Right Midfielder ■□

The position of Right Midfielder; right-most midfielder, closest to the sideline. See: Appendix 2: Player Positions.

Right of Way □

Two players on the same team going for the ball must determine who has precedence. Generally, the person heading toward the attacking goal, the person heading toward the sideline, or the person otherwise headed away from the defending goal has priority on the ball.

Right side (of the field), Right-hand side ◘ □

That part of the field to the right of the imaginary center line down the middle of the field of play, when facing away from the goal one is defending.

Right side net, Right side netting

That portion of the net behind the right goal post, when facing the goal from within the field.

Right side of the attack □

That part of the attacking third of the field to the right of the imaginary center line.

Right side of the body ■□

That half of the human body, to the side of the midline, which does not contain most of the heart.

Right Wing ■□

The position of right wing; right wing forward; right wing striker. See: Appendix 2: Player Positions.

Right wing back

Right fullback; the position of Right Fullback; right-side defender.

Right-footed ■□

A player who is naturally right-side dominant; a player who prefers to use his right foot to kick.

Right-wing striker

Right wing; right wing forward; the position of right wing. See: Appendix 2: Player Positions.

Rip it – ►

►***On-field Oral Communication:*** Tells a teammate with the ball to take a hard shot.

Rising ball

A shot which moves upward as it approaches the goal, usually causing the ball to go over the crossbar; often refers to a Penalty Kick which goes over the crossbar.

Rival

An opponent met for years-on-end which engenders special competitive fervor among players and fans with ensuing matches.

RM *(Abbrev.)*

Right Midfield; the position of Right Midfielder; right-most midfielder, closest to the sideline.

RMF *(Abbrev.)*

Right Midfield; the position of Right Midfielder; right-most midfielder, closest to the sideline.

Rocket

An extremely fast, well-struck, straight-line shot.

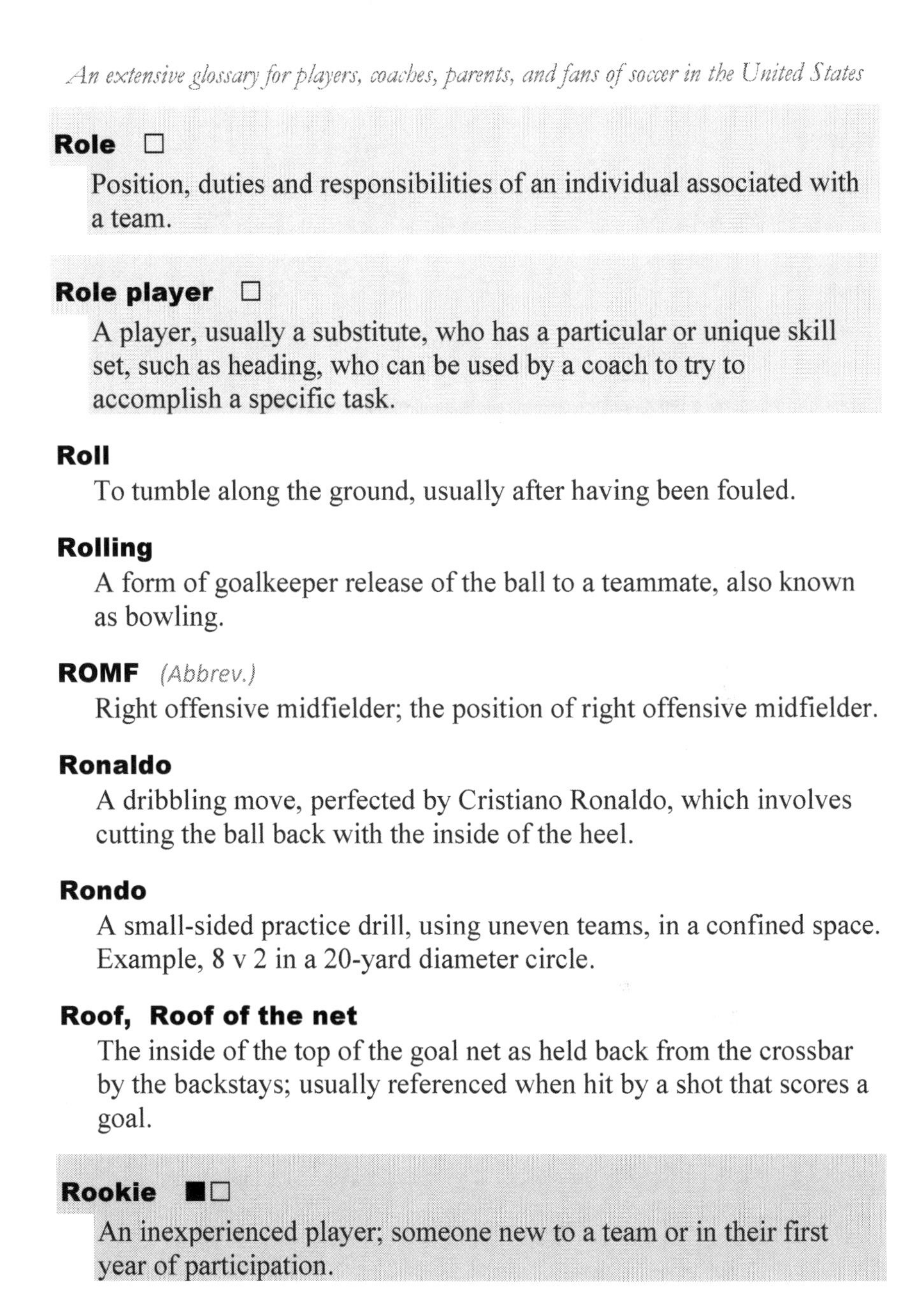

Role □

Position, duties and responsibilities of an individual associated with a team.

Role player □

A player, usually a substitute, who has a particular or unique skill set, such as heading, who can be used by a coach to try to accomplish a specific task.

Roll

To tumble along the ground, usually after having been fouled.

Rolling

A form of goalkeeper release of the ball to a teammate, also known as bowling.

ROMF *(Abbrev.)*

Right offensive midfielder; the position of right offensive midfielder.

Ronaldo

A dribbling move, perfected by Cristiano Ronaldo, which involves cutting the ball back with the inside of the heel.

Rondo

A small-sided practice drill, using uneven teams, in a confined space. Example, 8 v 2 in a 20-yard diameter circle.

Roof, Roof of the net

The inside of the top of the goal net as held back from the crossbar by the backstays; usually referenced when hit by a shot that scores a goal.

Rookie ■□

An inexperienced player; someone new to a team or in their first year of participation.

Rose, Rose up

Jumped very high to make a header (field player), or a catch (goalkeeper).

Roster ■□

The list of names of the players on a team.

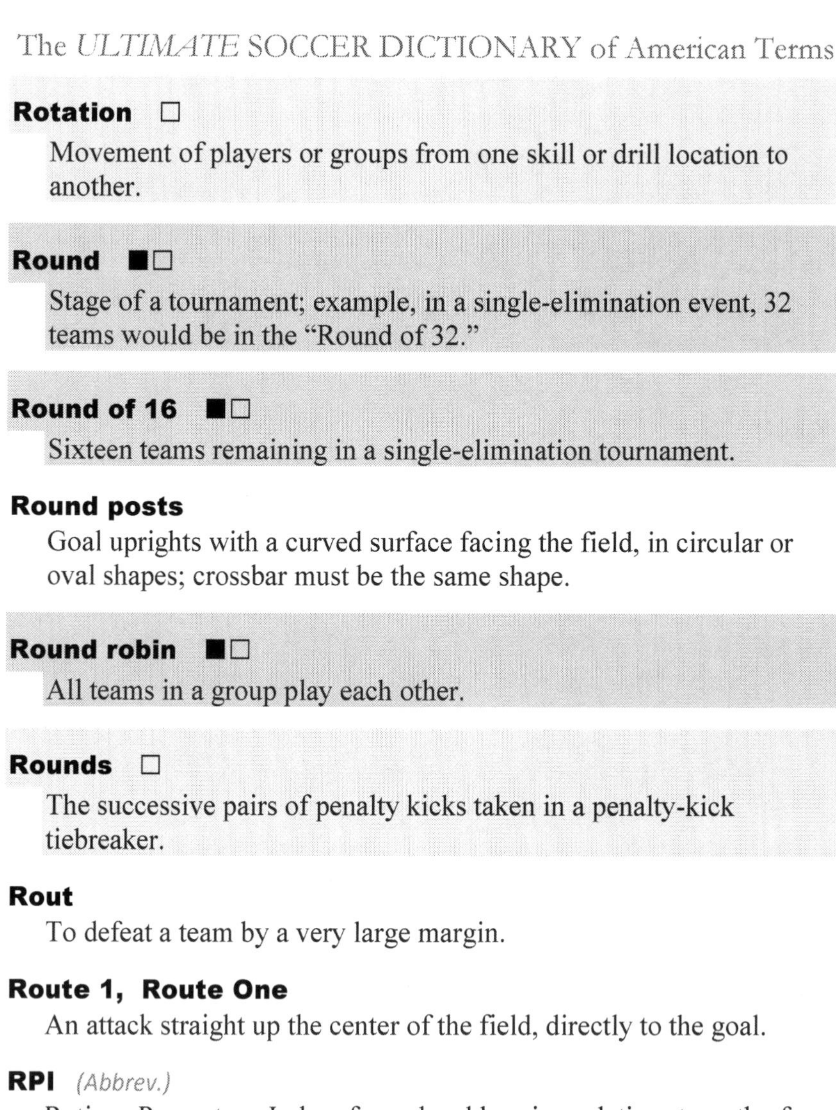

Rotation □

Movement of players or groups from one skill or drill location to another.

Round ■□

Stage of a tournament; example, in a single-elimination event, 32 teams would be in the "Round of 32."

Round of 16 ■□

Sixteen teams remaining in a single-elimination tournament.

Round posts

Goal uprights with a curved surface facing the field, in circular or oval shapes; crossbar must be the same shape.

Round robin ■□

All teams in a group play each other.

Rounds □

The successive pairs of penalty kicks taken in a penalty-kick tiebreaker.

Rout

To defeat a team by a very large margin.

Route 1, Route One

An attack straight up the center of the field, directly to the goal.

RPI *(Abbrev.)*

Ratings Percentage Index; formula addressing relative strength of teams, utilizing winning percentage and opponents' winning percentages.

Rub

See: Pick (1).

Rule book ◘ □

(1) The published Laws of the Game.
(2) Any recognized, formal, set of written rules governing the conduct of games as set forth by a competition organization, e.g., the NCAA.

Rules ■□

Any of the individual or collective explicit or understood regulations or principles governing the conduct of a game; Laws of the Game.

Rules changes

Amendments made once a year to the Laws of the Game; any changes made to the rules made by an organization before the start of a competition season.

Rules of the Road

A list of guidance provided to beginning players to learn where to run or who has priority on the ball while playing with the full team.

Run (1)

A winning or undefeated streak by a team.

Run (2) ■□

The act of running; to run.

Run (3) ◘ □

Moving to space where one might receive a pass.

Run around the ball

To take extra steps to set up the use of the dominant leg or foot before kicking.

Run at him – ► □

► ***On-field Oral Communication:*** Goalkeeper, defensive organizer, or defensive support player is telling a defender to go directly at the opponent with the ball in order to force the action, hopefully creating an error, dispossession, or a successful tackle.

Run down the ball

A player gets to a fast-moving ball and obtains possession before it can go over a boundary line.

Run of play

Normal free flow of a match in progress; not dead-ball situations or set pieces; having the better part of possession.

Run off the ball □

A successful shoulder charge by a defender that moves the offensive player and allows the defender to take the ball.

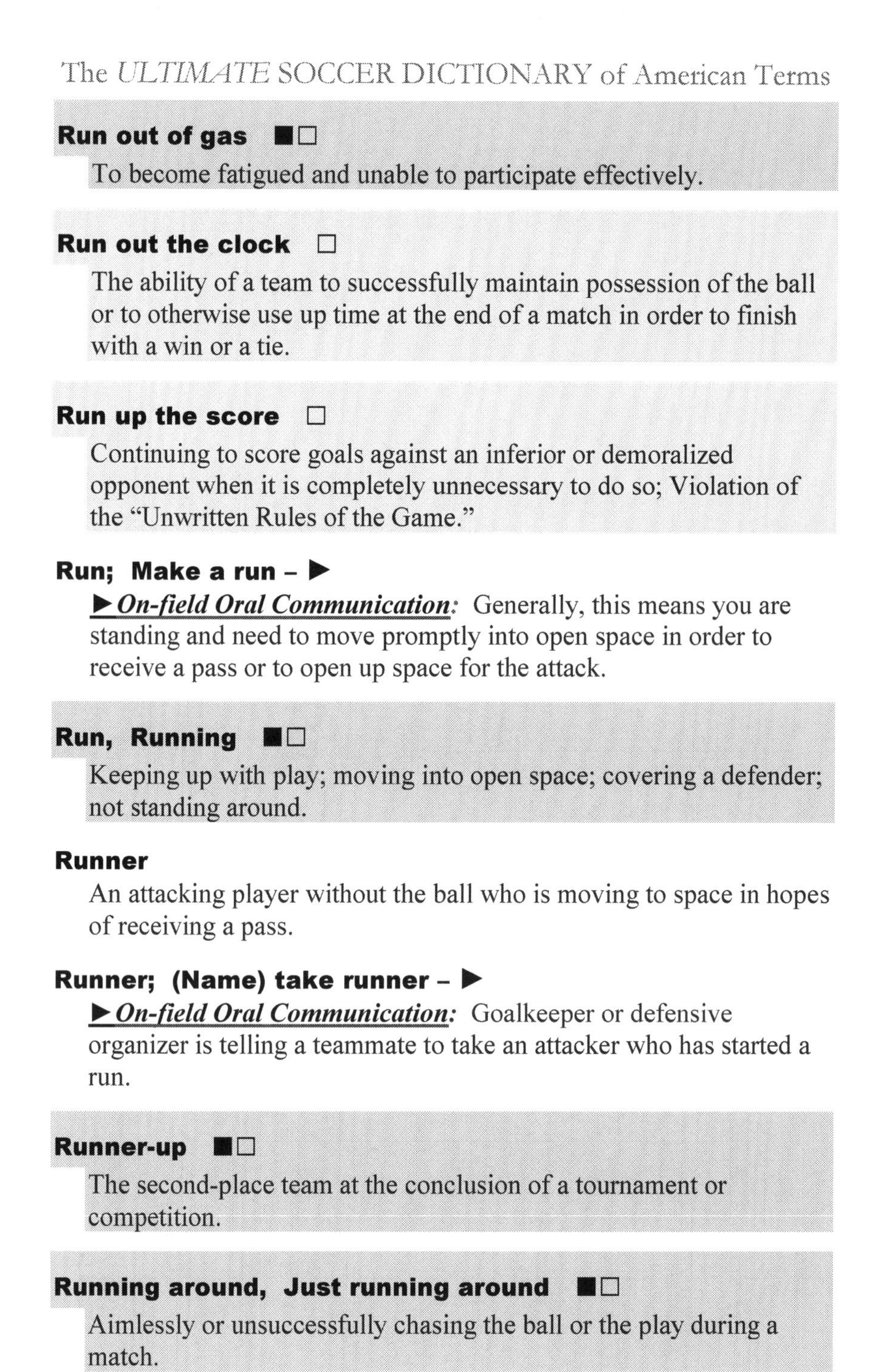

Run out of gas ■□

To become fatigued and unable to participate effectively.

Run out the clock □

The ability of a team to successfully maintain possession of the ball or to otherwise use up time at the end of a match in order to finish with a win or a tie.

Run up the score □

Continuing to score goals against an inferior or demoralized opponent when it is completely unnecessary to do so; Violation of the "Unwritten Rules of the Game."

Run; Make a run – ►

►***On-field Oral Communication:*** Generally, this means you are standing and need to move promptly into open space in order to receive a pass or to open up space for the attack.

Run, Running ■□

Keeping up with play; moving into open space; covering a defender; not standing around.

Runner

An attacking player without the ball who is moving to space in hopes of receiving a pass.

Runner; (Name) take runner – ►

►***On-field Oral Communication:*** Goalkeeper or defensive organizer is telling a teammate to take an attacker who has started a run.

Runner-up ■□

The second-place team at the conclusion of a tournament or competition.

Running around, Just running around ■□

Aimlessly or unsuccessfully chasing the ball or the play during a match.

Running free

Offensive player moving on the field without a defender marking him; unmarked.

Running shoes

Footwear designed for running; not cleats.

Running time

Local rule modification to Law 7 of the Laws of the Game, “The Duration of the Match,” which provides for no stoppage of the clock or added time.

Running with the ball

Speed dribbling.

Runover ☐

To step over the ball as part of a set piece. See: Set Piece.

Runs

Players moving into open space to set up a passing opportunity.

RW *(Abbrev.)*

Right Wing; the position of right wing; right wing forward; right wing striker.

RWB *(Abbrev.)*

Right Wing Back; the position of Right Wing Back; right fullback; right-side defender.

RWS *(Abbrev.)*

Right Wing Striker; the position of right wing striker; right wing; right wing forward.

S *(Abbrev.)*
Striker; the position of striker; center forward; single center forward.

SAC *(Abbrev.)*
State Assignor Coordinator; The person responsible for the coordination of assignors with regard to the assignment of **referees**.

Sackpack
A small backpack usually imprinted with a team logo.

Sacrifice ☐
To "give up one's body" in order to score, often placing one's head where a foot may appear or accepting the possibility of a collision.

Safe handling, Safe hands ☐
Goalie cleanly catches and holds on to the ball.

Safe play, make the ■☐
Passing the ball to an open teammate in a way that retains possession.

Safety ◘ ☐
Law 4 of the Laws of the Game; a player may not wear anything that is dangerous to himself or others, including jewelry.

Sag ☐
To slowly give up space in order to wait for support by retreating toward the defensive goal.

Sail, Sailed
The rise of a ball higher into the air than that which was intended, usually over the crossbar on a shot.

Salvage a point
To obtain a tie or a draw in a match, usually unexpectedly.

Samba soccer
Brazilian soccer, featuring creative and stylish ball handling.

Sanction □

The award or penalty resulting from a violation or infringement of the Laws of the Game.

Sanctioned tournament

For youth, a competition approved by the USYSA for participation by USYSA-registered teams.

Sanctions, administrative

The penalty to a player or team for failure to comply with team or league rules.

Sand bag anchors

Sacks filled with sand designed to hold goals in place, specifically for safety purposes so that they won't tip over.

Sandals

An open foot covering, usually consisting of one sole, for soccer generally made of synthetic, water-proof material; slides, flip-flops.

Sandwich □

To get caught between two defenders.

SAQ *(Abbrev.)*

Speed, Agility, Quickness; drills or activities to promote speed, agility, and quickness.

SARA *(Abbrev.)*

State Adult Referee Administrator.

Saucers

Small, colored plastic discs used by coaches to delineate practice space and drills.

Save □

Goalkeeper stops a shot from going into the goal, either by securing or deflecting the ball.

Save from the crossbar

Goalkeeper successfully stops the ball from hitting the crossbar and rebounding into the field of play.

Save from the post

Goalkeeper successfully stops the ball from hitting either upright of the goal and rebounding into the field of play.

Saved off the line

Defender at the goal-line keeps a ball from going into the goal after it has gotten past their goalkeeper.

SAY *(Abbrev.)*

Soccer for American Youth.

SC *(Abbrev.)*

Soccer Club.

Scarves, Scarf

Clothing worn by fans showing support for their team, printed or sewn with the team's colors, town, name and/or nickname.

Schedule ■□

The list of dates, times, locations and opponents for a competition season.

Scheduled water break □

A referee decision, made before the start of a game, to implement a stoppage of play in order for players to drink water due to hot, humid conditions.

Scholarship ■□

Administrative action, usually taken by a recreational or youth organization, to pay the fees for a player who cannot otherwise afford them; Fees paid by colleges and universities to attract talent.

Scissor kick, Scissors kick ◘ □

A ball skill whereby the non-kicking leg is thrust high into the air in order to raise the path of the kicking leg as it is thrust higher into the air to strike the ball immediately thereafter, above the original level of the head, with the player landing on his shoulders. The motion looks like a pair of scissors cutting. Also known as an overhead volley or a bicycle kick.

Scoop, Scoop pass □

To lift the ball with the foot, rather than kicking it, usually to flip it over an opponent's head.

Score (1) ■□

The number of goals made by each team during a match; the current score, the halftime score, the final score.

Score (2), Scoring ■□

To score a goal.

Score directly ■□

To score a goal, usually from a corner kick, but also from any other type of direct free kick, without the ball touching any other player.

Scoreboard ■□

Display sign designed to show spectators the current score of a match and possibly the game time.

Score Book

Official written record for the statistics and outcome of matches.

Scorebox

An area in front of the goal from which many goals are scored.

Scorekeeper ■□

Person who marks down and maintains the official written record for the statistics and outcome of matches.

Scoreline

Results of a match; internationally, home team is listed first; score of a game while it is going on.

Scorer

Player who scores or scored goals.

Scoresheet

Official written record for the statistics and outcome of a single match.

Scoring chance, Scoring opportunity □

An opportunity created during the run of play in a match that allows a shot to be taken.

Scout, Scouting

To observe an opponent to ascertain their strengths and weaknesses; to observe a player to be considered for acquisition.

Scramble goal
A score which occurs during a goalmouth scramble.

Scramble; Goalmouth scramble
A number of players contesting for a ball with no one in clear possession, usually in an area in front of the goal.

Scrambling, Scrambles
Goalkeeper having to quickly and furiously move along the ground, usually among a group of players, in order to obtain possession of the ball.

Screamer
A ridiculously high-speed shot.

Screen, Screening □
Keeping one's body between a defender and the ball while dribbling; taking a position in front of an opponent to discourage a pass or to keep him from seeing the ball.

Screw-ins
Replaceable cleats; soccer shoes with replaceable cleats or studs.

Scrimmage ◘ □
A practice session or unofficial game between two teams.

Scrimmage vests
Colored outer garments that can be pulled over existing clothing, used to visually designate members of a side, team or group; pinnies, practice vests, vests.

Scrum
A large number of players in a very small space all trying to get the ball.

Scuffed
Hitting the toe or side of the shoe into the turf while trying to kick the ball.

SDI *(Abbrev.)*
State Director of (referee) Instruction.

Seam (1) ■□
Space between two defenders which may be exploited with a run or a pass; a gap between two defenders, usually creating space for a through pass.

Seam (2) ■□

Stitching between two panels of a ball.

Season ■□

A designated timeframe to complete a schedule of competition against a set of opponents.

Seasonal year, Season year

Generally, runs from August 1 of one year to July 31 of the next year.

Seasoned

Experienced. E.g., An experienced player or coach.

Second attacker

Generally, the first player without the ball heading for goal; the next closest attacker to the goal.

Second ball □

The opportunity to shoot again due to a rebound from a first shot.

Second defender

Generally, the player on the defensive team who takes on the first closest attacker without the ball.

Second eleven

The next best group of players on a team; substitutes; backups; non-starters at each position.

Second half ■□

Playing time of a soccer match after halftime; Law 7 of the Laws of the Game, the Duration of the Match.

Second half of extra time, Second period of extra time □

The second portion of overtime play; under the Laws of the Game, the second of two equal periods, not exceeding 15 minutes each, after a tie during regulation play.

Second leg

Second game of a home-and-home (two-leg) series.

Second man running

Generally, the second player on the attacking team who sprints into the defense of an opponent in an attempt to get open and receive a pass from his teammate with the ball.

Second striker, Secondary striker, Supporting striker, Set-back striker
The trailing forward of a two-center-forward alignment which features a lead- or central-striker.

Securing
The goalkeeper takes firm and complete possession of the ball in his hands.

See, Sees the game
Word or phrase denoting that a player is able to get the big picture of what is going on during a match, is easily able to anticipate and react to changes, and otherwise has a "high soccer IQ."

Select ■□
(1) To choose a player;
(2) Select Soccer – higher level, competitive youth soccer where players are chosen for the team.

Self-confidence ■□
Confidence in oneself and one's abilities.

Self-control ■□
The ability of a player to retain composure, particularly to not retaliate after being fouled.

Sell the dummy, Selling the dummy
To run over or near the ball to create a distraction to make it look like it is going to be played, but to let the ball continue on its path to a teammate nearby who is ready to receive and shoot it.

Semi-finals □
Round of 4; four teams remaining in a single-elimination tournament with two games to be played before the final.

Send it – ► □
►On-field Oral Communication: Send the ball upfield. Kick the ball out of the defense into the attack. (Generally, this is used to tell a defender that there is immediate danger OR to tell an attacker that there is a fast-break opportunity.)

Send it in (1)

To cross the ball into the Penalty Area. ("…to the box.")

Send it in (2) – ►

►***On-field Oral Communication:*** Tells the ball handler to cross or otherwise pass the ball into the Penalty Area.

Send it through

To make a through pass.

Send off, Sent off

Ejected from a match; shown a red card; dismissal.

Sending players forward

More players move upfield to join the attack.

Sending-off offences

Law 12 of the Laws of the Game; a player is shown a red card and ejected from the game for serious foul play, violent conduct, spitting at a person, denying a goal-scoring opportunity by deliberate handling of the ball, denying a goal-scoring opportunity by a person with a foul punishable by a free kick or penalty kick, offensive language or gestures, or receiving a second caution in the same game.

Send-off match

A tune-up game, usually referring to an international friendly, played before a team departs for a tournament.

Separation ■□

Space between an offensive player and a defender; the ability to generate or create open space on the part of an offensive player.

Sequence

Series of passes and actions during a possession.

Serie A

Top division of Italian professional soccer.
[Pronunciation: SEH-ree-eh AH]

Serious Foul Play □

Conduct resulting in the issuance of a red card and ejection from the game.

Serve, Service ☐

To pass the ball to a teammate in a specific way designed to facilitate or maximize a specific skill, such as a header or a volley, usually a shot; providing a ball to a player as part of a drill.

Serves

Goalie releases, other than a punt, sent to a teammate following a save.

Set pieces, Set plays ☐

Designed actions for players to perform, including how the ball is to be served or shot, on a restart.

Set play situations

A restart location close enough to the goal that a set piece should be used.

Set up ☐

To pass to a teammate or create the opportunity for a teammate to score; assist.

Set, Sets, Sets the ball ☐

Places the ball down on the field, ensuring that it is not moving, at the spot where a free kick is to be taken.

Settle – ► ☐

► ***On-field Oral Communication:*** Player has time to control the ball on the ground, look up, and figure out what to do with the ball. This is the same as "Time."

Settle down – ► ☐

► ***On-field Oral Communication:*** Players are to stop getting overly excited and making mistakes.

Settled in the net

The ball stops moving, caught in the net, after a goal was scored.

SG *(Abbrev.)*

Soft Ground; soccer shoes with cleats designed to be used on soft ground.

Shackled

Forward marked so tightly as to be unable to get the ball, let alone to turn around and shoot.

Shadow

To mark an opponent man-to-man and go wherever he goes.

Shadow dribbling

Game, drill or warm-up exercise in which one player moves freely while another player tries to dribble the ball in contact with the first player's shadow.

Shadow play

Any number of drills or practice of tactics that do not utilize opposing players.

Shadowing

A type of man-to-man defense drill whereby players designated as defenders follow the actions of offensive players, while maintaining a goal-side position; marking.

Shank ☐

To miskick; to kick the ball in an unintended direction.

Shape

The proper positioning of defenders in a system of play.

Sharp; Looking sharp; Sharp play; Sharpness ☐

Usually the ability to conduct clean, crisp passing, receiving, and shooting on the part of a whole team; an individual who demonstrates crisp skill and technique during play.

Shelled

The goalkeeper or a defense has been under constant attack with numerous shots being taken against them.

Shelter

Overhanging structure, usually made of Plexiglas, covering the bench where the coach and substitutes sit during a match.

Shepherding *(Archaic)*

Jockeying and controlling a defender in an attempt to move him in a certain direction.

Shield (1), Shielding ☐

Keeping one's body between a defender and the ball while dribbling.

Shield (2)

Main part of a shin guard that provides protection for kicks; front plate.

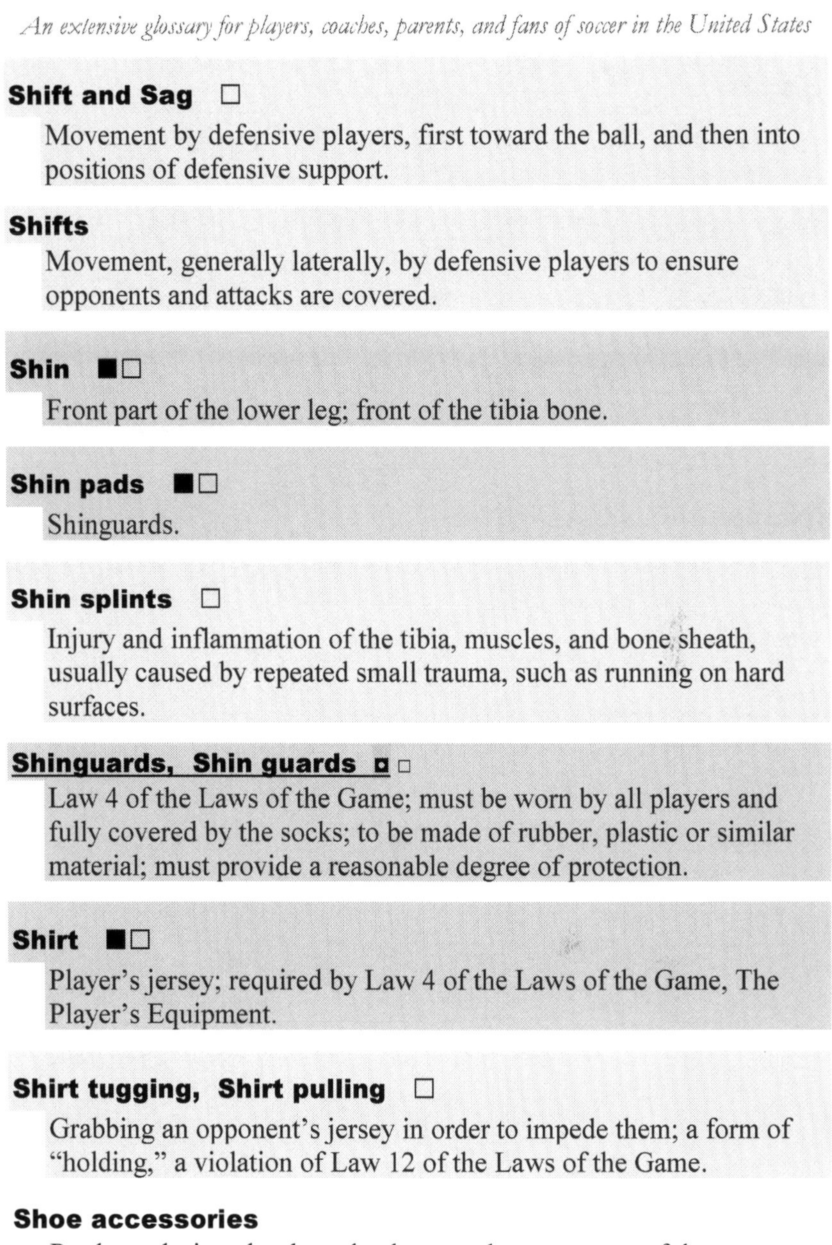

Shift and Sag □

Movement by defensive players, first toward the ball, and then into positions of defensive support.

Shifts

Movement, generally laterally, by defensive players to ensure opponents and attacks are covered.

Shin ■□

Front part of the lower leg; front of the tibia bone.

Shin pads ■□

Shinguards.

Shin splints □

Injury and inflammation of the tibia, muscles, and bone sheath, usually caused by repeated small trauma, such as running on hard surfaces.

Shinguards, Shin guards ■□

Law 4 of the Laws of the Game; must be worn by all players and fully covered by the socks; to be made of rubber, plastic or similar material; must provide a reasonable degree of protection.

Shirt ■□

Player's jersey; required by Law 4 of the Laws of the Game, The Player's Equipment.

Shirt tugging, Shirt pulling □

Grabbing an opponent's jersey in order to impede them; a form of "holding," a violation of Law 12 of the Laws of the Game.

Shoe accessories

Products designed to keep leather supple or waterproof; heavy rubber bands that can be slipped over the shoe to keep the shoe laces tied; stud keys, replacement studs.

Shoe bag

A player's small tote designed specifically to hold a pair of cleats.

Shoes

Soccer shoes; cleats; boots; footwear for games or practices. Must conform to Law 4 of the Laws of the Game, "The Players' Equipment."

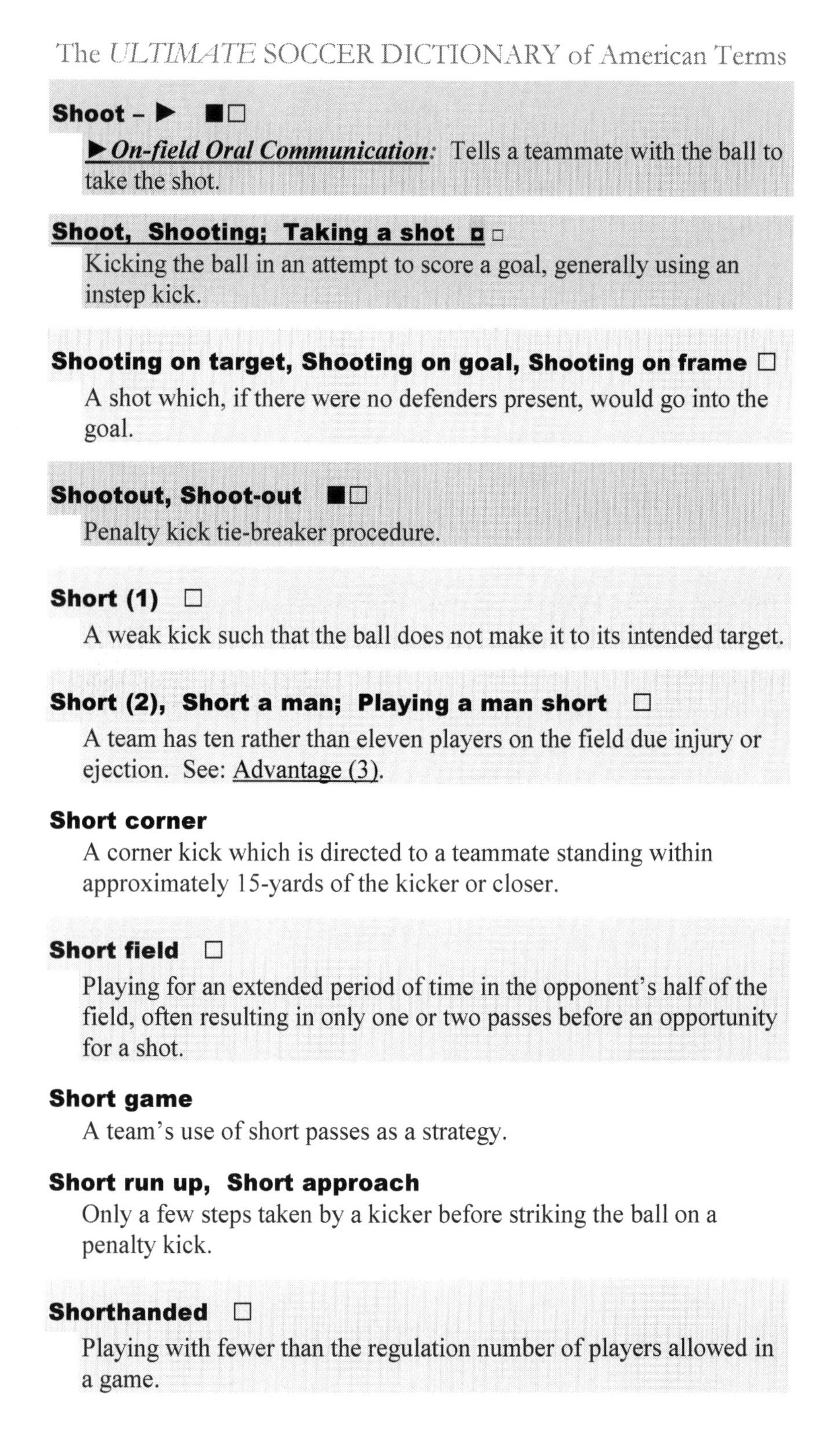

Shoot – ► ■□

► On-field Oral Communication: Tells a teammate with the ball to take the shot.

Shoot, Shooting; Taking a shot ◘ □

Kicking the ball in an attempt to score a goal, generally using an instep kick.

Shooting on target, Shooting on goal, Shooting on frame □

A shot which, if there were no defenders present, would go into the goal.

Shootout, Shoot-out ■□

Penalty kick tie-breaker procedure.

Short (1) □

A weak kick such that the ball does not make it to its intended target.

Short (2), Short a man; Playing a man short □

A team has ten rather than eleven players on the field due injury or ejection. See: Advantage (3).

Short corner

A corner kick which is directed to a teammate standing within approximately 15-yards of the kicker or closer.

Short field □

Playing for an extended period of time in the opponent's half of the field, often resulting in only one or two passes before an opportunity for a shot.

Short game

A team's use of short passes as a strategy.

Short run up, Short approach

Only a few steps taken by a kicker before striking the ball on a penalty kick.

Shorthanded □

Playing with fewer than the regulation number of players allowed in a game.

Shorthanded goal

A goal scored by a team playing with fewer players than the opponent.

Short-hop

A very brief bounce of the ball before being contacted; a pickup by the goalkeeper immediately after a brief bounce of the ball.

Shorts ◘ □

Player's pants; as specified by Law 4, The Players' Equipment.

Short-sided games ■□

Any scrimmage or match with teams of fewer than eleven players.

Shot (1) – ▶ ■□

▶ ***On-field Oral Communication:*** Shoot the ball on goal immediately. Don't hesitate; take one set-up touch at most.

Shot (2) *(noun)* ◘ □

A kick (or header) that directs the ball toward the goal in an attempt to score.

Shot (3) *(verb, past tense)*

To have kicked (or headed) the ball at the goal in an attempt to score.

Shot selection □

Choices by a player or team as to how, or from where on the field, to shoot the ball.

Shoulder charge □

A defender making legal contact, shoulder-to-shoulder, with a player in possession of the ball.

Shoulder pass

A pass of the ball, from one player to another, using forward movement of the shoulder, with contact coming above the chest and medial from the articulation of the upper arm joint (in order to be legal).

Shoulders

The space (at least two yards wide) just outside of the perimeter of the field of play. This includes the area along both touchlines (sidelines), from corner to corner, used by players for throw-ins, and the Assistant Referees' lanes in the diagonal system of control. This also includes the area along both goal lines, from corner to corner,

and the lanes used by the additional Assistant Referees. During a match, these areas must be kept completely clear to allow unobstructed use by players and Assistant Referees.
See: Appendix 3A – Soccer Field Diagram.

Shove ☐

Push, pushing, pushes; violation of Law 12. E.g., an (illegal) attempt to create separation.

Show – ►

►On-field Oral Communication: You will likely be a passing option if you move left or right from being on a direct line with a defender between you and your teammate with the ball.

Show the ball

A dribbling move where the ball carrier intentionally places the ball slightly farther in front of themselves in order to try to bait the defender to go for it. If the defender does try to get the ball, the ball carrier immediately pulls it back and attempts to go around the defender.

Showcase

Tournament designed to demonstrate the talent of teams and players, usually to college recruiters.

Showing

Moving to a position which lets a teammate who has the ball see that you are available to receive a pass.

Showing leadership

Providing credible instruction and motivation by word or deed.

Showing promise

Repeated attacks which start resulting in shots.

Showing the courtesy

Intentionally kicking the ball out of bounds to stop play so that an injured player may be attended.

Shutout ◘ ☐

At the conclusion of a match, to have kept the other team from scoring; no goals allowed.

Shutting down ☐

A defender is able to keep an individual opponent from doing what he wants to do; a team is able to stop the opposing team from starting or generating any form of an attack.

Shutting down the angle

The goalkeeper moves out toward a striker who has the ball in order to reduce the amount of the goal at which to shoot. See: Angles.

Side ◘ ☐

Team.

Side netting, Side panel

Those portions of the nets on the left and right behind the goal posts.

Side stitch, Stitch ■☐

A sharp pain in the lower side of the body, often attributed to a build-up of lactic acid or irregular breathing.

Side Tackle ☐

While moving in the same direction, an attempt by a defender to dispossess a dribbler of the ball by kicking it away or gaining possession; may involve a side-to-side shoulder charge.

Side volley

Kicking an airborne ball in a way that the kicking leg is essentially parallel to the ground.

Sidearm throw

A form of goalkeeper release.

Sideline ◘ ☐

Unofficial term for the touch line; see Touch Line; field marking delineating the right and left sides of a game field to identify the ball being in or out of play.

Sidelined ☐

Player unable to play, usually due to an injury; sometimes due to disfavor of the coach, poor play or misconduct.

Sides, 'sides – ►

►On-field Oral Communication: Tells a teammate to watch out to not go into an offside position.

Sidespin

"English" or rotation imparted to the ball causing it to revolve in a clockwise or counterclockwise direction, depending upon which side of the ball has been struck.

Sideways-on

A player's hip position, mostly as a defensive stance, on a diagonal toward the nearest sideline.

Sighted □

The ball is in view, particularly by the goalkeeper, while defending a re-start.

Signal (1)

The referee or other match official gives a physical indication, usually with whistle, arm or flag, of a decision or action to be taken.

Signal (2)

A player gives a non-verbal movement that indicates a choice of a play or indicates the start of a play.

Signature move

A dribbling fake or feint that is preferred by a particular person; a dribbling fake or feint that was originated and performed by a particular person.

Silent soccer

A procedure or rule sometimes implemented in youth games which mandatess no talking or yelling by parents and supporters.

Silly foul

A foul committed by a defender that not only had no benefit, but often results in the receipt of a yellow card.

Silver Ball

Designation or award to the person voted the second-best player in a tournament.

Silver Goal

A game ends after the full 15 minutes if a single goal was scored during the first Extra Time period.

Simple finish

To score in an uncomplicated or less-difficult situation; push pass the ball into the goal.

Simplified rules

For young players, soccer may be played with minimal explanation of the Laws of the Game. These are usually: (a) how a goal is scored; (b) ball in-and-out of play; (c) handling; and, (d) dangerous play.

Simulation

Faking being fouled.

Sin bins

The experimental use of players being sent off the field to a designated area for a given length of time, for certain infractions, who are then allowed to rejoin the match after the time expires. Similar to penalty boxes in ice hockey.

Single Elimination □

A tournament format where a team that loses a game is out of the tournament. Games in this type of format must be designed to create a winner.

Sinking ball

A kick, most often a shot, where the path of an airborne ball generally starts out parallel to the ground and then drops, either due to the effect of gravity or due to topspin.

Sit back

A team assumes a defensive posture tactically.

Sitting out □

Player not participating in a match due to card, injury or non-selection.

Situational awareness

The ability of a player to identify, process, and comprehend the critical elements of information about what is happening to the team; an example would include knowledge of the amount of time remaining in a match in order to try to score or to effectively defend.

Six

The outermost line of the Goal Area, parallel to the goal-line; 6; the six.

Six-second rule ■□

Violation of Law 12 of the Laws of the Game, Fouls and Misconduct, resulting in the award of an indirect free kick;

goalkeeper inside his own penalty area controls the ball with his hands for more than six seconds before releasing it from his possession.

Size 1, 2, 3, 4, and 5 ■□

Recognized ball sizes, from smallest to largest, with the largest being the standard for adult play; see Law 2 of the Laws of the Game, The Ball.

Skied

A shot that went very high over the crossbar; any kick unintentionally going way up into the air.

Skill ■□

A soccer technique; the ability to apply a proper soccer technique when required.

Skill on the ball

A players' level of ability to manipulate the ball, in the way he pleases, quickly and under pressure; contrast with movement off the ball.

Skill set ■□

A player's range of abilities and level of performance of techniques; acknowledges that some players are better at different things than others.

Skills ■□

Generally, the broad range of proper techniques and abilities required for effective play. E.g.: controlling, passing, and shooting the ball; goalkeeper skills.

Skills clinic ■□

The demonstration of multiple ball techniques to a large number of, usually young, players.

Skim

The bounding or skipping of a ball such that it does not take a usual bounce, generally on a wet surface; a ball skipping off the post or upright of the goal.

Skip

The bounding or skimming of a ball such that it does not take a usual bounce, generally on a wet surface.

Skip-header corner
The ball is kicked directly from the corner arc to the head of a teammate close to the near post who flicks it on with his head to a another teammate near the far post.

Skipper
Team captain; sometimes used to refer to the coach (trainer, manager).

Slalom dribble
A dribbling drill where cones or discs are placed in a straight line, a number of feet apart, and the player advances forward by weaving around them with the ball.

Slashing run
A fast run, generally on a diagonal, that cuts between and through defenders.

Slice
An “outward” curve of the ball after it is struck, left-to-right when coming off the right foot, and right-to-left when coming off the left foot; often used to describe an unintended result.

Slide pants
See: Compression shorts.

Slide tackle, Sliding tackle ◘ □
To propel oneself along the ground feet first in an attempt to increase momentum to reach the ball out in front of an opponent who has gone past.

Slide, Sliding
To propel oneself along the ground; slide tackle.

Slides
An open foot covering, usually consisting of one sole, for soccer generally made of synthetic, water-proof material; sandals, flip-flops.

Sling
Variation on goalkeeper’s “baseball-style” release.

Slip-in (shin guard)
A type of shin guard, without an attached securing mechanism, designed to be placed under a sock or held in place by a compression sleeve.

Slippery surface
Wet grounds due to rain, snow, dew or other moisture.

Slipping
Players not being able to keep their footing, possibly due to their studs not gripping the surface.

Slope
Angle of a field due to its design for water drainage.

Sloppy
A wet or rain-soaked surface; poor play.

Slot (1)
A gap or a space between the goalkeeper and a goalpost; a gap or a space between two defenders.

Slot (2)
Position.

Slot the ball, Slot home
To score a goal by placing the ball on the ground in the narrow space between the goalkeeper and a goalpost.

Small goals
Anything other than regulation goals as mandated in Law 1 of the Laws of the Game; Discs or cones set approximately two yards apart; portable goals; pop-up goals.

Small sided
Any type of practice game using fewer than the number of players in a regulation game.

Small Sided Game
A match, most often in youth games but also used in practice, between two teams generally using seven or fewer players each; SSG.

Smoke
To badly beat a defender with a dribbling move.

Smother, Smothered ☐
The ball is covered up completely by the goalkeeper's body as a result of a save.

Snake

A dribbling move using a quick touch with the inside of the foot, followed by a takeaway touch with the outside of the foot, creating an "S"-pattern.

Snap shot

Quick, hard shot where the shooter does not have the benefit of setting up the ball or the time to establish a full backswing of the kicking leg.

Snapping at the heel

A defender running behind an opponent with the ball nips at his heels or feet with the front of his shoes.

Sneak in behind

To get into an onside position between defenders and the goal without being picked up.

Sneak through

A pass barely makes it between two defenders; a shot barely makes it between the goalkeeper and a goal post.

Soccer ◘ □

A game played mostly with the feet using a ball and two goals; football; Association Football; commonly accepted that the word "association" was first abbreviated to "assoc." which then became "soccer."

Soccer gods, gods of soccer

"The Fates" that sometimes seem to determine the outcome of matches; bad luck or good luck.

Soccer intelligence, Soccer IQ (Intelligence Quotient)

The ability of a player to recognize, analyze, think about, and make proper decisions regarding the game of soccer.

Soccer is a Contact Sport

Soccer contains legal, illegal, and unfortunate physical contact.

Soccer mom ■□

A term that came into widespread (sometimes stereotypical) use referring to mothers who regularly transport their children to soccer games and practices; a mother acting as an administrative assistant.

Soccer-golf

A drill or fun game that combines aspects of soccer and golf.

Soccer-speedball

A drill or fun game that combines aspects of soccer and speedball.

Soccer-tennis

A drill or fun game that combines aspects of soccer and tennis.

Soccer-volleyball

A drill or fun game that combines aspects of soccer and volleyball.

Sock-like shoes

Next generation soccer cleats, with "compression-fit" features, designed to be extremely light-weight and to uniquely mold to the foot of the wearer.

Socks ◘ □

Commonly, game socks; player's stockings; required by Law 4 of the Laws of the Game, "The Players' Equipment."

Soft

Weak; usually a weak pass or shot; a ball with insufficient pace.

Soft cross

Usually, an unintentionally weak, lofted, centering pass not well directed to a teammate; Sometimes, an intentionally low-paced, lofted, centering pass intended to go over defenders and allow a teammate time to run on to the ball.

Soft free kick

A referee award of a free kick for a perceived foul or a foul that didn't really appear to happen.

Soft goal

An easy score as allowed by a goalkeeper; an easy score of any type, not really challenged.

Soft pass

A pass on the ground which does not have much pace, which can be: (a) a correct pass which is easily received, or (b) an incorrect pass which should have had much more pace and is intercepted.

Software

Computer applications designed for use by soccer coaches, including such things as video, graphics, data capture and analytics.

Sole plate

The pliable plastic, synthetic rubber, or proprietary mixture that provides the base for cleats on the bottom and attachment of uppers on the top of soccer shoes.

Solo
Performed by a player without any assistance, usually in scoring a goal; alone.

Space ◘ □
An area of ground on the playing field not otherwise occupied by anyone; open space.

Space to create
A player with the ball does not have a defender in close proximity, giving him the time to choose what he wants to do next.

Special Segments (of a game)
Occasions during a match which have been shown to have more goals scored.

Spectators ■□
Fans in attendance and watching a match.

Speed
Rate of movement or swift progression.

Speed chute
A small parachute attached at the waist to provide resistance for running training.

Speed dribbling ◘ □
Running fast with the ball out ahead with minimal touches to keep it within playing distance.

Speed endurance
The amount of time a player can maintain maximum speed.

Speed juggling
Rapidly touching the ball, with very little time between touches, while keeping the ball in the air.

Speed kits
Devices sold by sports-products companies designed to try to increase a player's speed.

Speed ladder
Flexible device resembling a ladder which can be laid out on the ground for speed and agility training.

Speed of play ☐

Quickness shown by a team in moving the ball around, passing, maintaining possession, and moving into the attack.

Speed of the game ☐

Generally, the pace at which a match is being contested, from slow-possession-style to fast-end-to-end running; a substitute acclimating to the pace of the game.

Speed of thought

Quickness shown by an individual in anticipating or reacting to changes in the game.

Speed rings

Multiple circular devices which can be laid out on the ground in different patterns for speed and agility training.

Spilled it

Goalkeeper stopped the shot, but did not cleanly catch or hold on to the ball, thereby putting the ball in a position where it might be obtained by an opponent.

Spin move, Spinning move ☐

A dribbling feint whereby the ballplayer drags the ball with the sole of the foot while turning his body 180 to 360 degrees in order to beat a defender.

Spirit and Intent of the Laws of the Game

The real meaning behind the written words of the Laws of the Game, recognizing that language doesn't always capture thought.

Spirit of the Game ☐

Two teams coming together in a sportsmanlike manner to enjoy the competition of a soccer match.

Spits, Spitting, Spits at an opponent

Violation of Law 12 of the Laws of the Game, "Fouls and Misconduct," resulting in the award of a direct free kick.

Sponsor ☐

An individual or business providing funds in support of a team.

Sports bra ■□

Article of clothing designed to be worn by women to restrict and constrain the movement of the breasts in order to better participate in athletics.

Sports drinks ■□

Liquid refreshment intended to supplement, improve or replace water and electrolytes during athletics.

Sportsmanship upon injury

Intentionally kicking the ball out of bounds to stop play so that an injured player may be attended.

Sportsmanship, Sporting behavior

Conduct which is ethical, appropriate, polite, and fair – before, during, and after a match.

Spot kick

Penalty kick (from the penalty spot).

Spot on the team; Get a spot on the team; Earn a spot on the team

To be accepted by the coach or organization to make the roster of a team.

Sprawling save

Goalkeeper scrambling along the ground before capturing the ball securely.

Spread out – ▶ ■□

▶ On-field Oral Communication: Teammate is announcing that their players are getting too close to each other, or bunching up, and need to move farther apart to create space for better play.

Spreading the ball around □

Offensive attacks which use the majority of attacking players and the majority of the space in the attacking end of the field.

Spring the trap, Springs the trap □

Defense calls for and implements an offside trap.

Sprint ahead □

To run at top speed into the attack.

Sprint back □
To run at top speed to get back into the defense.

Sprint, Sprinting ■□
To run at top speed, usually for a short distance.

Squad
Team.

Squad numbers
Numbers imprinted on players' jerseys or shirts.

Square (1) – ►
► ***On-field Oral Communication:*** You are open directly to the left or directly to the right of the ball-handler.

Square (2)
Flat defensive backs, all in a line, parallel to the goal-line.

Square pass
A pass made by a player to a teammate directly to his left or right such that the path of the ball is parallel to the halfway line; lateral pass.

Square posts
Goal uprights with flat surfaces presented to the field, in a square or rectangular shape; crossbar must be the same shape.

SS *(Abbrev.)*
Second Striker; Secondary Striker; Supporting Striker; Set-back Striker; the position of second striker; a forward trailing the center striker. See: Appendix 2: Player Positions.

SSG *(Abbrev.)*
Small Sided Game.

ST *(Abbrev.)*
Stopper; the position of stopper; a lead central defender or center fullback, usually designated to take on the opponent's center striker. (Can also mean the position of striker - must be recognized in context.) See: Appendix 2: Player Positions.

Stab
A quick thrust of the front of the foot at the ball to try to poke it away from a defender, pass, or shoot; toe poke.

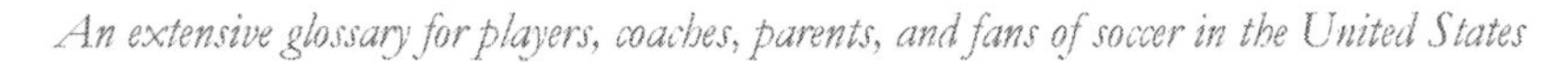

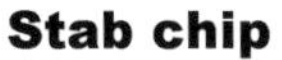
Stab chip

A quick thrust of the front of the foot under the ball to try to loft it over a nearby defender.

Stadium ■□

Building used to house spectators at a sporting event.

Stagnant attack

An offense that lacks creativity and produces few results.

Stalemate □

Usually a 0 - 0 tie, with neither team able to generate much offense.

Stalling ■□

Intentionally delaying getting the ball back into play in order to waste time.

Stanchion □

Goal post; upright of the goal.

Standing stretches

Exercises or activities, performed without getting down on the ground, designed to lengthen tendons.

Standing tall

Goalkeeper demonstrating strength, fortitude and resilience in defending the goal, resisting attacks, and absorbing contact.

Standing, Standing around, Stationary

Player(s) not making runs or otherwise not actively participating properly in a game.

Standings ■□

The position of teams in a group competition, relative to each other, usually based on the number of points attained from wins and ties.

Stands ■□

The seats, tiers, or terraces available to fans in a stadium.

Starters ■□

Players designated by the coach to take the field to begin a game.

Starting lineup ■□

The players and their positions as designated to begin a game for a team.

Starting XI

Starting eleven; the players designated to begin a game for a team.

State Association

Organization within a State approved by the USSF to administer soccer; National State Association; NSA; state associations are grouped into Regions.

State cup

Competitive structure established within age groups by a State Association, usually annually, to determine the best team in the state.

Statement; Making a statement; Statement game

Virtual domination of one team over another in a match.

States of the ball

The physical condition of the ball. This could include it being such things as light or heavy, soft or hard, or wet or sticky.

Static stretching

A flexibility process intended to lengthen muscles and tendons by the use of an extend-and-hold technique.

Statistics

The collection, tabulation and manipulation of data for analysis; for example, for a team in a tournament the total of "Goals For" minus the total of "Goals Against" equals "Goal Differential;" for example, for an individual player in a game, the total number of passes received by teammates divided by the total number of passes attempted equals the percent of successful passes.

Stay on your feet ■□

To remain on one's feet after contact, and not go to the ground; to resist the temptation to try to draw a foul when you can keep from going down.

Stay up (1)

To remain on one's feet after contact, and not go to the ground.

Stay up (2) – ►

► ***On-field Oral Communication:*** Tells a teammate to stay on their feet and continue to fight for the ball (and/or not be tempted to go to the ground to try to get a call).

Stay up (3) – ►

► ***On-field Oral Communication:*** Goalkeeper or defensive organizer tells his backs to maintain a high line.

Stay wide – ►

► ***On-field Oral Communication:*** Tells teammates that they are getting too bunched up in the middle of the field and to maintain their positions toward the sidelines in order to create space.

Stay with him (her) – ► ☐

► ***On-field Oral Communication:*** As a supporting defender, this tells a teammate who, during the flow of play, has taken on an opponent that may be making a crossing run or offensive switch, to continue to defend that opponent.

Staying in the keeper's range

The teammate setting up for a throwing release by the goalkeeper must not exceed the distance the goalkeeper can throw the ball (or be so far away that the ball is likely to be intercepted).

Staying with ☐

As a defender, running with an opponent to ensure that he remains marked; as a team, playing up to the level of a stronger opponent.

Steal, Stole ☐

To intercept or take away the ball in a way that was unexpected.

Steering

Defensively, to influence an opponent to move away from the goal; with very young player's, moving the ball slowly and deliberately without confident and controlled touches.

Step, Step Up, Step Out – ►

► ***On-field Oral Communication:*** Goalkeeper or central back is telling the defenders to move upfield.

Step-over ☐

A dribbling feint (move) whereby the player with the ball literally steps over and places a foot in front of the ball in an attempt to cause the defender to shift his weight in one direction so the dribbler can then proceed in the other direction.

Stepped on ■□

(1) To have a body part, typically the foot, contacted from above (and pressed down on) by an opponent's foot; (2) To contact the ball from above with the sole of the foot.

Stewards

Administrative support personnel, ranging from staff to police, who may surround and provide security for a field of play.

Stick it in the back of the net

To score a goal.

Stick, Stick the tackle □

To perform a solid, effective tackle.

Sticky

A ball with a surface that might cause the shoe of a player to seem to get stuck to it.

Stirrup

Sock-like device with a strap that goes under the sole of the foot designed to keep a shin guard in place.

Stitch, Side stitch ■□

A sharp pain in the lower side of the body, often attributed to a build-up of lactic acid or irregular breathing.

Stitching ■□

Thread that holds the panels of a ball together.

Stockings ■□

Socks; commonly, game socks required by Law 4 of the Laws of the Game, "The Players' Equipment."

Stolen (1) ■□

To have intercepted or taken away the ball in a way that was unexpected.

Stolen (2), Stealing the game ☐

Seemingly against the odds, scoring a winning goal with less than a minute remaining.

Stomp (on)

To violently and intentionally step on a body part of an opponent.

Stop ■☐

A goalkeeper save.

Stoppage

Times when the ball is not in play due to substitutions, injuries, time-wasting or other causes, including unexpected interruptions.

Stoppage Time ◘ ☐

Time added at the end of the first or second halves to compensate for the playing time lost while an injured player was accommodated during a match and other reasons; Law 7 of the Laws of the Game, Duration of the Match; allowance for time lost. Added Time. [Note: This is NOT the same thing as Extra Time.]

Stopper ◘ ☐

Primary central defender; center fullback; first to challenge in the back middle of a "Stopper/Sweeper" defensive scheme.

Stories, Soccer stories

Every coach has experienced some event which is amazing, strange, weird, funny, or instructive that can be related to other coaches.

Straight back – ▶ ☐

▶ ***On-field Oral Communication:*** Player who is open and available for a back-pass is telling his teammate who has the ball where his is located.

Straight lines ☐

Runs or passes that are made upfield, backward or square, parallel or perpendicular to the sidelines.

Straight time, Straight running time

Local rules modification to Law 7 of the Laws of the Game, "The Duration of the Match," which provides for no stoppage of the clock or stoppage time.

Strapping tape

Athletic tape when specifically applied for joint support.

Strategy ■□

The overall plan of a team's approach to play, including such things as the primary formation.

Strawberry

A surface abrasion to the skin, usually red in color.

Streak (1) ■□

Usually, a number of games won in a row - winning streak; often a number of games without a loss - non-losing streak; sometimes, a number of games lost in a row - losing streak.

Streak (2)

To run at great speed, usually down the sideline.

Strength ■□

Muscle power; durability; toughness.

Strength endurance

The amount of time a player can maintain maximum strength.

Strength of schedule □

The difficulty of beating a team's set of opponents.

Strength on ball

Ability of a player to maintain possession of the ball and not let it be taken away by a physical challenge.

Strengthening ■□

Activities and exercises designed to make muscles stronger.

Stretch out – ►

►***On-field Oral Communication:*** Informs an individual striker or other attackers to move as far upfield as possible.

Stretch them out, Stretching the play □

Spreading the defense from touch line to touch line across the width of the field due to the placement and movement of attackers.

Stretch, Stretching ◘ □

To reach out or extend one's body or limbs to lengthen muscles and tendons.

Stretched defense

Too much space between defensive players to be properly effective, which is an objective for the opponent's attackers and is to be avoided by the defenders.

Stretcher

Device used to carry an individual player off the field if the player is not able to move off under their own power, usually due to an injury.

Strike (1) ◘ □

To kick the ball, usually a shot.

Strike (2) □

A quick, almost unexpected shot, often resulting in a goal being scored.

Striker ◘ □

A forward in a system of play whose primary duty is to score goals; forward. See: Appendix 2: Player Positions.

Strikes from distance

To score from far away from the goal.

Striking, Strikes or attempts to strike an opponent □

Violation of Law 12 of the Laws of the Game, "Fouls and Misconduct," resulting in the award of a direct free kick.

Strip □

To take the ball away from an opponent; dispossess.

Strong foot ■□

The natural preference of which leg to use for a right-hand or left-hand dominant person.

Strong side □

The area of the field to the left or right of the imaginary midline that contains the most attackers or defenders at any given moment.

Stub Toe, Stubbed Toe *(may be used as a verb or noun)* ■□

To inadvertently catch the front of one's foot in the turf during the performance of a kick, most often an instep drive. ("I stubbed my toe on that last shot." Or, "She got a stubbed toe during yesterday's practice.")

Stud key, stud wrench

Device used to insert or remove different-length studs in shoes that have replaceable, screw-in, cleats.

Student of the Game

(1) Coaches need to learn the game in order to teach it and the only way to do that is by first being a student. (2) Any player seeking to excel at soccer must become a student of the game.

Studs ■□

Projections, grips, or knobs on the bottom of shoes; cleats.

Studs showing □

Making an illegal tackle with the sole of the foot directed at the opponent.

Studs up □

Sliding at or tackling an opponent with the soles of the shoe facing directly at him; illegal tackle; violation of Law 12 of the Laws of the Game; cleats up.

Stumble ■□

To lose balance and move in an awkward way, usually as a result of catching one's foot in the turf or getting it stuck on the ball.

Stunner

Last-second goal to win or tie a game.

Style

Manifestation of the overall type of play exhibited by a team; e.g., short-passing possession, long-ball, or defensive with quick counter-attacks.

Sub, Subs ■□

See: Substitute; substitutes.

Submarines

A player undercuts or "takes the legs out" from under another player who has jumped in to air to go for a head ball.

Subs allowed; Number of subs allowed □

By competition rules, the number of substitutes that may be used in a match.

Substitute, Substitutes ◘ □

Players who do not start the game and replace starters or other substitutes as the match progresses; must conform to Law 3 of the Laws of the Game.

Substitution Board; Added Time Board

Electronic device used by the Fourth Official in a match to show: (a) the jersey numbers of the players involved in a substitution, and (b) the amount of time (stoppage time) added to the game at the end of a half.

Substitution procedure

Law 3 of the Laws of the Game. With the approval of the referee, one player out and then one player in, at the halfway line. Ability and the number of players who may be substituted (or resubstituted) are determined by the competition rules.

Substitution; Make a substitution □

Taking the moment at a stoppage of play, and with the approval of the referee, to remove and then send on a player.

Success ■□

A high level of achievement with certain types of attack which result in good shooting opportunities; e.g., down the middle, crosses.

Sudden death ■□

The scoring of a goal in overtime that ends the game; golden goal; the period of playing time during which a golden goal could be scored.

Sudden-death penalty kicks; Sudden-death shootout □

Penalty kicks that go beyond five rounds of the penalty-kick procedure used to determine a winner of a game, whereby an unmatched score immediately produces the outcome.

Super sub

Talented player coming on as a substitute who routinely seems to score a goal, or set one up, after entering.

Support ◘ □

Offense: players who are behind the ball who are available for a back pass; Defense: players who are behind the defender who is taking on the offensive player with the ball who can come to the ball if the first defender is beaten.

Support in defense

Position of the next defender to the defender taking on the offensive player with the ball such that he is behind and nearer the goal in order to come to the ball if the first defender is beaten.

Support; or, You have support – ▶ ■□

▶ ***On-field Oral Communication:*** Tells defensive teammate that you are in a proper defensive position that if an unsuccessful challenge for ball is made, you have it covered.

Supporter (Athletic supporter, Cup) ■□

Clothing designed to support male genitalia; jockstrap; ("cup" or "athletic cup," made of plastic, for protection).

Supporters, Supporter ■□

Anyone who helps, encourages, facilitates soccer players, teams, and programs. E.g., fans; parents; helpers; volunteer coaches, linesmen, referees; backers and promoters; administrators and other staff.

Supporter's Shield

Awarded by MLS to the team with the most points in the regular season; presentation to the "winner" of the MLS regular season.

Supporting player □

On attack, generally a teammate closest to the ball handler and available for a pass; On defense, generally a teammate closest to and behind the defender taking on the ball carrier, available to take on the ball carrier if the first defender is beaten.

Surface (1) □

Type of playing field: natural grass or artificial turf; status of field: hard or soft, rocky or bumpy, wet or dry.

Surface (2)

The outer portion of the ball.

Surface (3), Surfaces of the body

The portion of the body used to contact the ball in the performance of a skill.

Surfaces of the soccer shoe □

Parts of the soccer shoe used to contact the ball during the performance of skills. See: "19 Surfaces of the Soccer Shoe"™

http://coachingamericansoccer.com/features/19-surfaces-of-the-soccer-shoe/

Surrender, Surrender a goal ■□

To give up a goal; to be scored upon.

Suspect

A defense that has holes or gaps or otherwise has difficulty defending properly; a goalkeeper that has difficulty stopping or holding onto the ball.

Suspend

To temporarily stop a match, usually due to weather, but sometimes due to injury where a player should only be moved by qualified professionals.

Suspension □

Player not allowed to participate in a match due to a prior (red card) ejection or an accumulation of (yellow card) cautions.

Suspension of game ■□

Delay or cancellation of a match, after it has begun, for such things as weather or other disruptive influences.

Suspension of player ■□

Administrative sanction against a player mandating loss of practice and/or playing time due to serious misconduct which may or may not have been committed while playing.

SW *(Abbrev.)*

Sweeper; the position of Sweeper; the trail central defender in a Stopper/Sweeper defensive alignment.

Swarm

The gaggle of youth beginning players all trying to get to the ball at the same time.

Swarming

Many players moving to the ball.

Sweeper ■□

Last central defender, another center fullback directly in front of the goalkeeper, without a marking assignment; moves left to right, to challenge anything that gets past the back defenders; usually in a "Stopper/Sweeper" defensive scheme.

Sweeper's in charge – ▶

▶ ***On-field Oral Communication:*** Goalkeeper is telling his defenders that he is ceding defensive oral communications to the central defender as the team moves upfield on attack; tells defenders that the sweeper or central defender is responsible for calling the offside trap.

Sweet spot

That part of the ball that, when struck, gets the optimum result and feels best to the kicker.

Swerve

Curling, bending, hooking or slicing path of a kicked ball in flight.

Swim move

While two players are running together in the same direction competing for the ball, the action by one player to swing the arm closest to the opponent from behind, over top, around, and in front in order to gain a positional advantage.

Swing the ball

The process of moving the ball from one side of the field to the other. In a direct style of soccer this is generally accomplished with a long cross or diagonal ball. In a possession style of soccer this is generally accomplished by passing the ball through the center midfielders; switch fields.

Swing, Swing it, Swing the ball – ▶

▶ ***On-field Oral Communication:*** Defenders are open in the back to use two or more passes to get the ball from one side of the field to the other.

Switch (1), Switch off, (Switch back) ■□

Defensive Switch – Two defenders trading marking assignments.
Offensive Switch – Two attackers exchange positions during a play.

Switch (2), Switch off, (Switch back) – ► ■□

►On-field Oral Communication: Tells a player to assume their position. There are generally two types of switches, offensive and defensive. The offensive type usually starts with a player dribbling at a teammate and the teammate moves into that player's position. The defensive type is usually made by a player that moves to cover an opponent expected to be covered by another teammate and the teammate now needs help to cover the space vacated. See: Switch, defensive; Switch, offensive.

> Remember: Each "***On-field Oral Communication***" term has this symbol ► and in the electronic versions is ***hyperlinked*** to Appendix 4, where all of these terms are listed together. Each term is ***linked back*** to its definition.

Switch back – ► □

►On-field Oral Communication: This is the formal acknowledgement that a switch which has occurred is being undone and the players are resuming their normal positions.

Switch fields – ► □

►On-field Oral Communication: Kick the ball from one side of the field to the other or get it there via a midfield player.

Switch, defensive □

An offensive player beats a defender, causing a teammate of the defender to have to cover his man, resulting in the original defender covering the teammate's man, effectively exchanging positions. A defensive switch is usually made by a player that moves to cover an opponent expected to be covered by another teammate and the teammate now needs help to cover the space vacated.

Switch, offensive □

An offensive player (with or without the ball) runs into the space occupied by a teammate and the teammate runs into the space vacated, effectively exchanging positions.

Switches

Substitutions.

Switching fields, Switching the ball, Switching play

Sending the ball from the right side of the field to the left side of the field, or vice versa, often via midfield players, in order to change the point of attack.

Swivel

Pivot.

SYRA *(Abbrev.)*

State Youth Referee Administrator.

System of play ◘ □

(1) Basic strategies to be employed within a formation.
(2) Sometimes used synonymously with "formation," a structure designating the positions of players on the playing field, establishing a basis for the strategy and tactics of a team's play; in common usage (with a goalkeeper assumed), identifies the players from the goal, outward, signifying the total number of back defenders (fullbacks), midfielders (halfbacks) and strikers (forwards), e.g., 4-3-3; always adds up to 10 for full sides.

T *(Abbrev.)*
Ties; number of games or matches tied or drawn.

Table
The list of relative positions of teams in a group competition; standings.

Tackle, Tackling (legal) ◘ □
To legally attempt to, or to actually, take the ball away from an opponent who has the ball; to dispossess the ball; may involve legal contact; takes a number of forms, such as “front block” tackle and “slide” tackle.

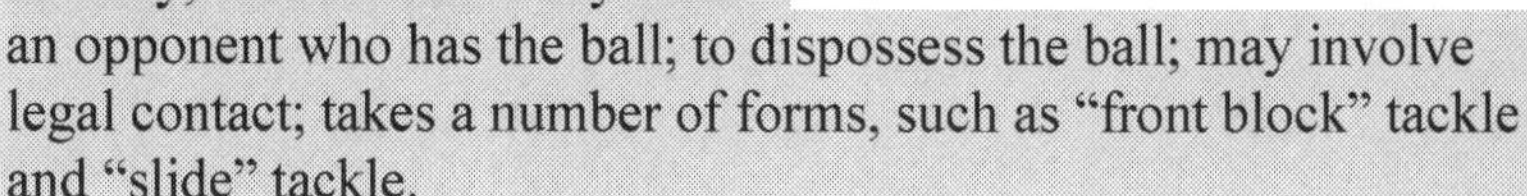

Tackling style
A player’s personal preference for block tackles or slide tackles, technical or hard.

Tackling, Tackles an opponent (illegal)
Violation of Law 12 of the Laws of the Game, “Fouls and Misconduct,” resulting in the award of a direct free kick; fails to legally contact the ball between himself and the opponent.

Tactical □
Shorthand referencing a range of activities from ball skills to set pieces.

Tactical Foul
A last defender intentionally trips, kicks, charges or otherwise brings down an attacker who has broken free outside the Penalty Area and is about to go one-on-one with the goalkeeper and has a high chance of scoring; professional foul.

Tactical substitution
(1) Usually, bringing on a player to bolster the defense or midfield near the end of a match; or, (2) Sometimes, bringing on a player to create a brief delay in the match.

Tactics (1) ◘ □
The approaches that will be used to attack and defend an opponent.

Tactics (2) □
One of the four components (“4 pillars”) of the game as taught by U.S. Soccer (Fitness, Psychological, Tactics, and Technique).

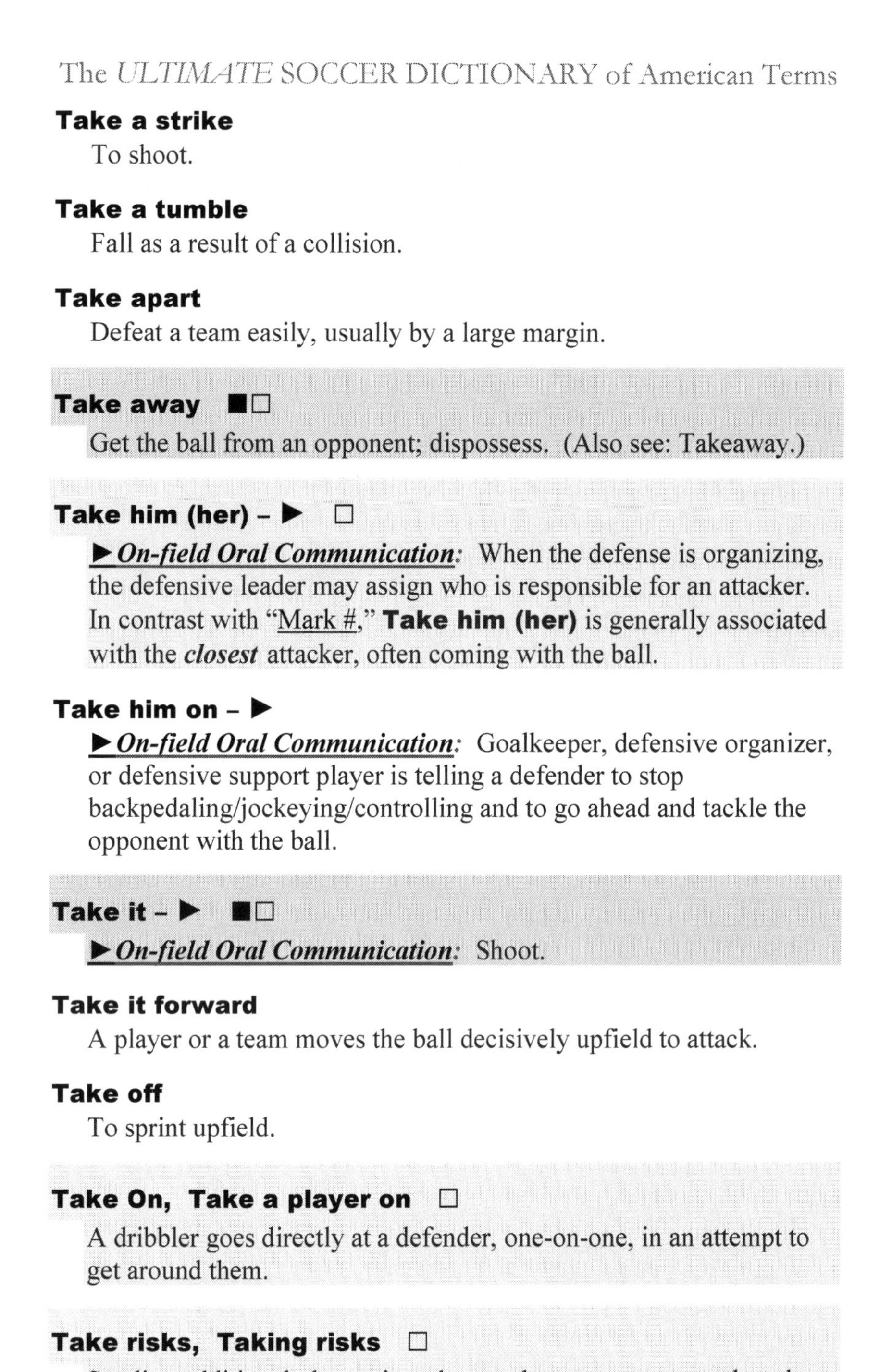

Take a strike

To shoot.

Take a tumble

Fall as a result of a collision.

Take apart

Defeat a team easily, usually by a large margin.

Take away ■□

Get the ball from an opponent; dispossess. (Also see: Takeaway.)

Take him (her) – ▶ □

▶ ***On-field Oral Communication:*** When the defense is organizing, the defensive leader may assign who is responsible for an attacker. In contrast with "Mark #," **Take him (her)** is generally associated with the ***closest*** attacker, often coming with the ball.

Take him on – ▶

▶ ***On-field Oral Communication:*** Goalkeeper, defensive organizer, or defensive support player is telling a defender to stop backpedaling/jockeying/controlling and to go ahead and tackle the opponent with the ball.

Take it – ▶ ■□

▶ ***On-field Oral Communication:*** Shoot.

Take it forward

A player or a team moves the ball decisively upfield to attack.

Take off

To sprint upfield.

Take On, Take a player on □

A dribbler goes directly at a defender, one-on-one, in an attempt to get around them.

Take risks, Taking risks □

Sending additional players into the attack to try to get a goal, at the expense of the defense if the ball changes hands.

Take someone down □

To send an opponent to ground, either as a result of a poor tackle or by holding.

Take the field ■□

To enter the field of play as a team; to enter the field of play as an individual.

Take the game to (the opponent) □

Attack often, regularly and decisively; having the majority of possession.

Takeaway, Take-away, Take away ■□

The ending part of a dribbling fake or feint that moves the ball away from, beside, or around the defender.

Taken down □

To go to ground as a recipient of a poor tackle or from holding by an opponent.

Taken down from behind □

To go to ground as a recipient of a poor tackle or from holding by an opponent who initiated contact from the back.

Taken off

Generally, a player removed from a match due to injury, possibly on a stretcher; a player is substituted, often after having recently received a caution.

Takeover, Take-over

A non-traditional form of a "pass," whereby the initial ball handler stops, leaves, or otherwise abandons the ball to a teammate who is moving onto the ball from another direction.

Taking

Receiving the ball against pressure.

Taking a dive

A player faking a foul, usually a trip, by stretching out and falling forward, landing sprawled on the ground, in an attempt to draw a penalty, usually within the Penalty Area. Illcgal and often ignored by the Referee; sometimes properly called as unsporting behavior.

Taking a peek

Striker takes his eye off the ball for a split-second look at the goal just before shooting.

Taking eye off the ball ■□

Player who looks in another direction right before he is supposed to concentrate on a ball skill, causing him to commit an error working with the ball.

Taking on, Taking a player on

Coming to meet an opponent in order to make an immediate tackle.

Taking the pace off the ball ◘ □

Reducing the ball's momentum, as in part of the act of receiving or trapping.

Talk (1), Talking – ► ■□

The use of oral communication among players on the field.
See: Appendix 4 – On-field Oral Communication.

Talk (2) – ► ■□

► ***On-field Oral Communication:*** Players have stopped using proper oral communications and must do so.

Talk trash, Talking trash, Talking smack ■□

Inappropriate verbal communication directed at an opponent with the intention of causing them to take their concentration off of the game or to do something wrong.

Tampering

Inappropriately trying to get a player from another team.

Tangled up □

Two opponents going for the ball who get their legs, arms, or both intertwined.

Tap

To touch the ball gently.

Tap-in

To score a goal by gently pushing the ball over the goal-line, usually as a result of play that has caused defenders and the goalkeeper to be out of position.

Tapped out

A player is physically exhausted; a team is unable to find any way to break down an opponent's defense; frustrated.

Target forward

Usually, a tall muscular center striker who is the object of passes in front of the goal.

Target player (1)

Usually, a tall muscular center striker who is the object of passes in front of the goal; Sometimes, any player who is the object of a pass in certain tactical situations, such as the start of a fast break.

Target player (2), Target, Target man

A player specifically designated to receive a pass in a given situation, often at a specific spot on the field; post-up player.

Target, targeting ◘ □

Often, a specific spot to shoot at on-goal.

TC *(Abbrev.)*

Technical Committee.

TCB *(Abbrev.)*

Trail Center Back; the position of trail center back; the trailing defender in a two-center-fullback alignment; sweeper.

TCF *(Abbrev.)*

Trail Center Forward; the position of trail center forward; the trailing forward in a two-center-striker alignment; secondary striker.

Teachable moment, Teaching moment ■□

A chance to stop, or "freeze" a practice, drill or scrimmage in order to provide coaching.

Teaching ■□

Instructing and training in skills and tactics. Coaching.

Teaching opportunity ■□

Any chance, at any time, to provide instruction.

Team ◘ □

Law 3 of the Laws of the Game; a group consisting of seven to 11 players while on the field, one of whom is designated as the goalkeeper; otherwise, all of the individuals collectively in a group playing on the same side in soccer games, including possible substitutes.

Team Administration

All activities, other than coaching, that relate to running or managing a team.

Team bag □

A player's equipment (kit) bag, which matches all of the other players' bags on a team, to be used at games.

Team list

Players, substitutes and team officials listed on a formal, official, team document.

Team Official

An individual such as a coach, assistant coach, trainer, manager or doctor, authorized by FIFA, according to Law 3 of the Laws of the Game, The Players, who are permitted to be in the technical area during a match.

Team parent, Team mom

Adult, often female and the mother of a player, who organizes, manages and directs the "extras" associated with a youth soccer team, including such things as snacks, pictures, and parties.

Team rules

Administrative requirements placed on players (and parents) for the smooth function of the team and for the safety of the players.

Team shape

Ability of players to maintain the team's formation during play, especially on defense. A team will attempt to cover certain areas of the field based on where the ball is located. When they are able to cover these areas, a team is keeping their shape or is in balance.

Teammate's name – ▶ ■□

▶ ***On-field Oral Communication:*** To get the teammate's attention for a pass or to recognize a situation.

Tease

A dribbling fake or feint where the dribbler appears to put the ball too far out in front to invite the defender to go for it.

Technical ability

Player's competence in performing skills and making proper decisions.

Technical Area

Law 1 of the Laws of the Game; coaches' box(es) near midfield outside the playing field.

Technical Director

Person in a soccer organization responsible for the management of staff and direction of operations, including player and coach developmental programs, competitions and leagues; a coach who teaches skills.

Technical play

Usually, team demonstrating excellent ball skills during the course of a match; any of the range of ball skills demonstrated by a team, from bad to good; performance of all aspects of the game.

Technical staff

Non-playing staff of a team, such as the coaches, trainers, and a doctor, identified by the team as team officials.

Technical training

Coaching and working on ball skills; coaching and working on all aspects of the game.

Technically competent

A player who has been properly instructed in, and can perform, ball skills; a coach who has been properly instructed in, and can teach, ball skills; knowledge and ability to perform all aspects of the game.

Technique (1) ◘ □

Ball skills.

Technique (2) □

One of the four components ("4 pillars") of the game as taught by U.S. Soccer (Fitness, Psychological, Tactics, and Technique).

Tee it up; teed up

Similar to golf, setting the ball up on a high tuft of grass in order to get the most out of a strong kick during a restart.

Telegraph, Telegraphing □

By looking at (or directing specific body movement toward) a teammate to whom one is just about to pass, such that a defender can "read" the intent and intercepts the pass.

Tempo □

Team speed while in possession of the ball, ranging from slow, as demonstrated by multiple back passes and moving the ball from side-to-side among the back defenders, to fast, with energetic runs and passes being sent forward.

Tendencies

A player's preferred and likely use of certain skills or moves, particularly when dribbling; a team's frequent use of certain tactics.

Tentative ■□

Indecisive; hesitant to make a move for the ball or to take a shot.

Terms, Terminology ■□

Words, phrases and "jargon" specifically related to, or unique to, soccer.

Territory

Generally, all or a portion of the half of the field a team is defending; any of a large area of ground within the field of play.

Test, Testing the keeper □

How shots or crosses are handled by the opposing goalkeeper during a match can be evaluated to determine if he has any weaknesses which can be exploited.

Testing

(1) Evaluation of a player to determine the status of their skills ability and fitness;
(2) Baseline evaluation of a player's skills, ability and fitness to determine future improvement;
(3) Evaluation of player's cognition for concussion comparisons.

The "50"

The Halfway Line of the field, as borrowed from American football.

The Assistant Referees

Part of Law 6 of the Laws of the Game.

The Ball

Law 2 of the Laws of the Game.

The Ball In and Out of Play

Law 9 of the Laws of the Game.

The Corner Kick
Law 17 of the Laws of the Game.

The Cup
The FIFA World Cup.

The Draw
Usually with seeding or random selection, or a combination of both, the placement of teams into groups for the FIFA World Cup; selection and placement of teams when used for a competition or tournament.

The Duration of the Match
Law 7 of the Laws of the Game.

The Field of Play
Law 1 of the Laws of the Game.

The Final
Championship game; the championship game of the FIFA World Cup.

The Goal Kick
Law 16 of the Laws of the Game.

The IFAB
The International Football Association Board, responsible for the Laws of the Game.

The Method of Scoring
Part of Law 10 of the Laws of the Game.

The Number of Players
Part of Law 3 of the Laws of the Game.

The Penalty Kick
Law 14 of the Laws of the Game.

The Players' Equipment
Law 4 of the Laws of the Game.

The Referee
Law 5 of the Laws of the Game.

The Spot
The penalty mark.

The Start and Restart of Play
Law 8 of the Laws of the Game.

The Throw-in
Law 15 of the Laws of the Game.

Theatrical
Play acting to try to draw the call of a foul.

Their end ■□
The opposing team's defensive half of the field of play.

Their goal
The goal that the opposing team is defending.

Thigh trap ■□
Receiving the ball with the inside, top, or outside of the upper leg.

Third attacker
Generally, the second player without the ball heading for goal; the second-closest attacker to the goal without the ball.

Third defender
Generally, the player on the defensive team who takes on the second-closest attacker without the ball.

Third kit
A player's third uniform option if a conflict arises between both home and away jerseys and/or the referees' jerseys.

Third man running
Generally, the third player on the attacking team who sprints into the defense in an attempt to get open and receive a pass from his teammate with the ball.

Thirds, thirds of the field
Dividing the field of play for discussion and coaching purposes into "Defensive," "Middle (Midfield or Transition)" and "Attacking."

Thrashing
A team is being thoroughly outplayed and outscored by an opponent.

Threaded pass, Threaded ball, Threaded in □
A pass which splits through defenders to reach a teammate such that anything other than a perfect path for the ball would have resulted in it being intercepted.

Threat ■☐

A challenging attack to a defense.

Three points for a win ☐

A system for establishing the relative positions of teams in a group whereby points are awarded for wins and ties and then accumulated and compared; usually involves one point for a tie and no points for a loss; alternative is two points for a win.

Three-man system

A single referee with two assistant referees officiating a game.

Three-on-one break ☐

As a result of the run of play, three attacking players rapidly take on just one defender.

Three-on-two break ☐

As a result of the run of play, three attacking players rapidly take on two defenders.

Three-sixty ☐

Dribbling move involving turning the body halfway, dragging the ball, and then turning the body again to face the original direction, creating a 360-degree turn; 360.

Through (1) – ► ☐

►***On-field Oral Communication:*** Pass the ball from the midfield between defenders into the open space behind the defenders so an attacker can run onto the ball.

Through (2); Going through ☐

Team advancing from a group stage to the second or knockout round of a tournament.

Through ball, Through pass ☐

The ball is sent from the midfield between defenders into the open space behind the defenders so an attacker can run onto the ball.

Through the legs ■□

Usually due to bad luck, but sometimes due to poor skills, a shot or a pass by an offensive player finds its way between the legs of a defender. See: Nutmeg.

Throw a match

The horrible notion of a team losing on purpose, possibly to place the team in a beneficial post-match position.

Throw-in, Throw in ■□

Law 15 of the Laws of the Game; re-start awarded to a team when an opponent last touched the ball and the whole of the ball has crossed the touch line, whether on the ground or in the air; puts the ball back into play at the point where the ball went out, according to a strict procedure.

Thumbs up □

Non-verbal communication by a teammate indicating what he was trying to do was a good idea even if it was unsuccessful.

Tie Breaker, Tiebreaker □

A procedure to decide a winner; penalty kicks, sudden death, golden goal; an administrative procedure to determine a champion or a team that advances in a tournament.

Tie Game ■□

At the conclusion of a match, both teams have the same number of goals.

Tied ■□

The number of goals is or was equal for both teams in a match.

Tight mark

A man-to-man defensive strategy where a defender tracks an opponent extremely closely with the intent of trying to deny him receiving the ball.

Tight spaces

During the run of play, an area approximately 15-yards square or less, which may involve as many as three attackers, the ball, and three defenders.

Tights

Compression shorts; full leggings.

Tiki-taka

A style of play associated with Barcelona and the Spanish national team involving short passes and ball possession. There are a number of different spellings, e.g., tiqui-taca.
[Pronunciation: TEE-kee-TAH-kah]

Time (1) □

The length of a game.

Time (2)

The status of the game clock.

Time (3) – ► ■□

►On-field Oral Communication: "You've got time." Player is telling a teammate that they have the time and space away from an opponent to control and then turn with the ball.

Time added on □

Law 7 of the Laws of the Game; at the discretion of the referee, playing time is extended at the end of each half for substitutions, injury, time wasting, or other events.
Also called Added Time, Stoppage Time. Includes Injury Time.
(Note: This is NOT the same as "Extra Time" or "Overtime.")

Time and Space

The physical components of ball and player movement; On attack, an objective is to create more time and space for ball movement and the generation of passes to create opportunities to score; On defense, an objective is to reduce the time and space available to an opponent.

Time lost

An event or the aggregation of time in a half associated with substitutions, injury, time wasting or other circumstances. Law 7 of the Laws of the Game allows the referee to account for these events by adding time at the end of the half.

Time of possession

The amount of time, in minutes, that a team controls the ball; See: Possession.

Time out ■□

The game clock is not running; local rules permit stoppages; only the referee can "stop the clock" (by adding time later); unlike American football, coaches may not call timeouts in soccer.

Time remaining ■□

The difference between the full match duration and current time elapsed.

Time wasting

See: Wasting time; the deliberate act of a player to keep from putting the ball back into play in order to let the clock run.

Timekeeper □

Usually the referee keeps the official time of the match; sometimes, other officials may be responsible for keeping time based on local rules, such as the NCAA.

Timing □

The ability to send a pass at the proper moment to beat defenders and connect with the teammate making a run.

Timing runs (into the box) □

Players sprinting into the Penalty Area in such a way as to permit teammates to pass the ball to them just before they may go offside.

Tipping

The act of the goalkeeper deflecting or parrying the ball around the outside of an upright, or over the top of the crossbar, of the goal.

Tired ■□

Inability to perform skills at peak level or to run well due to exhaustion.

Tired mind

Inability to think quickly due to exhaustion.

To feet □

The act of passing the ball to a teammate's feet instead of leading them.

To space □

The act of passing the ball to an area for a teammate to run on to it.

To take a touch ■□

To contact the ball with the foot, usually while dribbling; to contact the ball to set it up for a shot.

Toe down ■□

"Advice" or reprimand (usually not helpful) sometimes given to a player, e.g., after the player has skied a shot over the goal. Players need to be taught how to properly kick an Instep Drive.

Toe kick, Toe kicking, Toeing the ball ■□

Using the front tip of the shoe to kick the ball. Discouraged in favor of the instep drive.
(See photo, which highlights the front toe area of the shoe.)
(Also, see: "19 Surfaces of the Soccer Shoe™")

Toe poke ◘□

Generally, stretching the leg out as far as possible to tap the ball with the front tip of the shoe in order to get it away from an opponent or to score a goal.

Toe stub

Catching the front of the foot in the turf during the execution of a kick, usually an instep drive. See: Stub Toe.

Token pressure

Defender stays goal-side of the opponent with the ball, but only slows him up without attempting to tackle, winning the ball only after an error.

Too central; Getting or playing too central

A team or individual keeps the ball in the middle of the field a lot, at the expense of exploiting other space.

Too far □

A pass with too much pace goes past the intended recipient.

Too many touches □

A player misses the optimal opportunity to shoot or pass because of excessive dribbling.

Too muscular; a little too muscular

Too physical on a tackle, resulting in a foul.

Too physical □

Contacting an opponent with too much force, resulting in a foul.

Too slow a pace ☐

Moving the ball around without hurry in such a way that either opportunities are missed on attack or the opponent can easily intercept; lack of urgency.

Too strong ■☐

A ball hit too hard so that it goes beyond its intended recipient.

Too tall

A cross that goes over the head of the intended recipient.

Top corner ☐

The upper-right or upper-left area of the goal, where the goalposts and the crossbar meet.

Top of the area ☐

The outer edge of the Penalty Area; the Eighteen.

Top of the ball

That part of the ball seen directly from above.

Top of the box ☐

At the eighteen; the 18; the outermost line of the Penalty Area.

Top the ball ☐

To unintentionally kick above the mid-line of the ball.

Topped ☐

Kicking over top of the ball; kicking the ball into the turf; top the ball.

TOPSoccer® ■☐

US Youth Soccer TOPSoccer (**T**he **O**utreach **P**rogram for **S**occer) is a community-based program intended to help meet some of the needs of developmentally-challenged youth through the opportunities and rewards of learning and playing soccer.

Topspin ☐

A motion imparted to the ball that causes it to rotate forward in the direction it was kicked.

Toss (1) ☐

Coin toss.

Toss (2), Tossed, To get tossed

To be thrown out of a game; Ejected; Red-carded.

Total Football; Total Soccer

Introduced in the late 1960s and advanced by the Dutch in the 1970s, all players learned all skills and interchanged on the field as if there were no positions. Difficult to sustain due to fitness requirements; some of its features, such as all players learning all skills, and use of the overlap, remain.

Total goals decider

Home-and-home series where the outcome is decided by the total number of goals if each team wins one match.

Touch (1) ■☐

To contact the ball.

Touch (2) – ► ■☐

► ***On-field Oral Communication:*** Teammate is requesting a one-touch pass.

Touch (3) ■☐

Light control; to exert the minimum force to the ball to make it do what you want.

Touch (4) ■☐

The "feel" for the ball.

Touch (5), Touches ■☐

The number of times a ball is contacted.

Touch me – ►

► ***On-field Oral Communication:*** Teammate is requesting that the ball carrier perform a give-and-go or a "one-two" passing combination with them.

Touch pass ☐

A short, one-touch, pass that is little more than a deflection of the ball to a teammate.

Touches ☐

As a statistic, the number of times a player contacts the ball during a match or during a particular period of time.

Touches on the ball ☐

Number of times an individual player contacts the ball. In practices, it is assumed that an increased number of touches by a player increases his success rate at ball skills.

Touchline, Touch Lines ☐

Law 1 of the Laws of the Game; the two long sides of the rectangular field of play from corner to corner; sidelines; side lines.

Touch-tight

Extremely close, man-to-man, marking where the defender is at minimum arms-length or actually contacting an attacker with their hand, usually just before a free kick.

Tough tackling

Hard or harsh tackles; difficult tackles; illegal tackles.

Tournament ■☐

A limited-timeframe competition involving a small number of teams resulting in a champion.

Track, Tracks

To mark, follow, or maintain knowledge of the position of, an opponent in order to properly defend.

Tracking

A defender staying with an opponent, in a man-to-man scenario, even if the team is playing in a zonal defense.

Tracking back

Forwards coming back to help out in defense.

Traditional Jersey Numbering System

Historical player jersey numbering scheme, numbers one-through-eleven, where the goalkeeper was number 1 and then field players were numbered, fullbacks to the forwards, right-to-left, from number 2 to number 11, based on the old 2-3-5 or "W-M" formation.

Traditional number 6

Midfielder who remains central and generally provides equal support to the offense and defense; historically, the jersey number worn by a left midfielder.

Traffic ☐

A large number of players in a very small space, difficult to dribble, run, or work the ball through.

Trail center back

The position of trail center back; the trailing defender in a two-center-fullback alignment; sweeper.

Trail center forward

The position of trail center forward; the trailing forward in a two-center-striker alignment; secondary striker.

Trail, Trailing ☐

A player behind a player with the ball.

Trailing

A team is behind in the score.

Trailing – ►

►***On-field Oral Communication:*** You have a back-pass option.

Trainer ☐

Person who helps prevent, or promotes recovery from, injury (American); Coach (foreign).

Trainer's kit

Collection of equipment designed to assist the physical well-being or ability of players to participate in training or a match.

Training ◘ ☐

All of the work and practice, including skills, tactics, fitness, and scrimmages, that go into preparing for games.

Training Bib, Training Vest

Colored outer garment that can be pulled over existing clothing, used to visually designate members or a side, team or group; pinnie, practice vest.

Training Camp

Pre-season workouts.

Training goals

Portable, full-sized goals which can be stuck in the ground or mounted on standards, usually without backstays.

Training ground

Practice field.

Training jacket, jersey, pants, shoes, suit, top, bottom, clothes, outfit

Clothing used at practice, usually matched sets for members of the same team.

Training-ground finish

A simple, composed score of a goal.

Transfer

Formal movement of a player from one team to another which may involve administrative or contract changes and, in the professional ranks, possibly an exchange of money (transfer fee).

Transfer fee

Money paid from one professional club to another when a player switches teams.

Transition ☐

The switch from offense-to-defense or defense-to-offense when the ball changes hands.

Transition game, Transitional play ☐

The strategy and tactics used by a team when in transition.

Trap – ► ☐

►***On-field Oral Communication:*** Defensive coordinator is calling for the defenders to implement an offside trap.

Trap (1), Trapping ◘ □

To receive the ball and get it under control; receiving, collecting, controlling.

Trap (2) ◘ □

Short for Offside Trap.

Trap game

Match where one team is expected to defeat another, but the so-called better team may take the opponent lightly while the so-called weaker team is psychologically prepared, resulting in the very real possibility of an upset.

Trash

Scoring a lucky goal because the ball arrives at a player's feet after others have done all the work; garbage goal.

Trash talking ■□

Inappropriate verbal communication to an opponent, usually derogatory, intended to take the mind or focus of the opponent off the game.

Travel team

(1) Higher-level competitive team that plays games outside of its local jurisdiction, often in other States; (2) The selected group of players that represents a team at an away game – typically only a portion of the entire team.

Treatment, Treatment of injury ■□

Providing medical assistance or first aid to an injured player; providing therapy to assist in the recovery from an injury.

Treble

Team winning three trophies in a season (typically league season, league cup, and champions cup).

Triangle Midfield

The formation of a series of triangles by midfielders to promote possession; a formation of three central midfielders.

Triangles □

Three players on the same team coming together in a way that promotes open, short-passing opportunities; the position of three players on the same team that looks like they are at the points of the three-sided geometric shape.

Trickery

Clever, unique, or unexpected runs, movement or kicks designed into offensive restarts.

Tricks (1) □

Clever ball skills, usually as a part of juggling.

Tricks (2)

Clever movement of attacking players as part of a set play.

Trigger, Trigger player

A player, other than the kicker (or thrower on a throw-in) who initiates a re-start.

Trip (1), Tripping, trips or attempts to trip an opponent ◘ □

Violation of Law 12, Fouls and Misconduct, resulting in the award of a direct free kick.

Trip (2)

Travel to an away game.

Triple punishment

Being called for a foul, ejected from the match (shown a red card), and having to sit out one or more games.

Triple team

Rare occasion where three defenders take on the ball carrier.

Try one

To take a shot from distance on the odd chance that it might go in.

Try outs, Tryouts ■□

Evaluation of prospective players to determine if they are to be offered a roster position with a team.

Trying to squeeze it through

Attempting to force a pass between two defenders.

Trying to trick his way around the defender

Using a dribbling feint to beat an opponent.

Tumble ■□

To fall; to go down to the ground as a result of a collision; to go down to the ground as a result of a successful tackle.

Tune-up

A practice game or friendly just prior to the start of a tournament.

Tunnel

Enclosed path through a stadium from the locker rooms to the game field.

Tunnel vision □

Locking on to only one opportunity (e.g., for a pass) without seeing or recognizing some other developing opportunity.

Turf ■□

Playing surface, usually a grass field; shorthand for artificial turf; synthetic turf.

Turf burn □

Skin abrasion caused by sliding on artificial turf; raspberry; strawberry.

Turf monster

Mythical beast that causes a player to catch a shoe in the artificial turf, resulting in failed technique with the ball or even causing the player to fall.

Turf shoes

Soccer shoes with multiple small studs designed to grip best on artificial surfaces.

Turn – ►

►On-field Oral Communication: As you receive the ball facing away from the attacking goal, it is safe to turn the ball upfield without an immediate challenge from an opponent.

Turn the corner □

To get around a flank defender and head along the goal line toward the near post.

Turned □

Against their intent, a defender winds up having to face their own goal.

Turning an opponent

Using a run, dribbling fakes or feints, or a personal pass to get a defender to move out of a goal-side stance.

Turnover ■□

Loss of the ball to an opponent.

Turns □

While dribbling, the ability to quickly change direction.

Tussle

Two opposing players staying in contact with each other, usually hand and arm checking.

Two front

A formation using two strikers.

Two points for a win □

A system for establishing the relative positions of teams in a group whereby points are awarded for wins and ties and then accumulated and compared; usually involves one point for a tie and no points for a loss; alternative is three points for a win.

Two touch, Two-touch □

A player receives or traps the ball with the first contact and then passes it to a teammate or shoots with the second contact.

Two-footed tackle

Defender coming at the ball with both feet simultaneously, in an attempt to take it away; generally considered to be very dangerous and is usually called as a foul.

Two-leg stages

Home-and-home games (legs) used in a tournament to determine which team advances. (A.k.a. – "home-and-away.")

Two-man system

Two referees with no assistant referees or club linesmen, officiating a game; both have equal powers.

Two-on-one break ■□

As a result of the run of play, two attacking players rapidly take on just one defender.

Two-touch "rule" □

Reference to those portions of the Laws of the Game where players taking re-starts may not touch the ball a second time before it is contacted by another player.

Two-way midfielder

Extremely fit and skilled individual, playing in a midfield position, who is capable of both going into the attack and getting back in defense during the entire course of a match.

Two-way player

A player equally adept at, and willing to play, both offense and defense.

Tying laces

Securing and knotting the laces of soccer shoes so that the shoes will stay on the feet properly and so that the laces will not come undone during participation in practices or games.

Type of Match

Characterization of a game, such as Exhibition, Friendly, Scrimmage, Regular Season, Playoff, or Cup.

U#, Under-#, # and Under (U-System, U# Age Groups, Youth Age Groups) ■□

Classification system for youth soccer, based on birth year or birth date, used for age-appropriate competitions.

The "U" stands for "Under" and the "#" stands for an age in years. For example, for a player who is 10-years old or younger, the term is commonly expressed as "U-10," "Under 10," or "10 and Under."

There are two approaches to create age groups using the U-system:

- The first approach is the "calendar-year" system (a.k.a. "birth-year" system), used by U. S. Soccer, which is based on the player's birth year. (See: Appendix 6A: Age Group Charts)
- The second approach is the "school-year" system (a.k.a. "class group" system), used by many recreational programs, which is based on the player's birth date (from August 1 of one year to July 31 of the next year). (See: Appendix 6B: Age Group Charts)

In both of these approaches, the season year typically runs from August 1 of one year to July 31 of the next year.

See "Age Guide" tables in: Appendix 6: Age Group Charts.

UEFA *(Abbrev.)*

The Union of European Football Associations; the governing body of football in Europe; Confederation of nations in Europe.

Unbeaten, Undefeated

In a particular competition, a team has accomplished wins and ties without any losses.

Unceremonious

A clearance that goes to no one.

Uncomfortable

Generally demonstrating a lack of confidence in one's actions, usually as a result of playing out of position.

Uncontested ■□

A play, pass, reception, or shot that is not defended by an opponent.

Undecided

Inability of a player to quickly make a choice associated with a ball skill or action that needs to be taken quickly, usually resulting in a mistake.

Under pressure ■□

A player with the ball is being challenged aggressively by one or two defenders trying to thwart a move, pass or shot.

Under socks, Undersocks

First, usually thin, socks placed on the feet, followed by the shinguards, with the game socks on top.

Under the ball

Kicking or otherwise striking the ball below the midline such that it lofts, not always intentionally.

Undercut, Undercutting

To submarine an opponent or otherwise hit him low when he has jumped for a ball, usually causing him to crash to the ground.

Underdog □

Team not expected to win a match.

Underhit, Underhitting

Failure to kick a ball hard enough to achieve the intended result; striking the ball in a way that creates insufficient pace.

Under-inflated ■□

A ball with air pressure that is too low to meet the standard for its size and weight.

Underload

Area, created by design, with few attacking players; "resting" exercise during a fitness routine, intended to allow the body to recover.

Underneath

Trailing strikers or midfielders; space ahead of a set of defenders.

Underperforming

A player or team that is not showing the skills or abilities of which they are capable.

Underside of the crossbar

That portion of the crossbar immediately facing the goal-line.

Underspin

"English" or rotation imparted on the ball causing it to revolve in a direction around its horizontal axis from top to bottom toward the kicker.

Underway, Under way

Game has started; game is currently being played.

Unforced error

Player making a mistake in the performance of a ball skill while not being challenged by a defender.

Unguarded ■□

(1) A player who is not marked by a defender; unmarked;
(2) The goal is open because the goalkeeper is out of position.

Uni *(Abbrev.)*

Slang for "uniform."

Uniform

Clothing, usually just referring to the jersey, shorts and socks, worn by a player in conformance with Law 4 of the Laws of the Game, "The Players' Equipment."

Uniform ordering

Analyzing the need for, and acquiring, the proper clothing for a team.

Unintentional hand ball ◘□

Unconscious contact by the hand or arm, when struck by the ball, that usually does not rise to the level of being called as "handling" under Law 12 of the Laws of the Game, "Fouls and Misconduct."

United Soccer Coaches

Formerly the National Soccer Coaches Association of America (NSCAA), "…the world's largest soccer coaches' organization that serves members at every level of the game."

United Soccer Coaches Certificates and Diplomas

Awards for successful completion of the soccer courses offered by the United Soccer Coaches organization, formerly the National Soccer Coaches Association of America (NSCAA).

United Soccer League Pro Division

Third-tier professional soccer in the United States.

United States Soccer Federation (USSF)

The FIFA-recognized national organization and sanctioning body for soccer in the United States; USSF; U.S. Soccer; has a set of coaching licensing courses and programs with national licenses.

Unlimited Substitution

Based on the local rules of a match, the ability of a coach to move players in and out without restriction as to numbers.

Unlucky □

A good attempt at a pass or shot that just misses the intended target.

Unlucky call

Having a foul whistled against you that was incorrect.

Unmarked ■□

An offensive player not being covered by a defender.

Unorganized

A defense that lacks the discipline, control, communication, and/or coordination to cover an attack properly.

Unplayable □

(1) Ball is going out of bounds so quickly that it cannot be reached in time; ball goes over the head or wide of a teammate.
(2) Surface of the field or weather conditions are so bad that a match must be abandoned.

Unselfish □

A player who passes often and willingly.

Unsighted □

Shot which is not seen by the goalkeeper when it is taken, particularly difficult if it is a close-in free kick where a wall is used.

Unsporting Behavior, Unsportsmanlike behavior, Unsportsmanlike conduct ◘ □

Cautionable, yellow card offense; violation of Law 12 of the Laws of the Game, "Fouls and Misconduct."

Unwritten rules, Unwritten rules of soccer

Concepts demonstrating sportsmanship that go above and beyond those which are expected by the Laws of the Game.

Up (1) □

Leading in a game by one or more goals.

Up (2)

In the direction of the attacking goal.

Up (3)
To regain one's footing after going to the ground.

Up a player, Up 1, Up 2 □
Having a player or more advantage over the number of players on the field for the opposing team in a match. See: Advantage (3).

Up by # goals ■□
The goal differential during a match. E.g., a team leading 3-1 is ***up by 2 goals (i.e., "up by 2").***

Up top
A player positioned in, or playing, a lead or central striker position.

Up-downs
A fitness exercise during which a standing player goes prone to the ground and then immediately returns to a standing position.

Upfield □
In the direction of the goal a team is attacking.

Upgrade, Upgrading
A formal process for referees attaining a higher ranking.

Upper 90
The top-most corner of the goal, either left or right, just inside the upright and under the crossbar; 90 refers to the 90-degrees of a corner.

Upper left corner ■□
The top-most corner of the goal, to the left side as faced by an attacker.

Upper right corner ■□
The top-most corner of the goal, to the right side as faced by an attacker.

Upper V
Same as Upper 90; either of the top corners of the goal.

Upright ■□
Either of the two vertical posts of the goal; goalpost; stanchion.

Upset ■□

Game in which a lower-ranked or lower-regarded team defeats a higher-level team.

Urgency (or lack of urgency) □

The need to score a goal. Contrast with the lack of urgency shown when a team needs to score a goal but does not appear to be applying the effort necessary to do so; the need to win games.

US Club Soccer

USSF affiliate with alternative rules to USYSA; US Club.

U.S. Soccer ◘□

The governing body for soccer in the U.S. (A.k.a.: USSF)

U.S. Soccer Foundation

A 501(c)(3) organization serving as a national charitable entity for under-served soccer communities in the United States.
See: USSF; U.S. Soccer; http://ussoccerfoundation.org/

USASA *(Abbrev.)*

United States Adult Soccer Association (usadultsoccer.com)

USCAA *(Abbrev.)*

United States Collegiate Athletic Association.

usclubsoccer.org

U. S. Club Soccer is a national organization and sanctioning body for amateur soccer under the United States Soccer Federation.

Use him – ▶

▶ ***On-field Oral Communication:*** Pass the ball to the open teammate you see.

Useless appeal

An attempt by a player to get the referee to change his mind after making a call.

Using contact

A player taking advantage of being touched by an opponent to create the illusion a foul, to bait the referee or to take a dive.

USL *(Abbrev.)*

United Soccer Leagues.

USMNT *(Abbrev.)*

United States Men's National Team; MNT.

USOC *(Abbrev.)*

United States Olympic Committee.

USSF *(Abbrev.)*

United States Soccer Federation. Commonly referred to as U.S. Soccer (www.ussoccer.com). The USSF is the official governing body for soccer in the U.S. See: U.S. Soccer.

USSF Licenses

System of training and certification for coaches presented by the United States Soccer Federation, designated as "F," "D," and "E" at the State level and "C," "B," and "A" at the National level, with "A" being the highest level.

USWNT *(Abbrev.)*

United States Women's National Team; WNT.

USYS NL *(Abbrev.)*

U. S. Youth Soccer National League program.

USYSA *(Abbrev.)*

United States Youth Soccer Association, Inc.

Utility player ☐

Player possessing all-around skills and knowledge such that he could be used effectively in any field position.

v (v terminology) ◘ □

Versus; against; common usage during practice to denote squad or team strength in drills or scrimmages;
E.g., **2 v 1** generally represents a drill utilizing two offensive players against one defensive player.

Valve ■□

Device sewn or otherwise connected to the bladder of a ball to control air inflation.

Vanishing spray ◘ □

Temporary paint used by the referee on the field to mark the ten-yard distance from the ball required of defenders before a free kick is taken; sometimes also used to mark the location of the ball.

VAR *(Abbrev.)*

Video Assistant Referee (Video Assistance for Match Referees).

Varsity □

Top competitive team in high school or college. Implies the existence of a junior varsity.

Venue

Location for a match.

Verbal communication ◘ □

On-field talking among teammates in order to provide direction.
Note: In this dictionary, "***On-field Oral Communication***" terms are indicated by this symbol: ►.

Verbal cue

On-field Oral Communication either given by one's own team or overheard from an opponent to take a particular action.
See all entries marked with the symbol "►."
See also Appendix 4 – On-field Oral Communication.

Versus ■□

Against; opposing; v. or v -- E.g., 3 v. 1; 4 v 3.
See: "v terminology."

Vertical axis
The field from goal-line to goal-line, parallel to the sidelines.

Vests ◘ □
Scrimmage vests; colored outer garments that can be pulled over existing clothing, used to visually designate members or a side, team, group, or substitutes; pinnies, practice vests; performance measurement undergarment.

Veteran, Vet
Long-term player with a lot of experience.

Veteran soccer players
Per the IFAB, male and female players over 35 years old.

Video ■□
Visual record of players, practices, games, or the games of opponents.

Video Assistant Referee
An individual appointed to use video replay to assist a match official "with clear errors in match-changing situations." (IFAB)

Video games
Any of a number of animated software products for use on electronic screens with controllers. Example, EA Sports FIFA soccer.

Video technology
Use of cameras and replay to determine close calls, specifically if a goal has been scored or not.

Videographer
Person responsible for visually recording practices, games, or games involving opponents.

Violent Conduct
Violation of Law 12 of the Laws of the Game, involving an egregious act against a player, so severe that it results in the issuance of a red card and ejection from the game.

Vision ◘ □
The ability of a player to see, comprehend, and properly respond to as much as possible of what is happening on the field.

Visual cue

Non-verbal communication by a teammate indicating what he is going to do; an action by an opponent which tips off what he is going to do.

Volley, Volley kick, Volleying ■□

An instep or inside-of-the-foot kick of an airborne ball.

Volunteer, Volunteer coach ■□

An individual who provides services free of charge for the benefit of the team.

Vulnerabilities, Vulnerability

An individual's or a team's defensive weaknesses which can be exploited in attack.

Vuvuzela

Air horn noisemaker used by fans; term made common during the 2010 FIFA World Cup held in South Africa.

W (1) *(Abbrev.)* ■□

An abbreviation of "Win." Wins; number of games or matches won.

W (2) *(Abbrev.)*

Women's; soccer shoes designed with cleats intended for use by women.

W (3) *(Abbrev.)*

Wing; the position of wing or winger; a forward playing near the sideline.

W position

Proximity of the goalkeeper's hands prepared to catch the ball, such that the thumbs and index fingers appear to form the letter "W", Goalkeeper's "W."

WAGs

Wives and Girlfriends.

Waiting (1)

The deliberate act of a player delaying putting the ball back into play in order to let the clock run; wasting time; time wasting.

Waiting (2) ■□

Inactively standing around for someone else to do something.

Waiting for help □

Implementing delaying tactics on defense in order to create enough time for other defenders to arrive.

Wake Up! (or "Wake up, people!") – ►

►***On-field Oral Communication:*** - Player is attempting to get the whole team to increase its level of play or stop being lethargic.

Waking up □

A team demonstrates a higher-level of play, activity, or concentration after a period of lethargy; often comes about after being scored upon.

Walking

A player demonstrating tiredness or lack of endurance or fitness at a time when they should be running.

Walking it off ■□

A term for a player who is able to stretch or warm a minor injury by exercising the area in order to return to a game.

Walkover; Cakewalk

Winning a game by a very large margin due to playing an inferior team.

Wall ◘ □

A group of defenders lined up shoulder-to-shoulder to try to block the goal from a nearby free kick.

Wall building, Wall placement, Wall setting

The process of putting a wall in place based on the angle and distance from which the free kick will be taken.

Wall, (number) – ► ■□

► On-field Oral Communication: The goalkeeper calls for the defense to build a wall in response to an upcoming free kick and announces how many players he wants to be in the wall. The goalkeeper may also direct the players which way to move the wall. Example: "Wall, 4."

Wall pass

A give-and-go; "one-two"; 1 - 2; a pass resembling kicking a ball into a wall at approximately a 45-degree angle and then running to receive the rebound.

Wall player □

The player acting as the "wall" in a "wall pass" or give-and-go passing combination.

Warm down ■□

A brief period of light exercise and/or stretching after a strenuous practice or game, designed to gradually decrease the heart rate and promote a return to a resting state.

Warm up, Warm-up, Warm-ups ◘ □

(1) A period of gradually more challenging exercises designed to increase the heart rate and promote a level of activity appropriate for a strenuous practice or game. Usually includes stretching.
(2) A systematized approach to ensure that appropriate exercises and stretching are performed to prepare the body for a practice or match.

Warm up activities

The specific exercises, stretches or drills selected and used for warm ups.

Warming up ■□

Performing physical actions (e.g., exercises or stretching) by players preparing to enter a game (either as a starting player or as a substitute).

Warm-up suit; Warm-ups

Training clothes, consisting of pants and top, designed to retain body heat.

Warning ■□

The referee verbally admonishes a player that his foul or misconduct is just short of a yellow card.

Waste, Wasted ball, Wasted shot

An excellent opportunity to pass or shoot that either was not taken or was badly misplayed.

Wasted free kick

A re-start near the goal where the kick is played directly into a wall or shot wildly.

Wasting Time

The deliberate act on the part of a player of not putting the ball back into play promptly in order to run the clock down. Cautionable offense under Law 12 of the Laws of the Game.

Watch wide – ►

►On-field Oral Communication: Keeper or defensive organizer tells a defender that there is an opponent between him and the nearest sideline.

Watch your 'sides; Watch! – ► □

►On-field Oral Communication: Warns a teammate that he is in, or is about to go into, an offside position.

Watching ■□

Ball watching; a player is standing around instead of moving into a more productive location.

Watching; (Name) you're watching – ►

►On-field Oral Communication: Tells a teammate that they are looking at the play instead of moving into a more productive location. (E.g., "Craig, you're watching!")

Water break ■□

(1) An intentional stoppage of practice or a match to allow players to hydrate by drinking water or sports drinks; cooling break; hydration break.
(2) A FIFA-authorized procedure where a referee may determine before the start of a match, based on a formula involving temperature, humidity, and direct sun, if a hydration break will be used at the 30-minute mark or after, and at what stoppage of play, such as a throw-in.

Water kit

A collection of fresh water, water bottles, cups or ice to be made available to players for hydration.

Water-logged □

A soaked field or ball.

Waved off, Waves it off ■□

Referee moves arm or hand to indicate that a goal or foul is not going to be called and to play on.

Waves, Waves of attack

A team defense suffers repeated attack-after-attack from an opponent without being able to get and retain possession of the ball.

WB *(Abbrev.)*

Wing Back; the position of Wing Back; an outside defender closest to the sideline.

WC *(Abbrev.)*

World Cup; FIFA World Cup.

W-D-L *(Abbrev.)*

Wins-Draws-Losses.

Weak foot ■□

The opposite leg of a naturally right- or left-handed person.

Weak side ■□

The area of the field to the left or right of the imaginary midline that contains the least number of attackers or defenders at any given moment; the area of the field to the left or right side of the imaginary midline that does not contain the ball.

Weak, Weak effort, Weak shot □

Any contact with the ball that should have had much more force applied.

Weather conditions ■□

Part of overall field conditions, such as wind or rain, that will affect play.

Weight anchors

Bags filled with heavy metal designed to hold goals in place, specifically for safety purposes so that they won't tip over.

Weight lifting, Weightlifting, Weight training ■□

The movement of inanimate objects, usually made of metal, to increase muscle strength.

Weight of the pass

The speed, pace or strength of a pass. If the pass is too hard or goes long, you might say the weight of the pass was too heavy. If the pass is too soft or is short, you might say that the weight of the pass was too light.

Weight, Weight on the ball

The amount of force applied to the ball at the moment of contact.

Well defended □

An attack which was efficiently covered and possession of the ball was regained.

Well played □

Any of a number of skills or actions performed effectively and efficiently by an individual or a team.

Well-placed □

The accuracy and direction of the ball during a pass or shot in order to make it reach a teammate or score a goal.

Well-timed challenge

A tackle which is performed at the correct moment to get the ball, not too early and not too late.

Well-weighted ball

A pass which is performed with the correct speed or strength put to the ball to ensure that it reaches the intended receiver at the proper moment; proper pace.

Wet ■□

Water-soaked, usually due to rain; may include players, the field or the ball.

Wet ball

Water-soaked ball, which alters its performance, requiring recognition and special techniques.

Wet ball drills

Specific activities or exercises designed to familiarize players with how to alter their technique to play with a wet or water-soaked, ball.

Wet field, Wet grounds □

Damp to water-soaked grass or field of play which may alter the players' footing and the flight of the ball.

WF *(Abbrev.)*

Withdrawn Forward; the position of Withdrawn Forward; a secondary striker playing in a position behind a lead striker.

What you see – ▶ ■□

▶ ***On-field Oral Communication:*** There is no pressure from your back or sides and what you see in front of you as a dribbler is all you have to be concerned about for the time being.

Wheel kits

Devices designed to be inserted into holders usually welded to goals in order to assist with portability.

Whiff □

To miss the ball entirely when trying to kick it.

Whipped in

A particularly quick, fast, strong cross or pass to the area in front of the goal.

Whistle (1) ■□

The actual device used by referees to make sound to indicate states of play in a game.

Whistle (2), the whistle, the whistle has sounded ■□

A whistle has been sounded, usually denoting the beginning or ending of the half or the match.

Whistle (3), to whistle ◘ □

A foul has been called.

Whistling

Showing displeasure; International form of "booing" in the United States.

Whiteboard

A coaching device that can be written on with erasable markers.

Wide (1) – ► □

► ***On-field Oral Communication:*** Play the ball out toward the sideline.

Wide (2) ◘ □

Shot at goal which misses to the left or right.

Wide midfielder

A player in a midfield position closest to the sideline, right or left.

Wide open (1) ■□

(1) A player who is not being covered defensively;
(2) The mouth of the goal if the goalkeeper and nearest defenders have been caught out of position due to the run of play.

Wide open (2), Wide-open game

A game with equal possession where the ball goes regularly from end-to-end and either team is capable of scoring.

Wide striker

A player in a forward position closest to the sideline; wing; winger.

Widening the angle

Attacker moving away from a defender or toward the middle of the field in order to increase shooting or passing area.

Width ◘ □

The distance of a soccer field from sideline to sideline.

Width in attack

The ability of offensive players to create and maintain space between themselves from sideline to sideline.

Width in defense

The ability of defensive players to shut down space available on the flanks.

Win ■□

To have more goals that the opponent at the conclusion of a match.

Win it – ► □

► ***On-field Oral Communication:*** Encouragement to get to the open spot on the field where the ball is arriving; encouragement to win a 50/50 ball.

Win the ball, Wins the ball □

To come away with the ball after a successful tackle.

Wind sprints ■□

Fitness drill employing a series of fastest possible running over a short distance, intended to leave players trying to catch their breath.

Window

The momentary view that a striker sees just before shooting, showing him a clear trajectory for the ball to travel to the goal (unobstructed by defenders).

Win-draw-loss record, Wins-ties-losses record ■□

The summary of game results for a team in a competition season; note that for many sports in the United States the ties (draws) may be shown in the third position.

Wind-up □

Leg backswing before kicking the ball.

Wing backs, Wingback

Outside fullbacks; back defenders playing closest to the touchlines, right or left.

Wing, Wings (a.k.a.: Winger; Wing Forwards; Wide Forwards) □

Player(s) in a traditional attacking or striker position playing forward and nearest the touchline as either a "right" or "left" wing.

Wings

The sides of the field nearest the touchlines; flanks.

Win-loss-tie record, Wins-losses-ties record ■□

The summary of game results as usually recorded in the United States.

Winning goal ■□

Last goal scored to go one-goal ahead; can occur at any time during a match.

Winning Team

Law 10 of the Laws of the Game; the team scoring the greater number of goals during a match.

Winning the ball □

Using skill, technique, power, positioning, or sheer determination to wrest the ball away from the opponent; to get to the ball first before an opponent.

Wiped out □

A defender tackles or fouls an opponent so severely that the player's legs are taken out from under him and he is sent sprawling to the ground.

Withdrawn forward

A trailing center forward position behind that of a lead or central striker; secondary striker.

Withdrawn midfielder

A position utilizing a trailing, central midfielder, usually specializing in defense; defensive midfielder.

Within playing distance

A location of the ball in relation to a player, generally within two or three steps; concept associated with the application of certain rules.

Withstanding waves of attack

Sufficient numbers of defenders and the goalkeeper not allowing the opponent to score even though the opponent has extended periods of possession. Compare: bunkering; catenaccio.

W-L-D *(Abbrev.)*
Wins-Losses-Draws.

W-League *(Abbrev.)*
In the absence of a professional league, the highest level of women's soccer (semi-pro) in the United States.

W-L-T *(Abbrev.)*
Wins-Losses-Ties.

WM *(Abbrev.)*
Wide Midfielder; the position of a wide midfielder; an outside midfielder, playing closest to a sideline, who often moves into the attack.

W-M Formation, WM System
Old, traditional system of play, with players in a 2-3-5 alignment, where the fullbacks and halfbacks were in positions resembling a "W" and the forwards were in positions resembling an "M." Origin of both the basic field-player position-name designations and the 1-through-11 jersey-numbering scheme.

WNT *(Abbrev.)*
United States Women's National Team; USWNT.

Women's National Team
Top-level women's team representing the United States in international competition; United States Women's National Team; WNT; USWMT.

Women's Olympic Team
Team representing the United States in female Olympic competition.

Women's World Cup
FIFA World Cup for women's national teams, contested every four years.

Woodwork
The face of the goal (uprights and crossbar); common usage, "[his shot] hit the woodwork," from when the goals were originally made of wood.

Work ■□
Sustained physical effort to get better or overcome an opponent.

Work rate

The pace or level at which a player runs, attacks, defends, recovers, or pursues opponents during the course of a match.

World Cup; FIFA World Cup

International competition held every four years by the world governing body of soccer, FIFA, to determine the best national team.

Worry the goalkeeper □

Interfering with the goalkeeper's responsibility to release the ball from his hands in a timely manner, a cautionable offense.

Worthless □

An extremely poor shot or pass; a shot from a direct kick near the goal that doesn't even come close.

Wrap, protective ■□

Soft covering over an injury or device to protect the wearer and others.

Wrong foot ■□

An attempt to perform a ball skill with one leg/foot when proper technique calls for the use of the other leg/foot.

Wrong side □

Turned or otherwise defending from position or stance opposite of that which should be taken.

WS *(Abbrev.)*

Wide Striker; the position of wide striker; a wing forward.

W-T-L *(Abbrev.)*

Wins-Ties-Losses.

WWC *(Abbrev.)*

Women's World Cup; FIFA Women's World Cup.

XI ■□

Roman numeral for "Eleven", as in starting eleven on a full-side team.

YC *(Abbrev.)*
Yellow Card.

Yellow card ◘ □
Law 12 of the Laws of the Game; shown to a player who has committed a cautionable offense. (See: Caution.)

Yellow card offenses ■□
Law 12 of the Laws of the Game; a player is cautioned and shown a yellow card for unsporting behavior, dissent by word or action, persistent infringement of the Laws, delaying the restart of play, failure to respect the required distance when play is restarted with a corner kick, free kick or throw-in, entering or re-entering the field of play without the referee's permission, or deliberately leaving the field of play without the referee's permission.

Yes – ▶ ■□
▶ ***On-field Oral Communication:*** Go ahead and pass the ball to the open teammate.

YNT *(Abbrev.)*
United States Youth National Team(s).

You got it – ▶ □
▶ ***On-field Oral Communication:*** On offense, when two teammates could equally go for a ball, tells the teammate that the ball is theirs. (See also: "Yours", which may have a different meaning.)

You've got a drop
▶ ***On-field Oral Communication:*** There's a teammate behind you who is available and open for a back pass.

You've got me back – ▶ □
▶ ***On-field Oral Communication:*** I'm available and open for a back pass.

You've got time – ▶ ■□
▶ ***On-field Oral Communication:*** There is no immediate pressure from nearby and you have the time you need to settle or collect the ball and then look up to see your options.

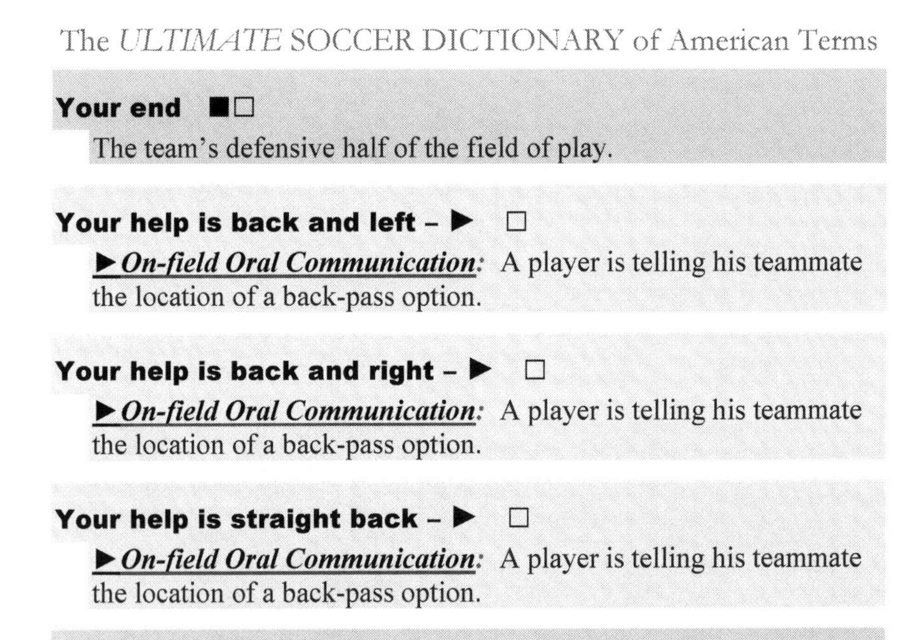

Your end ■□

The team's defensive half of the field of play.

Your help is back and left – ► □

► ***On-field Oral Communication:*** A player is telling his teammate the location of a back-pass option.

Your help is back and right – ► □

► ***On-field Oral Communication:*** A player is telling his teammate the location of a back-pass option.

Your help is straight back – ► □

► ***On-field Oral Communication:*** A player is telling his teammate the location of a back-pass option.

Yours – ► ■□

► ***On-field Oral Communication:*** You are telling your teammate that THEY must play the ball. (This is generally not a very good call and should only be used in case of injury or odd circumstance.)

Youth ◘□

Players under the age of 19.

Youth player

A male or female under the age of 19 before August 1, prior to the start of a seasonal year.

Youth World Cups

FIFA World competitions for youth national teams, by age groups.

Zero-to-ninety
Playing hard for a full match, start to finish, zero seconds to ninety minutes.

Zip ■□
Zero; Nothing; None; Nil.

Zone ■□
An area of a zone defense, usually manned by one defender.

Zone 1
Defensive third of the field.

Zone 2
Middle or transition third of the field.

Zone 3
Attacking third of the field.

Zone coverage, Zonal marking
The process by which defenders take on attackers who come into their zones in a zone defense.

Zone defense, Zonal defense ■□
A type of defense that starts with the defensive players assigned to an area of the field in front of the goal and covering any attacker who first comes into their area; contrast with man-to-man defense.

Zone of Defense
The area within a zone defense which a player is assigned to cover.

Zones of a field
An analytics or metrics approach which divides the field into 18 zones in order to focus on the characteristics and significance of each zone to the game and how it should be played.

Zones of a field – "Zone 14"
Of the 18 zones of a field, the zone determined to be the most significant - at the top of the Penalty Area.

’ (An apostrophe; *abbrev. for* **“minute”)** ■□

Shorthand representing “minute” for the time during a game when a goal was scored. Example: **9’ J. Smith** - John Smith scored in the ninth minute of play, sometime between 8:00 and 8:59.

+1

Plus One; Practice activity where the “+1” represents a player who switches to always be with the team with the ball; e.g., 2 v 2 +1; Plus 1.

1 v 1, etc. ■□

One versus one; One-on-one; See: “v terminology”; Practice drill with one offensive player versus one defensive player; number of offensive players is listed first.

1-shirt, 1-jersey

Jersey number worn by the goalkeeper under the old, traditional (numbers 1-through-11) numbering scheme.

1st Attacker

First Attacker; generally, the player with the ball heading for goal after a change of possession.

1st Defender

First Defender; generally, the player on the defensive team who first meets the opponent with the ball after a change of possession.

2nd Attacker

Second Attacker; generally, the first player without the ball heading for goal; the next most-dangerous attacker closest to the player in possession of the ball.

2nd Defender

Second Defender; generally, the player on the defensive team who takes on the first closest attacker without the ball and provides immediate support to the First Defender.

2-on-1 break ■□

A quick counter-attack marked by a sudden advantage of two attackers going against one defender, not including the goalkeeper.

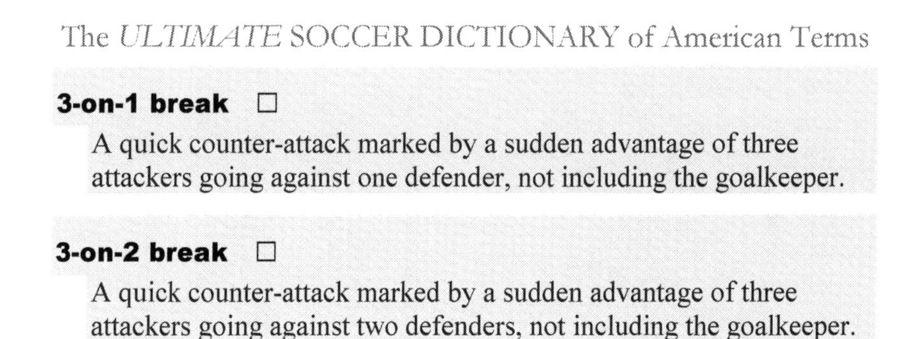

3-on-1 break □

A quick counter-attack marked by a sudden advantage of three attackers going against one defender, not including the goalkeeper.

3-on-2 break □

A quick counter-attack marked by a sudden advantage of three attackers going against two defenders, not including the goalkeeper.

3rd Attacker

Third Attacker; generally, the second or remaining players without the ball heading for goal expected to make runs which disrupt the defense; the next closest attacker to the goal.

3rd Defender

Third Defender; generally, the player or players on the defensive team who take on the second closest and remaining attackers without the ball.

4-2-3-1 □

Example of a formation, designated from the goal out, using four back defenders, two defensive midfielders, three attacking midfielders, and one striker (the goalkeeper is assumed and the total of the numbers always adds up to 10 for full-sides play).

4-3-2-1 □

Example of a formation, designated from the goal out, using four back defenders, three defensive midfielders, two attacking midfielders, and one striker (the goalkeeper is assumed and the total of the numbers always adds up to 10 for full-sides play).

4-3-3 ■□

Example of a formation, designated from the goal out, using four back defenders, three midfielders, and three strikers (the goalkeeper is assumed; the total of the numbers always adds up to 10 for full-sides play). See: Appendix 2 – Player Positions.

4-4-2 ■□

Example of a formation, designated from the goal out, using four back defenders, four midfielders, and two strikers (the goalkeeper is assumed; the total of the numbers always adds up to 10 for full-sides play). See: Appendix 2 – Player Positions.

6

The outermost line of the Goal Area, parallel to the goal-line, 6-yards out from the goal. The six; The 6.

6-cross

A lofted pass from the corner of the field delivered to the area approximately six yards in front of the attacking goal (the top of the goal area).

6-yard box □

The Goal Area.

9-shirt, 9-jersey

Jersey number worn by the center forward under the old, traditional (numbers 1-through-11) numbering scheme; nominally the jersey worn by the player considered to be in the most forward or lead striker position on a team.

10, 10 men, 10 players, 10 standing

To play or finish the game with only 10 players on the field; playing short; playing one man down.

10-shirt, 10-jersey

Jersey number worn by the left inside forward under the old, traditional (numbers 1-through-11) numbering scheme; nominally the jersey worn by the player considered to be the playmaker or attacking midfielder on a team; the number of the jersey worn by Pele; jersey number honoring Pele.

11 v 11 ■□

Practice scrimmage with two full teams, usually with full field and full-size goals; a regulation match with two full sides.

11+ Program

FIFA-designed effort to prevent injuries.

12

The Penalty Mark or Penalty Spot; an imaginary line, parallel to the goal-line, 12-yards out from the goal, that runs through the Penalty Spot. The twelve; The 12.

12-cross

A lofted pass from the corner of the field delivered to the area in front of the attacking goal at approximately the penalty spot.

12th man ☐

Twelfth Man: psychological and emotional benefit to a home team derived from an active and vociferous crowd of their fans.

12-yard spot

The Penalty Mark; penalty spot.
See: Appendix 3 – Soccer Field Diagram.

17 Laws of the Game

The rules of soccer; The Laws of the Game; The IFAB Laws of the Game. See: Appendix 5 – The Laws of the Game.

18 ◘ ☐

The outermost line of the Penalty Area, parallel to the goal-line, 18-yards out from the goal. The eighteen; The 18.

18-cross

A lofted pass from the corner of the field delivered to the area approximately eighteen yards in front of the attacking goal (the top of the penalty area).

18-yard box

The Penalty Area; the Penalty Box; the Box.

50-50, 50/50, 50-50 ball ◘ ☐

Fifty-Fifty; Fifty-Fifty ball; a ball which, during the run of play, is equidistant between two oncoming opponents and is likely to result in a collision unless one player is successful in getting to it first or the other player backs off.

90

Upper or lower corners of the goal, each a 90-degree angle; number of minutes in a full game.

(P) *(Abbrev.)*

Designation for a goal scored on a Penalty Kick.

#

Jersey number.

 # - all

Number of goals for both teams in a tie game, e.g., 1 – all, 2 – all.

APPENDICES

APPENDIX 1 – Soccer "Quick-Start Guide" ◘

This Soccer "Quick-Start Guide" is designed ***especially*** to help ***anyone who is new to the game of soccer*** – e.g., new players; parents and friends of soccer players; volunteer coaches; sports commentators; or any other new fans with little experience in soccer.

In addition to some ***easy***, introductory terms – like "ball" and "goal" – this "quick-start" list also includes a number of ***more-challenging*** terms (e.g., "offside trap," "advantage rule"). Some of these terms involve concepts and rules of soccer which may be unfamiliar to soccer novices but which are fundamentally important to understanding the game of soccer. In the ***electronic versions***, each "Quick-Start" term – indicated by the symbol ◘ – is ***LINKED*** to its definition. From within each definition, you may click on the symbol ◘ or the underlined term to ***return*** to this "Quick-Start" list. ***All*** "Quick-Start" terms appear in ***all*** versions of this dictionary.

Spending some time with this "Quick-Start Guide" will be an easy and fun way for you to quickly learn more about soccer.

The "Coach"

Page numbers are also shown for the BASIC and CONDENSED versions: **Page #**

REMEMBER:

In the ***electronic versions***, each "**Quick-Start**" term in this list – indicated by the symbol ◘ – is ***HYPER-LINKED*** to its definition.

From each definition, if you want to ***return*** to this "Quick-Start" list, simply **click the link**. This helps make it easy and fun to quickly learn more about soccer.

REMEMBER:
In the ***electronic versions***, each "**Quick-Start**" term in this list – indicated by the symbol ◘ – is ***HYPER-LINKED*** to its definition.
From each definition, if you want to ***return*** to this list, simply click the link.

REMEMBER:

In the ***electronic versions***, each "**Quick-Start**" term in this list – indicated by the symbol ◘ – is ***HYPER-LINKED*** to its definition.

From each definition, if you want to ***return*** to this list, simply click the link.

REMEMBER:
In the ***electronic versions***, each "**Quick-Start**" term in this list – indicated by the symbol ◘ – is ***HYPER-LINKED*** to its definition.
From each definition, if you want to ***return*** to this list, simply click the link.

APPENDIX 2

PLAYER POSITIONS AND FORMATIONS

- **PLAYER POSITION NAMES**

Specific position names, other than the **goalkeeper (G, GK)**, tend to be associated with the number of players involved in the general positions:

For the **back defenders (B, D)** or **fullbacks (F, FB)**, older three-back formations had a **center fullback (CFB)**, a **right fullback (RFB)**, and a **left fullback (LFB)**. As four-back formations evolved, the two players in the middle of the field have together been called **center fullbacks, central backs** or **center backs (CB)**. The central defenders may also be called the **right center back (RCB)** and the **left center back (LCB)**, or the **lead center back (LCB)** and the **trail center back (TCB)**. Depending upon their duties, a leading center back, often assigned to mark the opponent's best center striker, may be called a **stopper (ST)**. This player has also been called the **central defender (CD)**. A center back playing behind the stopper, who is often the last field player before the goalkeeper and may not have a marking assignment, can be given the ability to roam in order to support his other backs. As such, this type of defender is known as a **sweeper (SW)**. With possible other responsibilities, the sweeper has also been known as the **libero (L)** (Italian for "free"). The back defenders playing closest to the sidelines are also known as **outside fullbacks (OFB)**, **outside backs (OB)**, **right back (RB)**, and **left back (LB)**.

For the **midfielders (M, MF)** or **halfbacks (H, HB)**, older three-midfielder formations had a **center halfback (CHB)**, a **right halfback (RHB)**, and a **left halfback (LHB)**. As four- and even five-midfielder formations evolved, two players in the center, otherwise known as **center midfielders** or **central midfielders (CM)**, became an **attacking midfielder (AM)** and a **holding midfielder (HM)** or a **defensive midfielder (DM)**. The midfielders playing closest to the sidelines, or **outside midfielders (OM)**, are also known as the **right midfielder (RM)** and the **left**

midfielder (LM). In addition, there are a number of "hybrid" positions where outside fullbacks often move into the midfield, or outside midfielders move into back defense. These players are sometimes called **wing backs (WB)**. Outside midfielders moving into the attack are sometimes called **wide midfielders (WM)**.

For the **forwards (F)** or **strikers (S, ST)**, older five-forward formations had a **center forward (CF)**, **inside forwards (IF)**, known as the **right inside (RI)** and the **left inside (LI)**, and **wing forwards** (**wings, wingers** or **wide forwards) (W)**, known as the **right wing (RW)**, and the **left wing (LW)**. As the traditional wings and inside forward positions evolved into midfield positions, a single **striker (S)** or a **center striker** or **central striker (CS)**, a striker with a center forward, two strikers, two center forwards, as the **right center forward (RCF)** and the **left center forward (LCF)**, or the **lead center forward (LCF)** and **trail center forward (TCF)**, emerged. The trailing forward position has also been referred to as a **withdrawn forward (WF)**. A striker may also be paired with a **second striker**, **secondary striker**, **supporting striker**, or **set-back striker (SS)** or **wide strikers (WS)**, also identified as a **right wing striker (RWS)** or **left wing striker (LWS)**.

APPENDIX 2A – BASIC PLAYER POSITIONS CHART

BASIC PLAYER POSITIONS (in 4-4-2 vs. 4-3-3 formations)

APPENDIX 2B – Typical 4-4-2 Formation

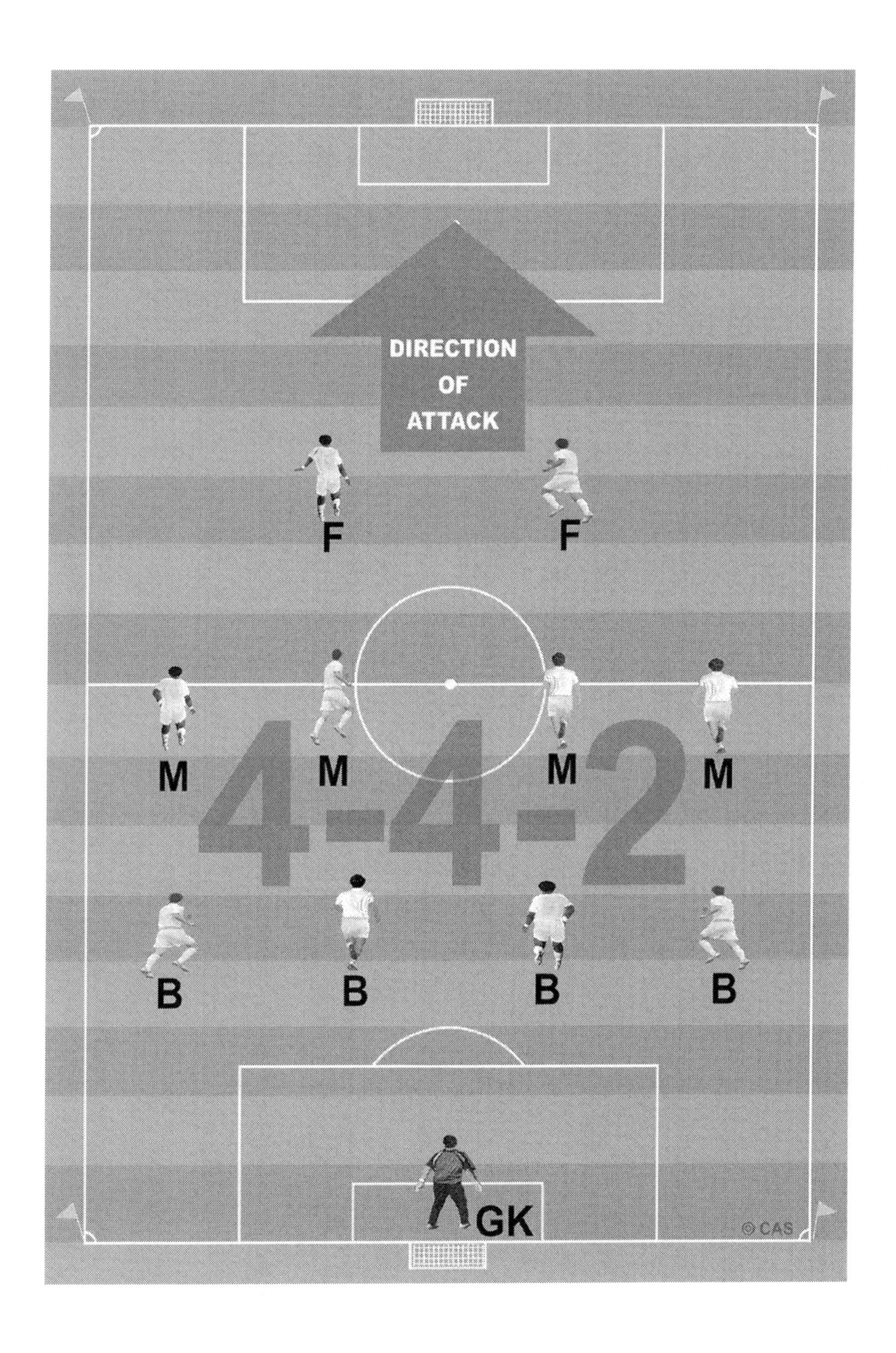

APPENDIX 2C – Typical 4-3-3 Formation

APPENDIX 3 – SOCCER FIELD DIAGRAM

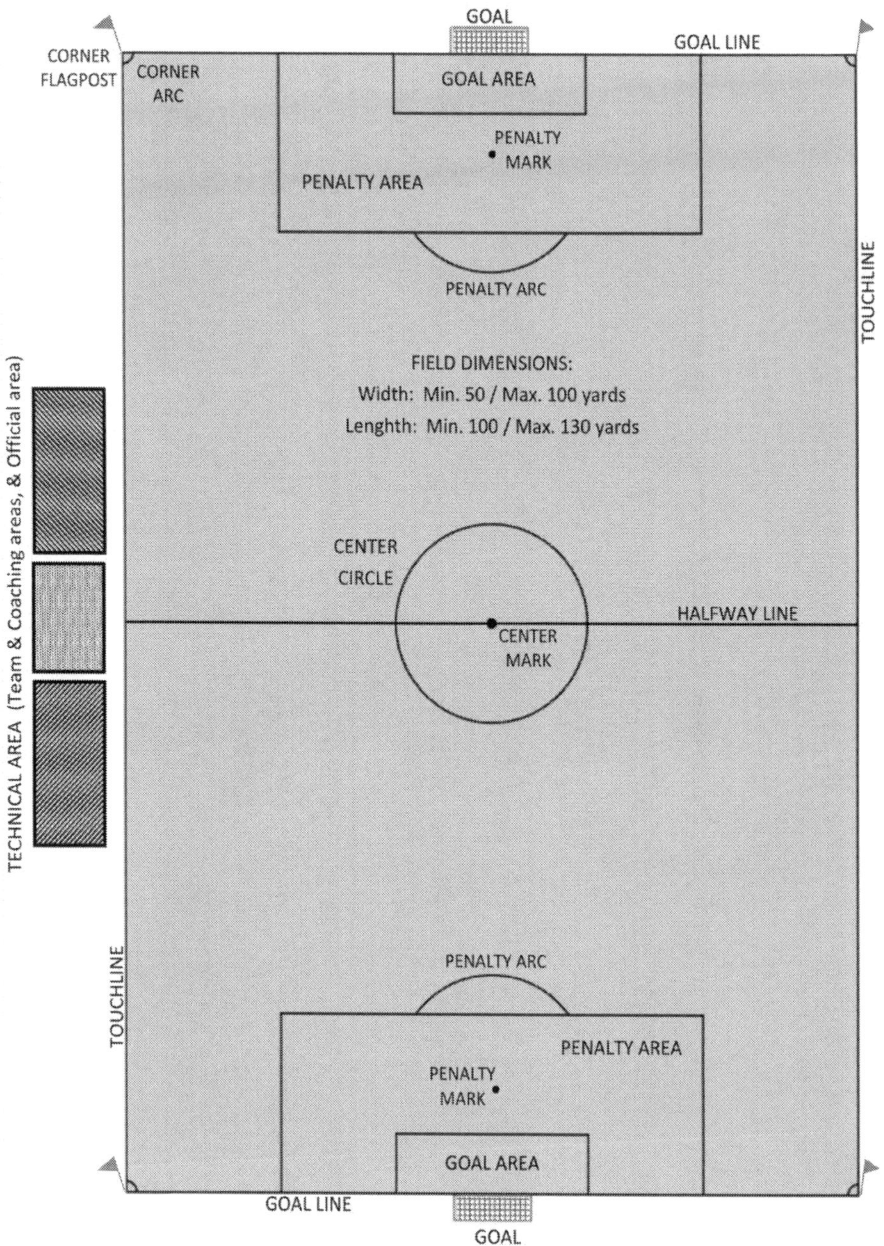

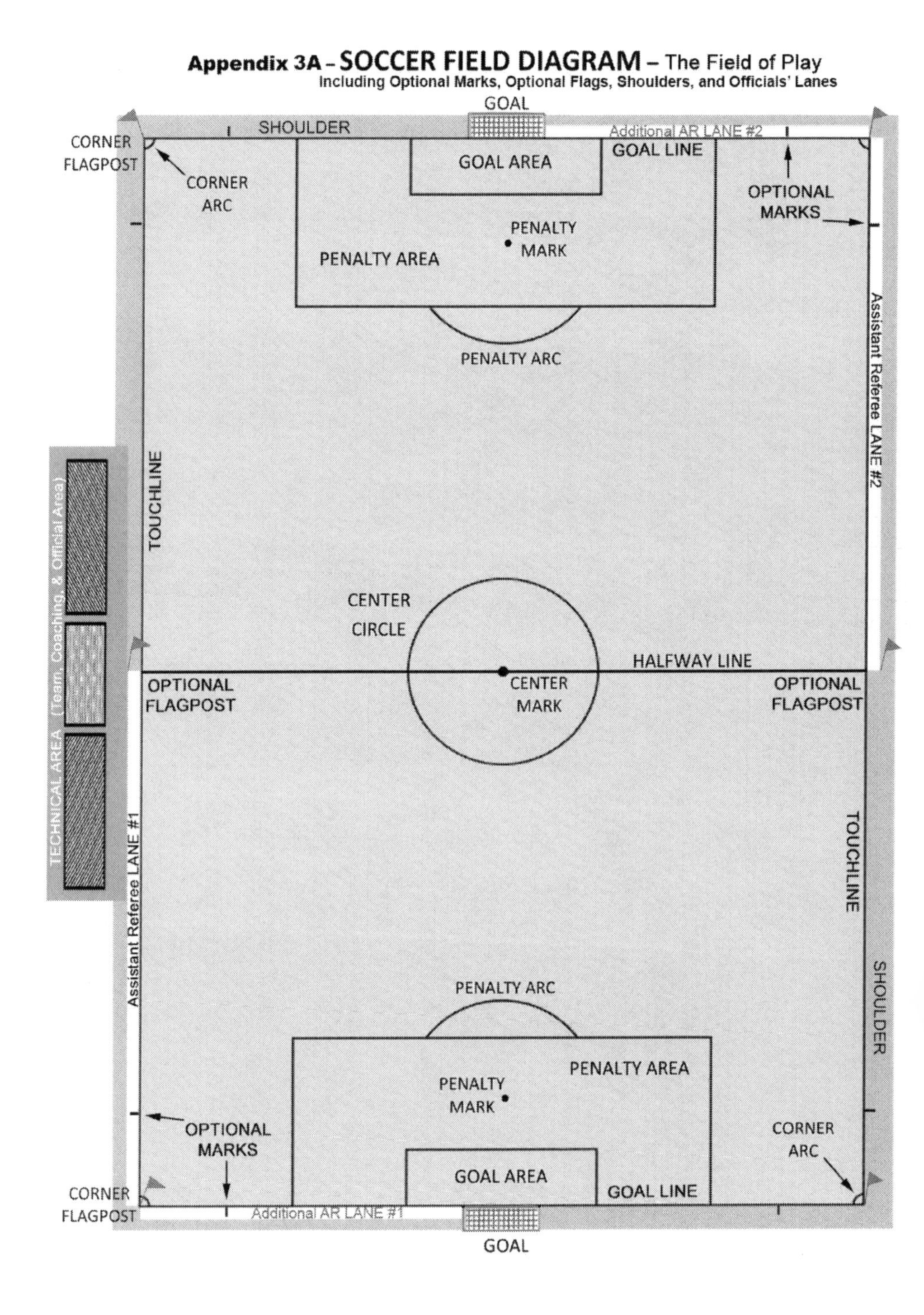
Appendix 3A – SOCCER FIELD DIAGRAM – The Field of Play
Including Optional Marks, Optional Flags, Shoulders, and Officials' Lanes
GOAL
SHOULDER
Additional AR LANE #2
CORNER FLAGPOST
CORNER ARC
GOAL AREA
GOAL LINE
OPTIONAL MARKS
PENALTY MARK
PENALTY AREA
PENALTY ARC
Assistant Referee LANE #2
TECHNICAL AREA (Team, Coaching, & Official Area)
TOUCHLINE
CENTER CIRCLE
HALFWAY LINE
OPTIONAL FLAGPOST
CENTER MARK
OPTIONAL FLAGPOST
Assistant Referee LANE #1
TOUCHLINE
SHOULDER
PENALTY ARC
PENALTY AREA
PENALTY MARK
OPTIONAL MARKS
CORNER ARC
GOAL AREA
GOAL LINE
CORNER FLAGPOST
Additional AR LANE #1
GOAL

APPENDIX 4: On-field Oral Communication ▶

This symbol: ▶ indicates "On-field Oral Communication" terms.
In the ***electronic versions***, each term is ***LINKED*** to its definition.

All "CONDENSED" version terms show ☐ with light shading.

Also, as usual, the black box ■ (and dark gray shading) indicates terms in the "BASIC" version, with ◘ for "Quick-Start" terms.
All "BASIC" terms are ***also*** in the "CONDENSED" version, so the BASIC terms always show ***both*** symbols: ■☐.

All other terms in the **complete** version show ***no*** symbols & ***no*** shading.

Page numbers are also shown for the BASIC and CONDENSED versions: **Page #**

REMEMBER:
In the ***electronic versions***, each "**Oral Communication**" term in this list – indicated by the symbol ▶ – is ***HYPER-LINKED*** to its definition.
From each definition, if you want to ***return*** to this list, simply **click the link**. This helps make it easy and fun to quickly learn more about soccer.

REMEMBER:

In the ***electronic versions***, each "**Oral Communication**" term in this list – indicated by the symbol ► – is ***HYPER-LINKED*** to its definition.

From each definition, if you want to ***return*** to this list, simply click the link.

REMEMBER:
In the ***electronic versions***, each "**Oral Communication**" term in this list – indicated by the symbol ► – is ***HYPER-LINKED*** to its definition.
From each definition, if you want to ***return*** to this list, simply click the link.

APPENDIX 5: Laws of the Game (Overview)

Law 1

(Laws of the Game) **The Field of Play.** Identifies the field markings and measurements and the size and types of goals.

Law 2

(Laws of the Game) **The Ball.** Identifies the size and construction of the ball.

Law 3

(Laws of the Game) **The Players.** Identifies the number of players on a team, the specific designation of a goalkeeper, and how substitutions are made.

Law 4

(Laws of the Game) **The Players' Equipment.** Identifies the specific apparel to be worn by players.

Law 5

(Laws of the Game) **The Referee.** Identifies the authority, powers and duties of the referee.

Law 6

(Laws of the Game) **The Other Match Officials.** Identifies the authority, powers and duties of the assistant referees, additional assistant referees, the fourth official and the reserve assistant referee.

Law 7

(Laws of the Game) **The Duration of the Match.** Addresses the length of games, halftime, and how to account for time lost due to such things as injuries.

Law 8

(Laws of the Game) **The Start and Restart of Play.** Addresses the coin toss, selection of ends, the kick-off and dropped ball.

Law 9

(Laws of the Game) **The Ball In and Out of Play.** Addresses when the ball is in bounds or out of bounds.

Law 10

(Laws of the Game) **Determining the Outcome of a Match.** "A goal is scored when the whole of the ball passes over the goal-line, between the goalposts and under the crossbar, provided that no infringement of the Laws of the Game has been committed previously by the team scoring the goal." Includes extra time and penalty kick tie-breakers.

Law 11

(Laws of the Game) **Offside.** At the moment the ball is passed, a potential receiver: (1) must be in an offside position and, (2) either interfering with play, interfering with an opponent, or gaining an advantage from being in that position.

Law 12

(Laws of the Game) **Fouls and Misconduct.** Identifies the offenses and the penalties to be imposed for violation of the rules. Also identifies those offenses which result in cautions (yellow card) and ejections (red card).

Law 13

(Laws of the Game) **Free Kicks.** Addresses the requirements for taking Indirect and Direct free kicks.

Law 14

(Laws of the Game) **The Penalty Kick.** Addresses the requirements for taking a Penalty Kick. "A penalty kick is awarded against a team which commits one of the ten offenses for which a direct free kick is awarded, inside its own penalty area and while the ball is in play."

Law 15

(Laws of the Game) **The Throw-In.** Addresses the procedure for putting the ball back into play after it has gone out of bounds over a sideline.

Law 16

(Laws of the Game) **The Goal Kick.** Identifies the procedure for placing the ball back into play after it has gone out of bounds over the end-line, having last been touched by an offensive player.

Law 17

(Laws of the Game) **The Corner Kick.** Identifies the procedure for placing the ball back into play after it has gone out of bounds over the end-line, having last been touched by a defensive player.

See the full Laws of the Game at: www.TheIFAB.com

APPENDIX 6 -- Age Group Charts

There are two approaches to create AGE GROUPS:

(1) The "CALENDAR-YEAR" system (based upon each player's "BIRTH-YEAR"). See Appendix 6A.

(2) The "SCHOOL-YEAR" system (based upon each player's birth date (Aug.1 of one year to July 31 of the next year). See Appendix 6B.

In BOTH approaches, the "SEASON YEAR" typically runs from August 1 of one year to July 31 of the next year.

APPENDIX 6A -- Age Group Chart
"BIRTH YEAR" and Season Matrix

Based on each player's BIRTH YEAR, U.S. Soccer now uses a "calendar-year" system. U.S. Club Soccer and USYSA use this format. The chart below is adapted from U.S. Club Soccer's website chart.

	SOCCER SEASON YEAR Each "season year" typically runs from August 1 of one year to July 31 of the next year for youth clubs.								
BIRTH YEAR	**2016-17**	**2017-18**	**2018-19**	**2019-20**	**2020-21**	**2021-22**	**2022-23**	**2023-24**	**2024-25**
2019									U-6
2018								U-6	U-7
2017							U-6	U-7	U-8
2016						U-6	U-7	U-8	U-9
2015					U-6	U-7	U-8	U-9	U-10
2014				U-6	U-7	U-8	U-9	U-10	U-11
2013			U-6	U-7	U-8	U-9	U-10	U-11	U-12
2012		U-6	U-7	U-8	U-9	U-10	U-11	U-12	U-13
2011	U-6	U-7	U-8	U-9	U-10	U-11	U-12	U-13	U-14
2010	U-7	U-8	U-9	U-10	U-11	U-12	U-13	U-14	U-15
2009	U-8	U-9	U-10	U-11	U-12	U-13	U-14	U-15	U-16
2008	U-9	U-10	U-11	U-12	U-13	U-14	U-15	U-16	U-17
2007	U-10	U-11	U-12	U-13	U-14	U-15	U-16	U-17	U-18
2006	U-11	U-12	U-13	U-14	U-15	U-16	U-17	U-18	U-19
2005	U-12	U-13	U-14	U-15	U-16	U-17	U-18	U-19	
2004	U-13	U-14	U-15	U-16	U-17	U-18	U-19		
2003	U-14	U-15	U-16	U-17	U-18	U-19			
2002	U-15	U-16	U-17	U-18	U-19				
2001	U-16	U-17	U-18	U-19					
2000	U-17	U-18	U-19						
1999	U-18	U-19							
1998	U-19								

APPENDIX 6B -- Age Group Charts

"SCHOOL YEAR" 2016-2017

Aug. 1, 2016 - July 31, 2017

AGE GROUPS "SCHOOL YEAR" 2016-2017 Registration Year: August 1, 2016 thru July 31, 2017

BIRTH MONTH \ BIRTH YEAR	1997	1998	1999	2000	2001	2002	2003	2004	2005	2006	2007	2008	2009	2010	2011	2012
JAN	U20	*U19*	U18	*U17*	U16	*U15*	U14	*U13*	U12	*U11*	U10	*U9*	U8	*U7*	U6	*U5*
FEB	U20	*U19*	U18	*U17*	U16	*U15*	U14	*U13*	U12	*U11*	U10	*U9*	U8	*U7*	U6	*U5*
MAR	U20	*U19*	U18	*U17*	U16	*U15*	U14	*U13*	U12	*U11*	U10	*U9*	U8	*U7*	U6	*U5*
APR	U20	*U19*	U18	*U17*	U16	*U15*	U14	*U13*	U12	*U11*	U10	*U9*	U8	*U7*	U6	*U5*
MAY	U20	*U19*	U18	*U17*	U16	*U15*	U14	*U13*	U12	*U11*	U10	*U9*	U8	*U7*	U6	*U5*
JUN	U20	*U19*	U18	*U17*	U16	*U15*	U14	*U13*	U12	*U11*	U10	*U9*	U8	*U7*	U6	*U5*
JUL	U20	*U19*	U18	*U17*	U16	*U15*	U14	*U13*	U12	*U11*	U10	*U9*	U8	*U7*	U6	*U5*
AUG	*U19*	U18	*U17*	U16	*U15*	U14	*U13*	U12	*U11*	U10	*U9*	U8	*U7*	U6	*U5*	U4
SEP	*U19*	U18	*U17*	U16	*U15*	U14	*U13*	U12	*U11*	U10	*U9*	U8	*U7*	U6	*U5*	U4
OCT	*U19*	U18	*U17*	U16	*U15*	U14	*U13*	U12	*U11*	U10	*U9*	U8	*U7*	U6	*U5*	U4
NOV	*U19*	U18	*U17*	U16	*U15*	U14	*U13*	U12	*U11*	U10	*U9*	U8	*U7*	U6	*U5*	U4
DEC	*U19*	U18	*U17*	U16	*U15*	U14	*U13*	U12	*U11*	U10	*U9*	U8	*U7*	U6	*U5*	U4

"SCHOOL YEAR" 2017-2018

Aug. 1, 2017 - July 31, 2018

AGE GROUPS "SCHOOL YEAR" 2017-2018 Registration Year: August 1, 2017 thru July 31, 2018

BIRTH MONTH \ BIRTH YEAR	1998	1999	2000	2001	2002	2003	2004	2005	2006	2007	2008	2009	2010	2011	2012	2013
JAN	U20	*U19*	U18	*U17*	U16	*U15*	U14	*U13*	U12	*U11*	U10	*U9*	U8	*U7*	U6	*U5*
FEB	U20	*U19*	U18	*U17*	U16	*U15*	U14	*U13*	U12	*U11*	U10	*U9*	U8	*U7*	U6	*U5*
MAR	U20	*U19*	U18	*U17*	U16	*U15*	U14	*U13*	U12	*U11*	U10	*U9*	U8	*U7*	U6	*U5*
APR	U20	*U19*	U18	*U17*	U16	*U15*	U14	*U13*	U12	*U11*	U10	*U9*	U8	*U7*	U6	*U5*
MAY	U20	*U19*	U18	*U17*	U16	*U15*	U14	*U13*	U12	*U11*	U10	*U9*	U8	*U7*	U6	*U5*
JUN	U20	*U19*	U18	*U17*	U16	*U15*	U14	*U13*	U12	*U11*	U10	*U9*	U8	*U7*	U6	*U5*
JUL	U20	*U19*	U18	*U17*	U16	*U15*	U14	*U13*	U12	*U11*	U10	*U9*	U8	*U7*	U6	*U5*
AUG	*U19*	U18	*U17*	U16	*U15*	U14	*U13*	U12	*U11*	U10	*U9*	U8	*U7*	U6	*U5*	U4
SEP	*U19*	U18	*U17*	U16	*U15*	U14	*U13*	U12	*U11*	U10	*U9*	U8	*U7*	U6	*U5*	U4
OCT	*U19*	U18	*U17*	U16	*U15*	U14	*U13*	U12	*U11*	U10	*U9*	U8	*U7*	U6	*U5*	U4
NOV	*U19*	U18	*U17*	U16	*U15*	U14	*U13*	U12	*U11*	U10	*U9*	U8	*U7*	U6	*U5*	U4
DEC	*U19*	U18	*U17*	U16	*U15*	U14	*U13*	U12	*U11*	U10	*U9*	U8	*U7*	U6	*U5*	U4

APPENDIX 6B -- Age Group Charts

"SCHOOL YEAR" 2018-2019

Aug. 1, 2018 - July 31, 2019

AGE GROUPS "SCHOOL YEAR" 2018-2019 Registration Year: August 1, 2018 thru July 31, 2019

BIRTH YEAR / BIRTH MONTH	1999	2000	2001	2002	2003	2004	2005	2006	2007	2008	2009	2010	2011	2012	2013	2014
JAN	U20	U19	U18	U17	U16	U15	U14	U13	U12	U11	U10	U9	U8	U7	U6	U5
FEB	U20	U19	U18	U17	U16	U15	U14	U13	U12	U11	U10	U9	U8	U7	U6	U5
MAR	U20	U19	U18	U17	U16	U15	U14	U13	U12	U11	U10	U9	U8	U7	U6	U5
APR	U20	U19	U18	U17	U16	U15	U14	U13	U12	U11	U10	U9	U8	U7	U6	U5
MAY	U20	U19	U18	U17	U16	U15	U14	U13	U12	U11	U10	U9	U8	U7	U6	U5
JUN	U20	U19	U18	U17	U16	U15	U14	U13	U12	U11	U10	U9	U8	U7	U6	U5
JUL	U20	U19	U18	U17	U16	U15	U14	U13	U12	U11	U10	U9	U8	U7	U6	U5
AUG	U19	U18	U17	U16	U15	U14	U13	U12	U11	U10	U9	U8	U7	U6	U5	U4
SEP	U19	U18	U17	U16	U15	U14	U13	U12	U11	U10	U9	U8	U7	U6	U5	U4
OCT	U19	U18	U17	U16	U15	U14	U13	U12	U11	U10	U9	U8	U7	U6	U5	U4
NOV	U19	U18	U17	U16	U15	U14	U13	U12	U11	U10	U9	U8	U7	U6	U5	U4
DEC	U19	U18	U17	U16	U15	U14	U13	U12	U11	U10	U9	U8	U7	U6	U5	U4

"SCHOOL YEAR" 2019-2020

Aug. 1, 2019 - July 31, 2020

AGE GROUPS "SCHOOL YEAR" 2019-2020 Registration Year: August 1, 2019 thru July 31, 2020

BIRTH YEAR / BIRTH MONTH	2000	2001	2002	2003	2004	2005	2006	2007	2008	2009	2010	2011	2012	2013	2014	2015
JAN	U20	U19	U18	U17	U16	U15	U14	U13	U12	U11	U10	U9	U8	U7	U6	U5
FEB	U20	U19	U18	U17	U16	U15	U14	U13	U12	U11	U10	U9	U8	U7	U6	U5
MAR	U20	U19	U18	U17	U16	U15	U14	U13	U12	U11	U10	U9	U8	U7	U6	U5
APR	U20	U19	U18	U17	U16	U15	U14	U13	U12	U11	U10	U9	U8	U7	U6	U5
MAY	U20	U19	U18	U17	U16	U15	U14	U13	U12	U11	U10	U9	U8	U7	U6	U5
JUN	U20	U19	U18	U17	U16	U15	U14	U13	U12	U11	U10	U9	U8	U7	U6	U5
JUL	U20	U19	U18	U17	U16	U15	U14	U13	U12	U11	U10	U9	U8	U7	U6	U5
AUG	U19	U18	U17	U16	U15	U14	U13	U12	U11	U10	U9	U8	U7	U6	U5	U4
SEP	U19	U18	U17	U16	U15	U14	U13	U12	U11	U10	U9	U8	U7	U6	U5	U4
OCT	U19	U18	U17	U16	U15	U14	U13	U12	U11	U10	U9	U8	U7	U6	U5	U4
NOV	U19	U18	U17	U16	U15	U14	U13	U12	U11	U10	U9	U8	U7	U6	U5	U4
DEC	U19	U18	U17	U16	U15	U14	U13	U12	U11	U10	U9	U8	U7	U6	U5	U4

APPENDIX 6B -- Age Group Charts

"SCHOOL YEAR" 2020-2021

Aug. 1, 2020 - July 31, 2021

AGE GROUPS "SCHOOL YEAR" 2018-2019 Registration Year: August 1, 2018 thru July 31, 2019

BIRTH MONTH / BIRTH YEAR	1999	2000	2001	2002	2003	2004	2005	2006	2007	2008	2009	2010	2011	2012	2013	2014
JAN	U20	U19	U18	U17	U16	U15	U14	U13	U12	U11	U10	U9	U8	U7	U6	U5
FEB	U20	U19	U18	U17	U16	U15	U14	U13	U12	U11	U10	U9	U8	U7	U6	U5
MAR	U20	U19	U18	U17	U16	U15	U14	U13	U12	U11	U10	U9	U8	U7	U6	U5
APR	U20	U19	U18	U17	U16	U15	U14	U13	U12	U11	U10	U9	U8	U7	U6	U5
MAY	U20	U19	U18	U17	U16	U15	U14	U13	U12	U11	U10	U9	U8	U7	U6	U5
JUN	U20	U19	U18	U17	U16	U15	U14	U13	U12	U11	U10	U9	U8	U7	U6	U5
JUL	U20	U19	U18	U17	U16	U15	U14	U13	U12	U11	U10	U9	U8	U7	U6	U5
AUG	U19	U18	U17	U16	U15	U14	U13	U12	U11	U10	U9	U8	U7	U6	U5	U4
SEP	U19	U18	U17	U16	U15	U14	U13	U12	U11	U10	U9	U8	U7	U6	U5	U4
OCT	U19	U18	U17	U16	U15	U14	U13	U12	U11	U10	U9	U8	U7	U6	U5	U4
NOV	U19	U18	U17	U16	U15	U14	U13	U12	U11	U10	U9	U8	U7	U6	U5	U4
DEC	U19	U18	U17	U16	U15	U14	U13	U12	U11	U10	U9	U8	U7	U6	U5	U4

"SCHOOL YEAR" 2021-2022

Aug. 1, 2021 - July 31, 2022

AGE GROUPS "SCHOOL YEAR" 2019-2020 Registration Year: August 1, 2019 thru July 31, 2020

BIRTH MONTH / BIRTH YEAR	2000	2001	2002	2003	2004	2005	2006	2007	2008	2009	2010	2011	2012	2013	2014	2015
JAN	U20	U19	U18	U17	U16	U15	U14	U13	U12	U11	U10	U9	U8	U7	U6	U5
FEB	U20	U19	U18	U17	U16	U15	U14	U13	U12	U11	U10	U9	U8	U7	U6	U5
MAR	U20	U19	U18	U17	U16	U15	U14	U13	U12	U11	U10	U9	U8	U7	U6	U5
APR	U20	U19	U18	U17	U16	U15	U14	U13	U12	U11	U10	U9	U8	U7	U6	U5
MAY	U20	U19	U18	U17	U16	U15	U14	U13	U12	U11	U10	U9	U8	U7	U6	U5
JUN	U20	U19	U18	U17	U16	U15	U14	U13	U12	U11	U10	U9	U8	U7	U6	U5
JUL	U20	U19	U18	U17	U16	U15	U14	U13	U12	U11	U10	U9	U8	U7	U6	U5
AUG	U19	U18	U17	U16	U15	U14	U13	U12	U11	U10	U9	U8	U7	U6	U5	U4
SEP	U19	U18	U17	U16	U15	U14	U13	U12	U11	U10	U9	U8	U7	U6	U5	U4
OCT	U19	U18	U17	U16	U15	U14	U13	U12	U11	U10	U9	U8	U7	U6	U5	U4
NOV	U19	U18	U17	U16	U15	U14	U13	U12	U11	U10	U9	U8	U7	U6	U5	U4
DEC	U19	U18	U17	U16	U15	U14	U13	U12	U11	U10	U9	U8	U7	U6	U5	U4

About the Author

John Harves grew up in Arlington, Virginia, where he played organized soccer for the first time at Yorktown High School. He founded a member club of the Arlington Soccer Association and started coaching youth soccer before graduation. His first youth team was composed of both boys and girls ranging in age from 6- to 15-years old. He went on to Virginia Tech, where he played for four years. He was the student-athlete there who successfully led the initiative to get soccer changed from club to varsity status. He was then the Men's Varsity Soccer Assistant Coach at Virginia Tech for one season.

During the summers and for three years after graduation from Tech, Coach Harves played for the Arlington Americans open team and helped found the Capital Soccer League of Washington, DC. In addition, he officiated for the Metropolitan Washington Soccer Referees Association and earned a United States Soccer Federation national coaching license. Also during this time, Coach Harves founded and directed the Arlington Soccer Association's youth referee program and their youth coaching instructional school. He is an inductee of the Arlington Soccer Hall of Fame.

Coach Harves was subsequently appointed the Radford University (Virginia), Men's Varsity Soccer Coach. He won his opening game after only six days with the team. This team finished their season with Radford's first winning record at 8-7. In his second season, Coach Harves lead Radford to a 10-3-3 record, at one point going 13 straight games without a loss. In his third and final year, the team finished the season at 11-6-1 and enjoyed Radford's first post-season play. Also in his third year, Coach Harves was President of the Virginia Intercollegiate Soccer Association (VISA). After Radford, he returned to the Washington area and resumed playing for, and then managing, the Arlington Americans.

Eight years later, he resumed coaching youth soccer with the Olney Boys and Girls Club and then Montgomery Soccer Incorporated (MSI) of Maryland. With the end of coaching youth soccer, Coach Harves has been presenting the information and experiences from his soccer career on his website, CoachingAmericanSoccer.com. During this time, Coach Harves was honored by his former college players with the establishment of the John Harves Soccer Scholarship fund at Radford University. Coach Harves is a member of United Soccer Coaches (formerly the National Soccer Coaches Association of America - NSCAA).

For Additional Information...

To learn more about ***soccer*** –
and about ***coaching soccer*** –
visit the author's main website:

CoachingAmericanSoccer.com

To each reader, soccer fan, and visitor to my website,

Thanks for buying the ULTIMATE SOCCER DICTIONARY! I love the game of soccer, and I'm sure you do too. It was a great pleasure for me to prepare this dictionary, and I've tried very hard to make it a beneficial and fun way to learn more about soccer. I hope you are enjoying using it and discovering its many useful features.

I look forward to receiving your feedback, and I would greatly appreciate it if you would take a minute to give the dictionary a 5-star rating on Amazon.com (if you think it deserves it). Also, your review of this dictionary would help others discover and enjoy this book. Thanks very much!

Have fun playing and learning more about soccer!

John H.

CoachingAmericanSoccer.com

Made in the USA
Columbia, SC
01 April 2021